MY TRICKLE-DOWN CHILDHOOD

A Journey from Panic to Peace

MARY DAVENPORT

BALBOA.
PRESS

A DIVISION OF HAY HOUSE

Balboa Press books may be ordered through booksellers or by contacting:

Balboa Press
A Division of Hay House
1663 Liberty Drive
Bloomington, IN 47403
www.balboapress.com
1 (877) 407-4847

Because of the dynamic nature of the Internet, any web addresses or links contained in this book may have changed since publication and may no longer be valid. The views expressed in this work are solely those of the author and do not necessarily reflect the views of the publisher, and the publisher hereby disclaims any responsibility for them.

The author of this book does not dispense medical advice or prescribe the use of any technique as a form of treatment for physical, emotional, or medical problems without the advice of a physician, either directly or indirectly. The intent of the author is only to offer information of a general nature to help you in your quest for emotional and spiritual well-being. In the event you use any of the information in this book for yourself, which is your constitutional right, the author and the publisher assume no responsibility for your actions.

Any people depicted in stock imagery provided by Thinkstock are models,
and such images are being used for illustrative purposes only.
Certain stock imagery © Thinkstock.

Print information available on the last page.

ISBN: 978-1-5043-8432-2 (sc)
ISBN: 978-1-5043-8433-9 (e)

Library of Congress Control Number: 2017910845

Balboa Press rev. date: 08/31/2017

DEDICATION

First I'd like to dedicate this to my husband and to my best friend, for not letting me stop. Next I'd like to thank everyone in my family for not telling me they were sick of hearing about my past. Also I want to thank my favorite uncle.

Thank you to all the authors for writing books filled with the exact knowledge I needed. When the student (me) was ready, the teachers appeared!

Also I want to thank you—the reader—for allowing me to share. If you are the student needing guidance, please take what you can from my journey. It is my hope you find some of the answers you might need.

CONTENTS

PROLOGUE

Just this year I have come to realize something profound. I've adopted the idea that everything that happens is an open door to a new life lesson. It's all in how I look at things. If I were to choose to look at my life in a negative way, I'd have to live with the trickle down that has been implemented into my life by those who came before. Fortunately, life changes at the speed of light when a new thought comes and more or less demands to become part of my thinking. I almost always accept it with open arms because this is the way I've always transformed myself.

The thought arrived in the evening and flashed into my mind like a comet. In many ways I had been awaiting its arrival even though I didn't quite know what to expect. This practice used to almost always take me by surprise when I wasn't really searching for enlightenment.

Let me explain how I see my new information and how I plan to implement it into my life. This realization seems to be softening my view as to why I've had such a difficult time in my life dealing with understanding my trauma. This information, I feel, will forever change how I am going to view both the traumas and the behaviors I implemented in order to deal with whatever ordeals I endured.

A month before I turned eight, my paternal grandfather died. He had stomach cancer, and it had definitely taken a toll on everyone. Family members had had a long time to adjust to the idea that he was going to die, so when it happened, they weren't surprised, only relieved his suffering was over. I didn't know what death was, so I didn't quite realize that death was forever. The concept of death had really never meant anything to me—at least not yet.

Three months later, when my father's truck was demolished by a train, my life changed. He hadn't been in pain. No one had expected him to die. One minute he was alive, and the next his dead body was trapped inside the still-steaming truck alongside the railroad tracks, and I was fatherless. It must have been difficult enough for family members to explain the death of my grandfather to me, let alone the death of my father. Death had no meaning because my mind wasn't psychologically to the point where I could cognitively understand what death meant.

Now put this together with the scene enacted during the funeral as my mother began to scream, run to the casket, and try to climb in or possibly drag him out. It must have been both frightening and confusing.

There's no way to really explain my thinking at the time because, according to current child psychology theories, I wasn't able to understand death. From what I've learned, comprehension of the reality of death happens at about age twelve. I was eight, and my brothers were ten and twelve. For me, my father had disappeared. The impact of this trauma doubled when my mother chose never to mention his name again.

At that point I didn't have enough personal experiences in life that would help me decipher anything other than the fact that my father was gone—maybe to the store or over to see his still-grieving mother.

I am certain someone probably tried to comfort me by saying he was in heaven. But hadn't the minister said he was in hell? Where were these places? I didn't know. Yes, I'd heard about them in Sunday school, but those were only words without meaning.

Now let's go one step further. A few months before my father's death, a man and his son came to our house for a visit. At that point I was seven. The boy started doing something to one of my brothers that I didn't understand. All I felt was discomfort at what the boy was doing. That discomfort locked itself into my memory in such a way that it would never make sense to me or stop haunting me. I hated him and wanted him to go home, but instead my father died. We moved, and I never saw that boy again.

Two years later, when I was nine, I had an encounter that even today I still call "the man by the river." I hadn't had, and should never have had, any personal experience with sex because I was too young. Even the slightest urges wouldn't begin to nudge their way into my life until hormonal changes began in my body.

Both of these things were brain openers, each inappropriately brought into my life—out of sequence of how they should have happened. That's just how it is in childhood development. If the information given to me was out of sequence, I wasn't going to be able to interpret what either of them might mean. This was both confusing and detrimental to my sense of well-being.

This is the point I want to highlight. I was doing the best I could at age seven through nine to decipher these unfamiliar messages in ways that could help me stay both sane and alive. That is one of the jobs our minds are conditioned for—to keep us alive. Because I was too young, my body remained alive, but my mind began to slip into an alternate universe in order to make sense out of what was happening.

When it comes to the man by the river, I can't definitely tell you he sexually abused me, but deep inside I know he did. I'm also almost positive it was my maternal grandfather. There were physical signs that it had happened as I began to mature, proving without a doubt I had lost my virginity early in life.

Let me go one step deeper. Since my memories are gone, but the melody of what happened has lingered on, it has become necessary for me to believe my internal knowing. I need that just as much as people with memory need others to believe what they actually remember about what happened to them. I know my truth because I feel it inside in a way that means I can't deny believing in my own truth.

Here is the gist of this thought: Take me at seven and nine when detrimental things were being done. I learned how to use my limited knowledge to try to understand what was happening. Since I had no way to do that, I simply split myself away from what was going on and made it about someone else. At that point I not only separated myself from my experience, but took it one step further and locked it away behind one of the doors of my childhood experiences and threw away the key.

Now think of the child I was at the time and the woman I am today. The child (me) took my memories and is still keeping them locked away. There is no way I can help myself retrieve something that is beyond my ability to understand or remember. Yes, I understand my predicament as the woman I am today, but living deep inside me is a wounded child who is still keeping secrets.

Now here is the quandary I'm left with. In order to finish my childhood issues, I needed the memories of what happened, but the child within has no way to explain or understand. In essence we are both lost in the situation I find myself in today.

I don't have actual memories, but the guilt, shame, fear, and confusion about what happened is still trapped in the mind of the child I used to be. Instead of "her" being able to consciously allow me, the adult I am today, to retrieve those memories, "she" gives me only the few thoughts and feelings she was able to attach to what she was seeing or physically experiencing.

Thankfully, as the woman I am today, I came to the realization that not knowing what happened was in my best interest. Instead, I find it is going to be necessary for me to abandon all thoughts of retrieving the keys that might open any doors to my memories.

Instead I am choosing to make new keys that open the doors—not to my past, but to my future. Even if I were to remember what happened, it would be with the mind of the child I was at the time. Since all that was left behind was her sense of confusion and panic, I need to allow her to melt into the heart of the adult I have become. I'm confident that every day I am becoming stronger and less afraid of what past demons might be lurking in the darkness of my mind. Instead I've chosen to turn the light of my truth into a new song that fills me with joy, acceptance, and peace.

CHAPTER ONE

The Creating and Keeping of a Child's Honor

July 2016

I wanted to take my mother shopping. The problem was that I'd have to leave her in the car, and it was hot outside. I had to think about it. Should I leave her behind or have her tag along? It was a hard decision. Even if I left her behind, I would be thinking about her waiting for me. After considering my situation, I decided to go get her. Soon I'd be taking her to another state, and I'd never see her again. In essence, this was going to be our last shopping trip, and I wanted to remember it. I knew she would not be missing me after I left her behind, and I felt sad.

Why is it important to tell you about this? What kind of daughter was I to leave her in the car on that hot day? The war had ended, but the dust hadn't settled. I was battling myself about how I felt about Mother and our circumstances. Why the hesitation? What was it I needed to buy that was so important?

I needed a pretty box and flowers for Mother. You might think that would be reason enough not to take her, but she didn't care about the flowers; neither would she complain if I left her alone in the hot car. Why? Because the box was for her cremated remains, and the flowers were for her grave.

Even though this admission might seem to be crass and uncaring, that is not a reflection of my feelings at the time. I was trying to make decisions. They would either give me comfort over the years or haunt me until my dying day. I wanted everything to be perfect. Every decision needed to be honorable. After all, this was my mother, and I'd never be given a second chance at doing this in the right way.

My story will tell you why I wrestled with all these decisions. You see, Mother and I never had a close relationship. Really, I can't even describe what we had as a relationship. Yes, we were related, but that changed the first time she held me and said, "I hate you. I wish you were dead. I wish you were never born."

I don't consciously remember her saying that. It was her sister—my aunt—who related what she'd heard hundreds of times from the day I was born and years afterwards. Why believe my aunt? When I was fourteen, Mother and I had an argument. It ended when she said, "I hate you." From that day forward, when I felt upset, I would go to the nearest mirror and speak Mother's words to myself. I made her words my own.

I'm going to be as careful as possible as I tell my story. I want to do it in the most honorable way possible. Even though my memories are scant, I feel sorry for the girl, forgetting I am talking about myself.

One of the things I tried to do was keep my information honest and truthful. Everything I was told, even though it could be classified as hearsay or allegations, comprised the truth I built my story around. I don't see myself as a victim, because I survived. My experiences did put me in a position in which I wasn't able to be the best daughter, sister, granddaughter, student, wife, mother, grandmother, or friend I would like to have been. By the time I realized I had a story, I was still young enough to make changes to my thoughts and behaviors but almost too old to do the same for our sons and their children. Fortunately I was able to realize I still had a chance to help with what had trickled down into their lives. It was with passion I finally screamed, "*Stop!* This can't go on."

It is my mission to relate this in a way that will warn others not to pass on their own trickle-down history. Even more, I want to help others become aware of how what they say or do to or around children stays with the children throughout their entire lives and is passed on for generations to follow. I hope my story makes you shake your head in disbelief or sickens you, because even now my past haunts me. My hope is that, by putting this story into book form and asking others to think about what happened, or what I firmly believe happened, they can realize how destructive behaviors and language can be to the most precious gift we can ever have—and that is our children.

How I Respected Mother's Honor While Keeping My Own

July 5, 2016

> My mother passed today. She was ninety-seven. I was sure I was going to treat the day she passed like any other day, and life would go on as normal. The wave I'm riding now is different than I expected.

The problem is that I don't feel anything, but consciously I know that can't be true. She was my mother, and like it or not, the child in me recognizes this. My inner self doesn't care about her misbehavior, but the adult I am now has a problem with our relationship as mother and daughter.

What I have done before when someone has died has been just to forget about it. Now, with my new thoughts, language, and behavior, I've had to deal not only with the confusion and panic I felt my entire life, but I must find a sense of compassion, not only for myself but for the ones who committed acts against me.

At the time I wrote this I still had two hurdles to jump over. The first was to go to the care center to pick up her things, and the second was to retrieve her ashes from the funeral home.

Shortly before her passing, a nurse called from the care center to say that Mother would probably pass in only forty-eight hours. I tried to recognize the sadness I might or should feel as I said good-bye to the nurse.

I was aware that Mother was slipping away and felt ready. She was the last of my original family, so now I could close the door on our past, and that would be the end of my struggle. You're about to find out that life wasn't going to allow this, which meant I'd been lying to myself about how unaffected I was going to be.

Since I hadn't felt the need to blame her, I thought this would end my problems. The child in me didn't agree. My inner child sees her as both a protector and a tormentor. I am aware that Mother was also a victim, so how do I regulate my feelings toward someone who also had a trickle-down past? It is similar to being blind and having a blind guide lead me into the brambles, then thinking the leader should have seen them coming.

On the evening of the call, I knew I needed to see her as often as possible before she passed. This event was something I needed to face, but I wasn't sure how I would react when the time came. This was a face-off between my past and present. If I did it correctly, I was positive I could accept everything the way it was, and then put it to rest along with her body.

When I entered the room, I saw how tiny and vulnerable Mother had become. Her eyes were open, but they were dull and blank. I went to her bed and took her hand. It was warm to the touch, but her fingers had a tinge of blue I hadn't seen before. This was a sign that her body was beginning to shut down.

Suddenly something inside me became filled with a warm essence of grace. I got on my knees so I could put my face close and look directly into hers. Mother's breathing was shallow and barely audible. I placed my hand on her side and felt the rising and falling of the blanket. Looking into her dull eyes, I began talking. As I did, her breathing became deeper, and I knew something in her was aware of my presence.

Over the past months I had seen her mind deteriorate. She always remembered her birthday. When I showed her a picture of her parents, she would say they were her mama and daddy. She couldn't remember their names, but she knew who they were. As for me, she had no idea who I was. First she said I was her mother, then her sister. I didn't feel upset because I knew this wasn't personal.

While I was there I caressed her hand and told her how hard her hands had worked. I mentioned the things I had seen her do as she struggled to keep our household together. I knew this wasn't the time to talk about anything other than positive things. The time for doing anything else had passed long ago, and I felt satisfied just letting it go. All I could do was listen to my internal spirit as I held her hand and talked about the dresses she had lovingly sewn for me to wear to school or for my own personal Easter parade. I thanked her for those things. The room seemed filled with warmth, love, and acceptance. I knew she was ready to be with Jesus and those who had gone before.

The next day I came again. This time I told her she would soon see Jesus, her sisters, her mama and daddy, her sons, my stepfather, and my father. I told her they were gathered waiting to usher her into heaven.

Mother constantly had prayed and talked about "going home to be with Jesus." Now she would soon be able to walk pain free as she left behind both me and the worn-out body that had carried her throughout her troubled lifetime.

I prayed with her, held her hand, and looked into her eyes. After I ended my prayer, she tried to speak. Even though I couldn't understand, I was sure she was trying to tell me she loved me. "Yes. I know you do," I said, "and I love you too." She tried three times with as much volume as she could muster to speak to me. Finally I left to get my family. I told her I'd be right back. I hadn't been home more than twenty minutes when someone from the care center called to say she had passed.

Several months earlier I'd made arrangements with the funeral home and with my uncle. I knew cremation would never have been her first choice, but I was going to take her ashes to another state, and this would be easier. I realized it wouldn't make any difference if I took a body or ashes to be buried as long as I did it in a respectful way.

My husband suggested I put both my father's last name as well as my stepfather's on the stone. My brother, who had died in 1956, was buried at the same cemetery and carried my father's name. This would enable others to see the connection between them as mother and son.

I felt apprehensive when I went to the center to pick up her things. When our sons were little, my aunt gave my mother a sheepskin. Mother carefully cut out the words *Joy in Jesus* using red velvet ribbon. She put them on the skin and hung it above her fireplace. It was the first thing visitors saw when they came to see her. Later I hung the words in her room at the center so anyone coming knew where she had placed her heart and mind throughout her life. I also bought hot pink letters spelling her name and put them on the wall above her bed. It may have seemed silly, but I did it to humanize her. This made it clear to every visitor that people cared for her.

On the day she passed, we came into her room to see her body for the last time. Even though it felt sad to say good-bye, I knew it was a cause for celebration. She was now free to move on to that place she had longed to be so long ago. I kissed her still-warm forehead and told her spirit to go free.

You'd think that, after that experience, everything would be sadness, sunshine, and roses but it wasn't. I was happy for her freedom, but waves of emotion swept over me in a way I hadn't expected. I felt a sense of displaced anger slamming into me. It was hard retaining that feeling of grace and peace one minute and anger the next. I finally recognized that my sense of anger didn't need to be over analyzed. I just need to allow it to be part of the process I was going through.

When I came for her things, I talked with the woman who worked at the center who was always singing "Jesus Loves Me" with Mother. She told me she'd sat with Mother the night before. Shortly before her next shift someone sent her a text telling her, "Your little songbird has passed."

That reminded me of a memory from childhood. I was eight, and Mother had taken me to evening services at church. Half asleep, I lay my head against her chest as services came to a close and the congregation sang: "God be with you till we meet again." I remember hearing the words echoing in mother's body; I remember the sense of peace and joy I felt.

When I talked to the woman at the monument company about Mother's stone, she asked what I wanted put on it other than the normal things. I wasn't sure, and then suddenly the words the caretaker used came to mind, and I asked if they could put "Little Songbird." Thinking the story was sweet, she asked if I would like a small bird etched alongside those words, and I told her that was perfect.

So now when I think of Mother, I will remember her singing when I was eight and how only a few weeks before she passed she smiled as she sang her last song to me: "You Are My Sunshine." It is my hope that, when I am finished with my grief and Mother's ashes have been placed in her grave, I will be able to tell myself "well done" and be pleased with how I honored both my mother and myself.

July 27, 2016

Mission accomplished!

CHAPTER TWO

Finding—Discovering—Then Becoming the Adult I Was Meant to Be

Traces of Pain

Traces of pain
Run deep in our souls.
When we dig it out
It makes us whole.

An Overview into My Past

When I see the words *trickle down*, I first think about politics because that's where we've mostly heard the term used. At a second glance, I see something different. Before each child come parents, grandparents, great-grandparents, and so forth. There are some aspects of personality that can't be changed because they come from nature. Others come from our nurturing. That was what I built my life on. It was supposed to have been a solid rock, but unfortunately I found it was nothing more than shifting sand. It had been exhausting to pretend everything was all right. When I realized this was untrue and there was something wrong, I froze. Finally I had to remove the blindfold I had worn throughout my life; otherwise, I would crash into every wall and fall into every ditch set in place by my original family.

Another word to think about is *perception*. This book is about my sense of what was happening to me as a child, as well as what was happening around me. I filtered what was happening to me through my own experiences, my own lens, and then tried to make sense of it. My lens was distorted like a fun house mirror because my mind couldn't afford to see the truth. Everything was out of focus, giving me a constant sense of confusion and panic. That was the only way I could continue living—or not living—in my world.

Having a degree in psychology would have helped me to share my perceptions. It isn't that I didn't have the brains to become a psychologist, because my self-study happened over a twenty-eight year span of time. During this period I studied a great number of books, many of which were college texts. I could have worked for and received a PhD. But why? I'm standing too close to the mirror to have a clear vision of what happened to me as a child. Even with a degree, I could experience any unresolved issues beginning to surface. If this happened, there would be a chance for over identification.

When I began talking to counselors who worked in the field of rape and incest, I encountered the healthiest, most understanding, under-recognized professionals ever. Each seemed capable of hearing things that would make others throw up, and yet they were willing to wait as stories unfolded. I never found anyone trying to make comparisons. To this day I stand in awe of how well they do such a difficult job.

I'm not planning to tell who did what, because this information is unavailable to me. My story is about the impact the abuse of others had on me over the years. And it did not affect just me; it affected anyone who came in contact with me. This is where the term *trickle down* comes into play. The things people did to me followed me into every aspect of my life. It might appear to others that I was the only victim. Not true. Everyone I touched became a sideline victim. Explaining this is the goal of my book! I hope to show the impact that abuse had on me as a child and how it has stayed with me.

What was said or done to or around me stayed tightly intertwined in my life until I had to attempt to remove, repair, or lessen the damage. This is what my story is about—my valiant, focused, determined effort to regain and reshape my life so I could become more of what I was originally meant to be. I'll share what I've learned because I know I'm not alone. There are others just like me who are unaware of how what happened can be passed on.

What to Do

I don't know what to do.
I don't know what to say.
I have no idea the reasons

That makes me quite this way.

I've tried and tried again
My memories to regain,
But all I find is emptiness
It makes me feel insane.

I filled the voids with memories
Of varied lengths and kinds
So I could find the peace desired
In this thing I called my mind.

In 1988 I was forty-six and knew I had choices I needed to make. If I was careful about the directions I followed, I was sure I could make serious alterations in my life. I'm thankful I didn't know how many years this was going to take, or I might have decided to leave well enough alone and do the best I could with what was left of my life.

It came down to making one of four choices: One, I could continue to live a life that was less authentic and ignore the urges I was beginning to feel. Two, I could ask for medication and live a spaced-out life oblivious to everyone and everything. Three, I could take my own life and be done with it. Or four, I could look for ways to make the changes I needed.

The last was the path I chose—so I could live my life rather than exist. By now I knew living my life the way I had been was going to be as difficult as it would be to remain the same. I needed to face the music, get fully into my life, and learn to dance to whatever tune life played.

Dancing

I'm dancing.
Can't you see me twist and turn?
But am I really dancing?
Or is there something to discern?

My arms were flailing
As if keeping to a beat,
But was I really dancing
When I couldn't move my feet?

The Dance

Whatever the tune
I'll dance the dance
No matter what
The circumstance.

So if my life
I would enhance
I listened to God
As I danced life's dance,

And when my days
On earth are o're
I'll heed God's music
And dance no more.

Throughout my life, on one hand, I had an inner quality that was strong, but on the other hand, I was a frightened mouse. Alone I was strong; with others I was afraid. When I was alone, I knew what to expect, but when I was around others, I felt as if I was in constant danger.

I knew from the beginning it was going to take work to change a lifetime of thoughts, behaviors, and language. I recognized that my life was becoming easier as I addressed and changed each detrimental issue. If I had never changed throughout those years, I wouldn't be any different mentally, emotionally, or spiritually than I was as a child. Eventually I would die without ever tasting the joy, hope, and peace I have found these past years.

I am going to write about some of the things I confronted in order to make transformations. One of the first is that I don't feel the need to blame anyone. Yes, maybe some people in my life could have behaved differently, but they didn't do so. When I investigated their childhoods and realized what had happened to them, I knew I needed to be the one to stop the trickle-down drama of our family. My regret is that, by the time I realized my story, I was married and we had raised our family. Had my issues trickled down into their lives? Absolutely!

As a child, I had one thing going for me that seemed to make me different from others. I had the ability to move between realities to lessen my burdens so things seemed less frightening. Changing my reality has been difficult. To do this I flexed the muscles of my thoughts and behaviors. It's like everything else—the more I did this, the easier it became.

It has been terrible to see myself and my way of thinking in an unbiased fashion. I didn't like discovering my unhealthy sense of reality. I especially didn't want to be labeled as bizarre or crazy, even though I fit the bill. It seemed nice to take non-reality mini vacations when I needed a break from the heaviness of living in the real world.

After learning my story, I was grateful not to be emotionally connected to so much tragedy. Then again, this meant I could never really get over it. If I didn't know what it was, how was I supposed to put behind me? I finally decided it wasn't about getting over it; rather, it was about learning how to live with it so it would have a less-crippling effect on me in the future.

Studying the science of how the mind works has allowed me a reasonable amount of insight. It has been enjoyable to see how a behavior that may have seemed insane wasn't insane, but was rather a way to remain sane as I traveled through difficult times.

One thing I noticed about mental wellness—or illness—is that it can be defined by a combination of labels. It would have been easy to cling to them so I could convince myself that was just how I was, and then stay that way. I had to learn to accept the fact that what I was doing may not appear to be realistic or sane, but it was my world, and I was used to it. What I do is respectfully address labels as a cowboy would address, in passing, a woman in a western movie. I see myself tipping my hat to acknowledge them. I smile, nod my head, and move on. I recognize that labels contain only the power I choose to give them. At that point they become powerless to keep me locked within the grip of any diagnosis or description.

As for generations who came before me, our stories intertwined in a way that made it clear why I wasn't being protected. One of my problems was sexual abuse. Who did this? It was more than likely my maternal grandfather. I can't swear one hundred percent that he was the one, but all the evidence pointed to him.

Mother was ninety-seven when the care center where she resided placed the words *sexually abused as a child* on her chart. When they told me, I coldly said, "Well, that's what happens when your father is accused of being a pedophile." Even Mother once shared with me that her father had "probably" abused her. She wasn't willing to talk about it, but her sister was. My aunt had memories of what had been done, not only to her, but to my other aunt and sometimes to friends when they came to play. She said it was well known that her father touched young girls in a sexual way. And adult women—well that's another story. Did that stop anyone from moving me into the home of my grandparents after my father's death? No! I was eight, and even now you might hear me coldly refer to myself as "a convenient piece of child." That may sound crass, but no matter how you paint it, it is more than likely true. It didn't matter that I was his granddaughter any more than it mattered that Mother or her sisters were his daughters. When the urge hit and he had a chance to meet his needs, he evidently took advantage of anyone with the right equipment.

This was happening in the late forties and early fifties. Back then no one vaguely imagined that a child might be able to remember what happened or what was said. Not only that, but it wasn't common to confront a perpetrator or bring him up on charges.

I mentioned how messages given to me in childhood convinced me I didn't have a right to live, let alone be loved or happy. These things followed me in a negative way, especially after my brother's death in 1956. One thing I learned was that, even as my conscious mind pushed memories away, my body made it plain I had problems. My subconscious mind tried to bring what happened back in a way I could deal with so I could put it behind me like toys from my childhood. Ignoring or doubting what had happened to me as a child trickled down into every facet of my life until it became impossible to stop the health issues it created.

One major issue hit in 1985 shortly before I became aware of my childhood. It was uterine cancer. Fortunately it was found early, and a dilation and curettage was performed. (This is a procedure in which the cervix is dilated and the endocervix is scraped to remove cancerous tissue.) Afterward the doctor told me he was almost positive he had been able to scrape away the affected tissue. He remarked that my progesterone and estrogen levels were extremely high, which meant I wasn't anywhere near going through menopause. Something in me strongly disagreed. He presented me with two options: regular screenings or a hysterectomy.

Hysterectomies were still being done on a regular basis at that time, and since I felt I was still in danger, I opted for surgery. After it was over, the doctor told me a different story. My internal sense had been right. Upon removing my uterus he said it was evident I had finished menopause years earlier. During that time, however, I continued having regular periods, but suddenly the bleeding became abnormally heavy and almost continuous. Because of that, I was anemic and began sleeping eighteen hours a day. I was sure something was wrong, but never imagined it was cancer.

As terrible as it sounds, I was thankful for the cancer. Without it, I never would have learned how distorted my body had become because of stress. I had lived my entire childhood under extreme anxiety, and that had changed everything I experienced. It not only happened through my childhood but through my entire adulthood—and would have until the day I died.

Soon, all our sons were grown, and our house was empty. Before they left I could stay busy, which enabled me to keep the gnawing in my mind at bay. Now, even though there was a silence in the house, my mind would not be still. My days were filled with even more panic and confusion. I felt as if I was being chased by a wild animal, and if I stopped or slowed down I'd be consumed. I had absolutely no idea what else might be wrong. When I was given the diagnosis of cancer, as horrible as it may sound, it felt like a way out. It was a form of medical suicide by way of nontreatment. If I did nothing, the cancer would take its course, and all the madness would end. It took courage to not only face the disease, but to fight.

After the cancer was in my rearview mirror, I still felt a mounting sense of panic and confusion, and I knew I needed a distraction. That was when I decided to look into Mother's genealogy. Both her parents had been one-quarter Native American, and I found this fascinating. With all my new freedom it seemed reasonable to see if I could find the tribes with which they were affiliated. Mother's parents both had passed, and the only paperwork available had been given to one of my aunts. The problem was that she too had passed, and every scrap of family paperwork had been burned. To find the connections should have been adventurous, but instead it turned dangerous. After months of working on our family's history, I remembered my father. He had been dead forty years, and I suddenly realized I didn't know anything about him or his family's history. It seemed reasonable that, if I was going to research Mother's family, I should also look into his.

This is how my slide down the rabbit hole began. I didn't realize how desperately I needed to research both sides. I thought it was only about my parent's genealogy, but instead it began stirring more panic and confusion, and I suddenly knew I was heading for trouble.

Doing battle with your mind is like taking fresh kill from a lion. Finally I wrote every small detail I could remember about my family. There were scraps of memory I began calling "slips." Why? Somehow these had slipped past my mind's ability to forget. Not one of these had a beginning or end; they just dangled like Spanish moss from a tree. Nothing made sense.

I thought the first reasonable thing to do was talk to Mother. The reaction I got when I asked about my father was explosive. It was as if, instead of dying, he had run off with another woman and was still alive. Her hatred of him spewed out in an unimaginable way. Later she tried to tell me that the reason she hadn't told me about him was that she had decided that, if she didn't have anything nice to say, she wouldn't say anything at all. At that point my curiosity turned into intrigue.

I decided that, instead of dealing with her, I would ask my brother. He was four years older and hopefully had a better handle on our childhood. Now my research started to change from genealogy into a mystery. With my newly awakened detective mind I cautiously began to question my brother about our father. I was aghast when he exploded the same way our mother had done.

Your core family (father, mother, and siblings) is known as your original family. There wasn't anyone left in this group who could talk to me about my father without exploding. By now there wasn't any way I was going to stop. I had one other option, and that was talk to Mother's sister. She may not have been part of the original family, but she was close enough. She was twelve when I was born and was with our family on a daily basis during my early years. I had no reason to feel she wouldn't be willing to talk about the family dynamics she witnessed. I had always seen her as being as honest, so I knew she would tell it like it was. If her reaction was the same as theirs, I decided I'd need to accept that my father was a SOB and wipe him out of my mind. When I called to ask if I could speak to her about my family, she said yes.

It really wasn't until I remembered that I had a flesh-and-blood father that I began to have newer problems. I realized that the same thing that had enabled me to forget my childhood must have been what wiped away memories, not only of him, but of everything and everyone. Strangely enough, as terrible as it sounds, after he passed, I don't feel I missed him. Instead, my life went on; I was oblivious to his death or to any abuse happening. My mind seemed to be using whatever it needed to keep me alive. It didn't' seem to matter that it wasn't being handled in a healthy way; it simply had to do with staying alive.

My memory slips served as a foundation on which I could build questions for my aunt. I was desperate to put my life together. I was able to piece a few things together, but there were still gaps in the seams. Finally, when I found these gaps, I brought out my inner cowboy, noticed them, and moved on. This made it easier than trying to fill in the gaps with what I thought may have happened.

Almost immediately after my father passed, we moved in with our grandparents. Soon after that, I was introduced to a new Father, and He became the only father I needed. I understand that, shortly before my father died, Mother had become involved in church. At one point she told me she asked God to resolve her marital issues, and He did by so through father's death. I could hardly believe she wanted to take credit for something so vile.

I became involved in church when my aunt took me to her church where she was teaching a group of children called Sunbeams. I loved it! In class I sang about how Jesus loved me, and I was told I was one of God's children. I loved to recite the Lord's Prayer with the other children. I was supposed to be saying "Our Father which art in heaven" but instead I was saying "My Father which art in heaven." By using the word *my* instead of *our*, I made my earthly father and God the Father the same.

I was eight when my earthly father died. I'm sure someone tried to console me by telling me he was in heaven. I put two and two together as I spoke those words, and instead of four came up with five. Now God was my Father—not the man killed when his truck was hit by the train. It remained that way for the next forty years.

Now, let's go to my questions in 1988. Every answer I was given was like puzzle piece that had long ago been scattered across the years. Most of the missing pieces given to me by my aunt fit perfectly with my slips of memory, but there were still huge chunks of information missing. In some ways I felt the life of the child she was describing couldn't have been mine.

Did I feel angry at those who had participated in creating my problems? No! Instead I felt angry with myself for forgetting my story. Something deep within became determined. I was going to force my mind to give me back what it had stolen. This sounds easier than it turned out to be. To pry something from a mind used to keeping secrets is extremely difficult. I tried one thing after another. When one door closed, I found another. All I wanted was to free myself from, of all things, the hidden secrets in my mind.

I never imagined that such a simple thing as researching my family tree would have so many twists and turns. In the beginning, genealogy wasn't anything other than a shiny object to distract me. It eventually became more than a look into my past; it became a mission. It wasn't only about who my family had been; it was about who I had been as well as who I had become and why.

After driving seven hours and talking with my aunt, I felt shell-shocked. On the trip home, I knew I needed to decide what I was going to do. In answer to my every question she had described abuse. By now I had a list that went like this: sexual, verbal, physical, emotional, psychological, and spiritual. Under each were different people doing different things oblivious to what someone else might be doing.

Very early I evidently began constructing methods that would help me deal with what was happening. One of my methods was known to me as "my internal family." This actually might be something akin to split personalities. Evidently I began assigning each abuse to a member of this imaginary family as a way to protect myself. I know this might sound intriguing, but even this will be made clear as my story unfolds. For me it became a simple thing. I'd pass not only the memory but my emotion to an invisible family member and go on my way as if this was perfectly normal. Imagine my surprise when I found this wasn't true. Memories and emotions were well hidden from everyone, so no one questioned what I might be doing, and I saw no reason to volunteer their presence in my mind.

When I arrived home from my visit with my aunt, I wasn't sure I needed to talk about my new information. After all, I was grown and felt the same way a lot of people did. It had all happened way back then, and this was now. The idea of addressing our past in 1988 was just becoming trendy. Before, the message had been to leave the past in the past because that was where it belonged. The problem was that this hadn't been working for me. I felt traumatized and overwhelmed by what I had been told, and it merely made the ravenous animal in me even more determined to have its meal.

Finally, after several days, I decided to tell my husband. We were going through our own issues in our marriage and had been for years. I wasn't sure he would care about my past. It took all the courage I could muster to speak to him about something even I hadn't been able to deal with yet. One day when he came home for lunch, I decided to tell him. As he filled his plate, I told him my story. I could tell he was listening, and I could hardly wait to hear what he had to say. When I finished, he looked at me and calmly said, "Well, that explains a lot of things." That's it! That's all he had to say.

After that he calmly sat down to eat. When he came home that evening, I could tell something had changed. I wasn't sure what, but his behavior was different. This wasn't the first reprieve we'd had in our marriage, but before it had never lasted more than a few weeks. This time our issues began to subside as his behavior toward me stayed in place. It took a year before I talked to him about what he meant when he said, "That explains a lot of things." I was shocked by his answer.

From that point on, I began to tell people that our marital issues had been a misunderstanding. By that time we had been married twenty-seven years, seven of which had been really good. I can't imagine how much happier our lives and the lives of our children might have been if we had known sooner what had happened to me as a child. After we talked he told me he felt I should talk to a therapist.

Before I go further, let me tell you about my husband. He is an extremely intelligent, caring person. We started dating in 1961 shortly before we graduated from high school; in fact we were classmates. He had a full-ride scholarship to engineering school but decided that wasn't what he wanted to do. He did, however, want to go to college so he enrolled and started classes. After his first semester, he was still uncertain about his major so he joined the military. Before he left for training, we became engaged. We decided, if he was sent overseas, we would wait until he returned to get married, but if he was sent somewhere in the United States, we would be married, and I would go with him. After he finished basic, he was sent to California, so off we went to start our new life together.

You know the adage about when you get married it isn't just between the two of you but also involves both sets of parents as well? When we were married, we had all sorts of people intruding into our lives, including my "internal family." My husband's past plus my past later made for a messy marriage, but we hadn't seen anything yet. By the time he was discharged, we already had our first two sons. He went back to college full time, still not willing to admit, even to himself, what he really wanted to study. He convinced not only me but himself that he was going to become a math/science teacher at a nearby high school or local college. I thought that sounded great and was set to do everything I could to help. I worked full time while he was in college. After school he worked a part-time job so we could pay bills. After a year I became pregnant with our third son. At that point he became a part-time student with a full-time and a part-time job. Needless to say, he was exhausted and hardly ever home. A few years later I gave birth to our fourth and final child. By now I was busy taking care of kids, cutting corners, and finding ways to make ends meet while keeping our family intact.

In 1972, as my husband approached his final semester in college, he dropped the bomb. He had changed his major to premed and wanted to go to medical school. This was going to involve another three years of college plus residency and internship. I was numb. This meant moving away from our families, friends, church, and our dumpy heaven of a house. Now we would be venturing out with our four sons aged four, six, eight, and nine. What we were going to attempt to do was insane, but we did it anyway. How did we manage to stay together? Simple—it had to do with the same behaviors that had helped me keep my life together as an abused child. The amount of panic and confusion, however, was continuing to build year after year until I felt I truly might explode.

My husband and I loved each other, and we both felt we needed to consider not only ourselves but our sons. We weren't willing to throw in the towel and end our marriage. Neither of us realized our lives were about to become even more complicated. At one point in 1977 we almost divorced, but my childhood method of taking care of business was still in full force and kept us together.

In 1988, several months before I found out about my childhood, things became intolerable both in our marriage and in my mind. It was then I finally began to see that things probably weren't going to change. We were again contemplating divorce, and I was considering suicide. Something in my mind, however, kept screaming at me to stop, look, and listen to what was really causing our problems. I was trying to make sense of things, but my mind was so muddled it was difficult to stay focused.

By that time I felt as if I was really going insane, and something had to be done if I was going to stay alive. At about that time something unbelievable happened that not only cleared my mind but hinted at something I wouldn't realize until twenty-two years later. This part of my story deserves its own place, so I'm going to do that in detail later. Of all things, it has to do with epilepsy.

It all started in October of 1988. In November I made an appointment to see a psychiatrist. He had me take a Minnesota Multiphasic Personality Inventory test (MMPI). This had to do with my mental evaluation. Upon reviewing it said, "Well, I see you're depressed." I immediately corrected him and said, "No! I'm confused. I have all this information, and I don't remember any of it. I've been depressed before, and this isn't it." At the time I didn't realize I had what is known as chronic depression. This happens when someone is in a state of depression for a long time—like all of my life!

I had to wait until January of 1989 to begin formal therapy, and I was sick the entire time. If I ate without feeling hungry, I wasn't able to digest my food. I had two choices: First, put up with the stomach cramps and hope I'd keep my food down. Or, second, put my fingers down my throat and throw up. I guess my internal family members were keeping me alive, but they just weren't hungry.

One of the issues was my internal family. Until then I had never talked about them. I didn't realize this might need to be brought up in therapy. All I know is they kept me going with their antics. As long as that was happening, I was in familiar territory. If anything else happened, they'd be there to take care of me. Later I realized they were part of my problem. They were helpful and harmful at the same time, but they were still doing their duty, which was to keep me alive.

From the beginning, talking about myself as an individual (saying "me") was another glitch in my view of the world. At that time I didn't realize anything was unusual, and I saw no reason to change my behavior. Instead, I did something akin to manifesting a separate personality to deal with each new issue.

Between 1989 and 2000 I met several professionals who wanted to work with me about the way I was using pronouns like *she, her, they, we, our, us,* and so on when referring to myself. Believe it or not, using other personalities seemed to make perfect sense. They were and still are my family. Even after all this time, they are still at times an intricate part of my behavior. They are like the close-knit family I never had. Today they still hang around, but have I taught myself to ignore them. Sometimes I treat them like naughty children and make them sit in the corner of my mind until they agree to behave.

In March 1989 I began writing poetry and what are known to me as psychological stories. I have placed the poetry within this book. The psychological stories are something I may mention here and there, but never reveal in their entirety. This type of writing has a very powerful core that can be explosive if not handled properly.

This is not my first book. It is actually the ninth. I've tried six times to put my personal story into readable form. Each time I finished, things changed, and I'd set aside my last book and try again.

For quite some time I remained neutral about my life's story—no anger, just the feeling of how sad it seemed. In 2001 my original family began to die. Within four years everyone was gone but Mother, and her demands were high. In 2007 I had to start dealing with changes in Mother's life, and at that point anger did show itself. I hadn't been able to grieve for the loss of my support system, and now I was trapped with Mother living in our house.

In some ways, the only grief I felt was the loss of my freedom. Before Mother came to live with us, I could visit her, touch base, then return to the safety of my home. I hadn't been around her 24/7 since 1962, the year I was married. When she became a constant in my life, I found myself being swallowed by all the things needing my attention. Not only was I tending to Mother and her needs, but our grandson was living with us. I wanted his childhood to be as calm as possible, but now that was becoming more difficult. I would cringe as Mother screamed at her dog and shoved my grandchildren with her walker. My behavior was less than honorable during the next few years.

If Mother shouted at her dog or shamed it, something deep inside felt as if she was yelling and shaming me. I taught myself to not take things personally, but the child within wanted nothing to do with what I had accomplished. Mother living in her own home was one thing, but living in mine was quite different. Instead of feeling anger toward Mother, I was angry at myself. I knew I should be handling things better, but remember, I have no memory about my complicated story so I wasn't able to recognize what nerves she touched. Even under the best of circumstances, I'm sure others know how difficult it can be when roles are reversed and suddenly you are your mother's mother. Add in a home, a husband, and a small child, and I can guarantee that will bring the best of people to their knees.

She lived with us for over a year before we moved her into an apartment we built just across our driveway. When she was ninety-four, we had to move her to a care center where she seemed quite content. Everyone there loved her and treated her with even more love and respect than I could. She sang "Jesus Loves Me" to the staff members and never failed to tell them she was praying for them. She sweetened with age, and I am thankful for that. I only wish we could have connected earlier so we could have done things together and enjoyed one another's company. My philosophy is that mothers don't intend for their children to be harmed in any way. I find it hard to believe she truly wanted me to suffer. Because she also, more than likely, was molested, something in her had to turn a blind eye. At ninety-seven she often had dreams of someone coming to harm her. I found it sad to see her trying to deal with her own trickle-down childhood.

When I visited her, I kept things calm and uncomplicated. I'd kiss her hello and good-by, help her eat, and coax family members to visit. I talked with the staff, monitored her needs, took her little gifts I knew she might enjoy, then leave with the knowledge she was safe, clean, fed and, as I said, content. She never missed me when I wasn't there but always smiled and recognized me as someone she should know when I visited.

When it comes to my story, I don't want sympathy for what I went through because, at the time I had no idea what was happening. As a child, I felt I was writing my life's story with one hand and erasing it with the other. I have no emotional feelings about what happened. What I care about is how things trickled down into the lives of others. I have been able to help some in our family change their thoughts, behavior, and language, but that's not how I wanted it to be. One of the things I would like to accomplish by writing this book is to take some of what I might earn and reinvest it in my family. This way they can have the opportunity to live the genuine life they were meant to live instead of the patched-up one I gave them.

This is what I'm trying to say. Even at ninety-seven my mother was still confronting her childhood. As you can see, it isn't over until you put an end to it or die. I chose the first option, but Mother chose the second. I've never been sorry for the amount of time or expense my own journey has taken. I hope that, by sharing, I can enable readers to see it doesn't matter what your age might be. If you hope to truly live in the now, you have to finish the cold meal left on the plate of your childhood and chew it for all it's worth. You may choke on parts of it, but when you've been able to swallow as much of it as possible, then you can spit it out or let it go. That's when you begin your life over. I know that's true because that's what I've done.

In this overview I've shared stories that may come up again. Be patient. If I tell it twice, then it is because I need to do it that way. Each replication has a different slant with different thoughts and feelings.

Battles

Battles rage within my mind
When answers I had sought to find.
The past and present interlaces
With unheard voices and unseen faces.

When I try to make sense of this unknown past
It runs from me until at last
I put my mind to the test
And do for myself what I feel best.

If it has to do with my present world
Then 'tis best to let my mind unfurl
And expose things which I know not
Until I find the very spot.

When emotions separated from my heart
And left me with these unknown parts
I'll piece together until I'll be
Living now—from my past set free.

A Full Blow-By-Blow Family History:

The Blame Game

The blame game is not for me.
What I want is accountability,
Not from someone from my past,
But from myself is what I ask.

Too many times we shift the blame
Just so we can play the game,
But this is what you should ask,
How can I get beyond my past?

My plan is to first explain story by describing the people who played the most important parts in my trickle-down life. It is important to tell how my grandparents and parents were raised. When I learned this I could tell how difficult it was for them to overcome their own childhood issues. Even theirs had trickled down from their parents and grandparents. This enabled me to see how great-great and even great-great-great grandparents had a hand in what eventually happened to me. Even though I didn't like what happened, I was able to see how our family issues had been passed from one generation to the next. It is difficult to feel angry with the children they were and how they were being raised. Instead of being angry with them, the only upset I feel is that they made my job of parenting more difficult. Who did this hurt? Yes, it hurt me, but even more than that, I've seen the effect it had on not only our sons but their children as well. Life is difficult enough without being saddled with a past that you don't know. Just because I hadn't been told about earlier family issues didn't mean they didn't take a toll on my life. Trying to understand helped. They became real people with real problems. Their solutions didn't resolve their issues; instead, they just filtered their own mishandled solutions into the lives of everyone yet to come.

It helped to attempt to understand the childhoods of not only my parents but past generations. Life is seamless. I always tried to remind myself to not only ask questions without judgment but to accept the answers that way as well. It is astounding how damage is passed from one generation to the next. I tried to remain quiet when I asked my questions so people felt comfortable. Doing that helped them to be more willing to share. I made sure I left blame out so I could see the whole picture.

I don't see any members of my family as monsters. It would be easy to try to paint them in a way that might make someone think they were terrible, but this isn't true. Everyone was behaving the way people did long ago. We've heard family stories about how children were disciplined and how wives and children were seen as property, how hard times were, and how scarce money might have been. I used to hear people use the phrase "the good old days," but some of those days really weren't good for everyone. We all phase through times of scarcity as well as times of plenty. Entertainment was simple: family reunions, Sunday meals, and children playing tag or catching lightning bugs. School was often held in a one-room schoolhouse with all classes sharing the same space. Our pace was slow, and we took time for each other. It isn't like that today.

Now time seems to fly. Almost every minute of the day is filled with activity. Children don't play outside the way we did; instead, their days are full of not just school but a list of programs—ballet, gymnastics, track, football, basketball, clubs galore. And the list goes on. We travel miles to go to the store. In days past, we had corner groceries if you lived in the city. Or, if you lived in the country, there was a grocery/feed/hardware store where you could buy most anything from nails to marshmallows. In the country, going to the store was something families did together. Sometimes they made a day of it. People sat outside after dark visiting with families or neighbors. Now some of us hardly know our neighbors, and even if we do, there isn't enough time or interest to sit and visit.

Back then, if they were fortunate, families sat down for mealtimes of meat, potatoes, something green, and of course bread and dessert. We never heard of pizza or ate spaghetti at my house. We drank milk or water with our meals. Sodas were an unheard of unless it was a treat. Now it's about fast food and meals eaten in front of the television or on the run.

Fathers used to work, and mothers stayed home taking care of the never-ending list of tasks she was expected to accomplish. Now it takes two parents just to make ends meet, and it's hard to make family time.

Kids wore hand-me-down clothes and were happy to have them. Now they want what's in fashion. The first time my grandson bought a pair of jeans with rips in the legs it, was all I could do not to patch them. I finally gave in and bought what he wanted, but the urge to mend them never faded.

So now let's go back in time and look at the "good old days" in the lives of my ancestors. I don't think you'll be surprised to see that some of the very same issues happening in my family are still happening today. Life seems to repeat itself generation to generation until somewhere someone decides to make changes. This wasn't the case in the lives of our great-great grandparents. Change was slow, and families lived by the rules of the husband, the government, or the church.

As I tell about each significant person in my life, I'll explain how he or she measured into mine. I was surprised how everything trickled down over generations.

At one point I told my husband that I didn't like it when I read in someone's book that the author felt that writing the book was worth it if it helped even one person. My husband didn't hesitate before he told me that my book had already helped that one person I was talking about, and that was me. He told me it had been important for me to change myself and make the journey. If other people benefitted from the process, that was great, but what was important was how writing this book helped me.

"Just doing that," he explained, "is part of your healing. Because it allowed you to step back and look at your amazing progress without judgment, and that's enough."

I can't imagine where I would be today if I hadn't taken the time to make sense of my life. Others might see what I'm doing as a self-absorbed endeavor, and maybe it was to a certain extent, but it was truly more than that. I admit I'd probably be six feet under by now had I not written this book. I would have died without ever having had a chance to be alive, and that really does seem a shame. Not only that, but it doesn't seem fair.

"Well", you might say, "who says life is fair?"

That is a good question, but I think you should have a life first. I didn't consider just breathing in and out and putting one foot in front of another as being much of a life. I existed; I didn't live.

Next I asked my husband, "How can I justify spending all the time and money it has taken to do my self-study?"

Again without hesitation he told me, "It would have taken more time and money if you had done it through formal therapy." He continued by telling me that what I had accomplished was nearly impossible, and for that reason alone I should write about my findings. He said, if I was able to change my behavior and thinking from panic to peace, it should be shared so others could see what could be done.

I find my husband to be an astounding person. How many people do you know who will support a loved one who gets down and dirty in exposing their lives together? I was determined to dig up anything and everything I could about myself and hold it to the flame so I could see my truth. Even if it became too personal and included some of our dirty laundry, he never flinched. He just patiently allowed me to work through my issues without taking any of what I was saying, doing, or exposing personally. Never once did I seem to cause him to question himself; instead, he courageously encouraged me to continue until I was able to find a peaceful answer that satisfied my sense of well-being.

It has been hard to understand how my mind could have ever betrayed me the way it has. After all, didn't we enter this world together, my mind and me? Aren't we supposed to be of one mind inside our bodies? Evidently mine wasn't. My mind split or splintered in a way that will never enable me to see the world the same way others do. To top it off, my mind took most of my personal experiences and removed them from my memory. Which leads me to the question: is my mind a friend or a foe?

Maternal Family

Their Impact

I feel as if I was doomed from the beginning to fail in one way or another. If not fail, then struggle constantly with the feeling that something was dreadfully wrong. It has been hard to convince myself that anyone would care because, like many other self-deceived children, I wasn't able to see that anything was different for me than it was for others. I thought everyone's world was just like mine, so I didn't find it necessary to change or even ask for help.

I learned that deceiving myself as a child set me up for an uphill struggle. I've heard it said that I've always been in charge of my own destiny, but there were things I had to do as an abused and traumatized child if I was going to succeed. These things were not necessary for others.

Grandfather

When my grandfather molested me, he destroyed the part of my mind that told me I had the ability to control what happened to my body. He probably lied about what he was doing. He may have tried to blame or threaten me to make it seem normal. When I was eight I had no idea what was normal, so I had to take his word about what he was doing to me and why.

A child doesn't know what is happening when sexual acts are involved. I didn't have enough worldly information to understand that wasn't how I should be experiencing things. It probably confused me, especially if I was told it was okay or if I was threatened that something bad would happen if I told. Maybe I was convinced this was the way adults showed children love. It wasn't about romance, but simply how the word love was contorted.

Remnants of Rape

Remnants of rape left scars on my mind,
A more difficult task than I could find.

They never heal, they seep and bleed
With memories blind I never heed.

Raping the child was a simple thing;
No one to fight what they have to bring.

For a frail little body without any shape
Was theirs for the taking for committing of rape.

You know she can't fight you, even though she might try
So her body stays living, but her mind starts to die.

My paternal grandfather's parents did something that was almost unheard of in those days—they divorced. On one of my trips to cemeteries in the area where my grandfather lived I found not only his mother's grave, but that of her parents and grandparents. In one fell swoop I was able to locate family as far back as my great-great-great grandparents.

His father then married a nice woman who not only finished raising his children but gave birth to their own. The only one available to talk to me was his half-sister.

I was eleven the last time I had last seen her. When I returned forty years later, she was happy to see me. The last time I saw her was in the summer of 1953 when I was being taken to spend time with my father's family. The ride had been long and hot, and I was excited to finally arrive. I stuck my head out the window and yelled, "We're here! We're here!" As I brought my head back into the car, I probably had a grin from ear to ear. About then Mother turned around and smacked me across the face. I wasn't happy to be there after that. Instead, I held back, tipped my head down, and hoped no one would see the bright red mark Mother's hand had left across my face. Little did I know that would be the last vacation I was going to be taking to see my father's family.

When I came back to the area as an adult, I was nervous because I hadn't really known why I had never been allowed to return. I had suspicions, which were later confirmed, but that's another story. During our conversation, I cautiously asked about my grandfather.

My grandfather's half-sister began telling me about the boy he had been and how mysterious his life seemed to her. He would be gone for days or weeks living in the woods with some of his friends. They didn't call him by his given name, but instead called him "Zeke." When he did come home, she said he would climb the ladder into the loft where he slept and pull it up after him. It seemed strange his family would have allowed him to be gone without knowing where he was or what he was doing, but they did. From what I was told, he continued to go away for long periods of time even after he married my grandmother. I hoped my grandfather's half-sister would tell me more than she did, but she was from an era when things like that weren't discussed.

In 1989, my husband and I spent the night with her, and this was the first time I woke up hearing gunshots. I looked at my husband, who was still soundly sleeping, and even went to the window to see if I could see where the noise had come from. Later I tried to piece together why

I might have awakened to gunshots. I found several recollections from my childhood that might have created that sound, but I was never sure exactly what my mind might be remembering.

Finding information about my grandfather was difficult. I was told his life with my grandmother had also been filled with weeks and sometimes months of his absence without a clue as to where he had been or what he had been doing. My mother's sister and I began to suspect he may have had another family. We never had a chance to investigate because she passed before we had the opportunity. Being able to acquire any type of reports on him would have been helpful, but they were impossible to locate

According to family history, one of his childhood friends disappeared, and the police interviewed my grandfather. It was said they were sure he knew what happened, but he wouldn't tell. It was rumored the friend might have run away with another woman. And then there was another rumor about him being killed. No one knew, except my grandfather.

My aunt had her own story about her father. It took place the day she was to be married. She and my grandmother had to bail him out of jail for attempted rape. From everything I was told, this hadn't been the only time this happened. I talked to people who said they knew him to be not only a pedophile, but a sex offender. It would have been hard to believe just by meeting him, but we've all heard about the terrible things seemingly nice people have done.

It is well known how most of the time the offence isn't about abusing a random person; rather, it is about abusing someone the abuser knows. It's a matter of convenience and availability. That's why I referred to myself as "a convenient piece of child" in my story. He could easily find a reason to be near me. I remember my grandmother wouldn't allow him take me anywhere in the car. That was probably the only effort she made on my behalf to protect me from him. When my aunt was a girl, she tried to tell her mother what he was doing, but the minute she started my grandmother told her, "Oh, honey, we don't talk about those things." And they didn't.

There had been one other piece of information I was able find that began to make sense. When I was ten I overheard the adults talking about a seventeen-year-old girl who worked in my grandparent's corner grocery store. They were whispering about how she had committed suicide. I wasn't sure what the word meant. I heard she'd hung herself, but at that tender age I didn't know what that meant either. Later, when I went back to gather the pieces of my story, I asked my aunt what had happened. She informed me that the girl had been pregnant with my grandfather's baby. Back then having a child out of wedlock was horrible. Rather than having the child or face the shame, she took not only her life, but the life of her unborn baby. Do I think my grandfather cared? I doubt he ever felt responsible for her decision to end her life, but he should have.

Basically, what I'm trying to say is that my grandfather wasn't a nice person. He is the only one I feel was responsible for purposely harming others. Was he the man known to me in a memory I called the man by the river? I'm not sure, because even though I remember looking into the face of this man, I wasn't able to remember it. That is always where the memory ends. I was later able describe the surrounding area to my aunt, and she took me to the spot where we believe it happened, It was my grandfather's favorite place to go.

Here is that memory: I was standing on the banks of the Mississippi River looking at the water. A man approached me from behind, turned me around, took my hand and placed it on the front of his pants and said, "I'll bet you've never felt anything as hard as this before." That was when I looked at his face. Since it was so far from where we lived at the time, I couldn't have gotten there alone. I don't remember what happened. I tried to write a psychological story about it, but in the story I didn't write about what happened to me but about how she focused her attention on a bird singing in a nearby tree.

Incest

The hardness of his flesh
Cut deep into my soul
Penetrating in body ways
That left me less than whole.

Once Mother remarried, we moved. Each time we returned for a visit, after everyone had gone to bed, I would wake up with a headache that felt as if my head was exploding. The throbbing was so loud I was positive everyone could hear it. Later, after finding out about my story, it made sense why I might wake everyone in the house with my screams about a headache. If I did this, he couldn't touch me in the night. I thought it was a clever way for my mind to make him stay away.

I also have a memory of something that happened after I was married. We had driven a long way to visit our families. While Mother and Grandmother were finishing dinner, I decided to visit my grandfather. He had Parkinson's and was quite frail, so much so that he had to be helped to move.

When I entered the apartment, he was sitting in a chair staring blankly at the television. I sat on a footstool in front of him and began talking. At first he didn't seem to know I was there, but then suddenly his eyes found me, and he said something I couldn't understand. Without warning, he lunged forward and grabbed for me. I can't tell you how startled I was or how frightened I felt. I never went into a room alone with him after that. It was almost as if something in me awakened, and a long-ago fear struck a memory I had forgotten.

Before I move on, I want to share an experience that, at the time, seemed nice. It wasn't until I began going to incest therapy that this experience took on a different meaning. In November of 1958, a week before I turned sixteen, I went on a hayride with my youth group. The boy I asked was involved with someone else, but still took me up on my offer. I don't think I was nearly as interested in him as a romantic interest so much as I was choosing the person I wanted to give me my first kiss. Did I receive my kiss? Yes! At that age I was naïve and innocent, or so it seemed.

Once I started therapy having to do with sexual molestation, I discovered something that ruined the entire experience. Because of an emotional tie-in, I wrote the poem I offer below.

Sweet Sixteen

I was sweet sixteen
Never been kissed
Never quite knew
What I had missed.

Then later I found
To my great surprise
An astonishing fact
That opened my eyes.

My innocence gone
My mouth opened wide
My tears over flowed,
It was then that I cried.

It seems sad, I thought
Never to be
That innocent girl
I thought had been me.

I find it quite ugly
To think of me then,
That I had been raped
But I didn't know when.

How do you deal
With life's cruel blows?
I haven't decided.
I guess no one knows.

If I had it to do
All over again,
I think that forgetting
My sure vote would win.

So that for one moment
And it was sublime
I'd know my first kiss
Frozen in time.

If I had remembered,
It would not have been right
I'd lost the enchantment
Of that wonderful night.

Of hayride and giggles
Of snuggles and such
Were the thoughts I'd remember
That would help me so much.

When my life wouldn't glimmer
Like lights on a tree,
It had happened to her
And it happened to me.

The first kiss is best,
Or so they do say.
I'm not sure if they're right,
But it's better that way.

A kiss is a kiss,
And mine was so sweet.
Ahead to a future
I knew I could meet.

I think that my childhood
Was quite out of shape,
Not for the kissing
But for the rape.

After I found out about being molested, an entirely different picture was painted of something that had a special meaning to me. I found that, long before that event, quite unrealized by my conscious mind, my innocence had been stolen. When this psychological poem surfaced, I had to face the truth. This person who should have loved me like a granddaughter had changed my future with his trickle-down selfishness. No wonder they imprison people who commit incest or other sexual abuse. They steal something more valuable than gold or diamonds. They steal our love, innocence, and humanity.

Now I want to explain how I began to view my grandfather when it came to his alleged behavior. It took years for me to see this connection. Eventually I began to see how what he had done wasn't personal. Now, put the top back on your head and hear me out. It softened how I began to see him as my abuser. It is in no way meant to be an excuse; it's just something I have to think about. It helped me see how truly sick this man was. I'm supposing my grandfather had a deep-seated need to sexually abuse females. I'm not going to entertain the idea that he abused boys, because I was unable to find any evidence of that. I doubt seriously if the women and girls he abused mattered to him. It had nothing to do with age. All that seemed to matter was that they had the right equipment. I don't feel anyone he molested registered in his mind as having a name or a face. Each was just a convenient body to be taken advantage of, whether compliant or not.

He had an internal need that demanded to be met, and I fit that need. Some say it isn't about sex, it's about power, but I see it as an overwhelming addiction. It was a case of his needs over mine, and because he was more powerful, he was able to take what he wanted at my expense.

If you think about the word *power* in this way, you'd be right. I doubt seriously he felt powerful when this urge triggered his behavior. Instead it became a horrendous need that demanded to be met. My grandfather, as terrible as it sounds, was probably in many ways powerless when it came to choosing not to do those things. I think in his mind he didn't feel guilt, only satisfaction.

Deep inside I really do want to hate him, but how can I do that when I can't remember what he did or how often? There must have been a deep cruelness to him that that was more important than any love he might have felt for me as his granddaughter. I finally stopped trying to understand why he was the way he was and let it go.

When it comes to my grandfather, I was able to get the last laugh. This is a story I love to think about. It happened a year after I found out about his behavior. It is supposed to be empowering for a victim to confront an abuser, even if he is dead. That's what I did. I decided to go back and confront people on Mother's side of the family who had passed and have a talk with them. The first one was my grandfather.

Mother's sister lived a few miles from the little country church cemetery where my brother, grandparents, stepfather, and aunt were buried. Because my grandfather was the first one on my list, I looked for his grave. Little did I know I wasn't going to be able to go further because of what happened when I found his headstone.

It was almost dark when I stepped out of my car to find his grave. I knew where he was buried, so I moved quickly toward it. Guess what I found. A pile of dog poop piled appropriately on his side of the headstone. In my mind I could almost see God directing the dog to the spot I would be visiting. I could hear the words spoken by a power greater than yours truly: "Right there. Do it right there, and hurry up because she's going to be here soon."

When I spotted the pile of poop, I felt justified that notice had been given to what he had done. I took a picture and laughed all the way back to my car. I don't think I said anything toward his body, which now thankfully lay six feet under. The dog had already met my need.

After I got back to my aunt's I told her about it, but she seemed upset. I thought she'd enjoy the humor since he had done the same thing to her when she was a child, but at that moment she wasn't seeing him for what he had done but for who he was—her father. I thought about how my aunt felt and decided that, even though I thought the scene was perfect for his behavior, I didn't like the look on my aunt's face. Because of that I decided to go back.

It was pitch black when I returned to the cemetery to confront the cold, brown pile of poop directly below his name. I thought he deserved it, but my aunt's feelings were more important than the universal joke I saw. I pulled out my flashlight and found my way back to his grave and gave the cold dried poop a kick with the side of my shoe and watched it roll away. Even that felt good. It was as if I was kicking his crap out of my life.

By the time I got back to my aunt's and told her what I'd done, she almost seemed sorry. She had finally allowed herself to participate in the joke played by the Universe, but also liked the new way I described my own feelings. Hating him or what he had done was a complete waste of energy. No amount of kicking dog poop was ever going to change history. That didn't mean I had to like the thought of what he had done; it just meant that I no longer was going to allow his behavior to molest my mind.

That reminds me of a story I heard during my senior year of high school in an assembly held by military personal talking to our class about the armed forces. The draft still applied, but if you waited for it, you had no choice as to which part of the armed forces you were going into.

This was his story: It seems there were two young brothers, one a pessimist and the other an optimist. One Christmas the boys' parents decided to turn the tables. They decided to give the pessimistic boy piles of wonderful toys and the optimistic boy piles of horse manure. Come Christmas morning they went to the door of the pessimistic boy's room, opened it, and saw he was clutching a toy and crying uncontrollably. They asked what the matter was and why he wasn't happy with his toys. The boy, clutching the toy closer, looked at them and told them that, if he played with them, they'd break and then he'd have nothing. They were aghast.

Now they were going to have to face the son to whom they had given the manure. The father put his shoulder against the door and with effort shoved it open. Prepared for the worst, they were surprised when they found their son whistling as he shoveled their smelly gift out his window. He stopped what he was doing and smiled. When they asked how he could be so happy when all he had gotten for Christmas was a smelly mess, he grinned even wider and told them that, with all that horse shit, there had to be a pony in there somewhere.

I quite often think about this story when something happens. Not long ago I heard it said that we don't always get what we want; rather, we get what we need. I don't know if I really needed all the things that happened to me, but I am the first to admit that, in the long run, it worked out as far as learning goes.

Grandmother

Now let me tell you about my grandmother. Her story always seemed sad. Mother said when she was a girl and Grandpa would be gone on one of his mysterious journeys, Grandmother would sit in a rocking chair and sing "If I had the wings of an angel, over these walls I would fly." All of her attention was focused on Mother. That means that Mother was about as spoiled as the day was long. Grandmother never taught her to do anything, but instead did everything for her. This created a definite problem after Mother married. Since my father was from a staunch German family, which trained their children to work, her inability to cook, clean, or do menial chores was a shock.

My grandmother was five feet tall, and in my memories of her, she seemed sweet. They may not have had much money, but she was always well put together. I never remember her raising her voice, but then again that doesn't count because I may have just stored such behavior away with my other lost memories. I'm of a mind that she was a well-liked, pleasant person. When it came to getting what she wanted, I don't think size mattered. She was stubborn and wasn't one to give in easily. I guess you might call her the quiet ruler of the family. That applied to everyone but my grandfather. He wasn't about to let anyone rule him, so whatever she might want to say she probably kept to herself.

Grandmother's mother died when she was small. She had an older sister and a brother. Her baby brother had died. Not long after her mother's death, her father remarried and began another family. Her stepmother gave birth to two girls plus a boy born with hydrocephalus (water on the brain). My grandmother and her sister were nothing more than added baggage in the marriage; they were treated in a lesser manner than the woman's biological children.

It seems one day my grandmother was rocking in a chair while the baby boy was lying on a blanket on the floor. Rockers are known to "walk" as they rock (move across the floor), and one of the rockers touched the boy's head and left an indentation. Shortly after that, the boy died. The stepmother blamed Grandmother for his death and told her husband she refused to live in the same house with the person responsible for her son's death. If he didn't remove the child, she and their daughters would leave.

Rather than have his wife and daughters move or my grandmother sent away, he decided to acquire the house next door. He reached out to his former mother-in-law and asked if she would move into the house and take care of his daughters. That was how my grandmother was raised. It wasn't as if she wasn't allowed to go next door, but instead of going there as a member of the family, she went there to work. She ironed, scrubbed floors, washed, mended, cooked, and did anything else the stepmother needed done. In other words, she was more of a servant than a daughter to anyone in the house, even her father.

Not only was my great-grandfather maintaining two houses, but allegedly had a third. This was for his mistress. So, as you can see, our-present day issues don't have anything over what was happening in days gone by.

My grandmother went to college for two years and became a teacher. I even have a picture of her standing with her students. If you didn't know it was my grandmother, you would have thought the woman in the picture was Mother. I was amazed at how much they looked alike.

Grandmother's life was on track. She was not only teaching, but she was engaged to be married to a missionary. What a different direction our family would have taken if she had done that. Instead, she met my grandfather and told my aunt, "I just had to have him." She broke her engagement, stopped teaching, and married him.

Once, after my grandfather's death, my aunt and grandmother were talking, and Grandmother shared this story. She told my aunt that her new husband had done unspeakable things to her the night of their wedding. My aunt didn't ask what those things were, and

Grandma didn't say. What he might have done leaves you to wonder, but remember, what might be classified as unspeakable things in their era might be extremely commonplace now.

Very shortly after they were married, Grandpa did one of his disappearing acts and was gone for a long time. They told me a year, but that seems far-fetched. Once I went to see Mother in the care center and asked about her father. She told me he would go away for a long, long time, but then he would come back.

Mother had two younger sisters, born ten and twelve years after she was born. Mother had never really shared anything before that time, and sharing wasn't in her nature. She saw her sisters as more of an intrusion into her misshapen world.

I recognize as an adult that Mother and Grandmother had a codependent, enmeshed relationship. When my grandfather went away on his trips, they had each other. When I was born, I don't feel Mother was as interested in me as she was in her mother. Because of that, we never bonded. As long as they had each other, they were both satisfied.

My grandmother and other enablers kept the secret. She, as the adult, decided to protect herself and her place in the world rather than me, the innocent child. This wasn't unusual then. The man ruled the family, and everyone else followed his rules and protected him so he would protect and provide for them in turn.

After my father's death, we moved in with my grandparents. If I wanted to go somewhere, I'd go into their corner grocery store and ask if it was okay. I can still hear the ring of the cash register as Grandmother popped it open, reached inside, handed me money, and said, "Here's a dollar, honey." Believe me, this was far different from the way it was when my father was alive. Then I was given only a nickel when we went to the store. Those are the only memories I have of my grandmother.

Like many people, she was a good person caught in a bad set of circumstances. She was doing her best, but what may have seemed best for her certainly wasn't going to trickle down in a very good way for me.

Maternal Aunts

Mother had two younger sisters, and she seemed to have a palpable sense of jealousy toward them that lasted throughout their lifetimes.

Shortly before my father died, my younger aunt was married. After that she and her husband never moved. Their children grew up in the same house, attended the same school and church, had the same friends, and lived close to family. I always thought it must have been wonderful to have grown up like that. I hoped our children would have the same opportunity, but that never happened.

Instead we moved from town to town so their father could complete his education. People used to tell me to think about his potential earning power, but I always pointed out that I couldn't pay bills or feed our children on potential; neither would the power company leave the lights on because of it. Between my husband and me, we were able to accomplish all of those things, but it wasn't easy.

My cousins played sports and went to college. Our oldest son was gifted in sports, but we moved around a lot, and it was the local kids picked to play ball. When it came time for college, our sons all screamed "No!" All they'd heard their entire lives was that we needed to move so their dad could continue his education. What about grandchildren? They were able to stay in the same school system where they started. I was happy when at least that part of the trickle-down ended.

It was the aunt who stayed in the same place that I became close to as an adult. After my father's death, she offered to take my brothers and me off Mother's hands. Mother told her she could have either or both of the boys, but she could never have me. That comment let me know I wasn't really anything more than property to my mother. I can only imagine how different my life would have been if had I been allowed the privilege of living with my aunt and uncle.

The Chair Girl

My mother loved me like a chair.
She'd put me down, and I'd stay there.

In that chair I would remain;
I did not move till nighttime came.

Finally in slumber my head would fall;
I'd dream sweet dreams of nothing at all.

When morning came somehow I'd find
I was a chair girl in my mind.

I'd sit so silent and whisper prayers;
She'd soon remember I was still there.

I'd hear a noise and think—at last
She's come for me; my time is past.

I was content to merely stay
Happy to fade and go away.

I don't like being a chair;
Please don't ever put me there.

This aunt and uncle did help raise my brothers, both of whom were older than I. The younger of my brothers was sent to live with them when he was ten. He lived with them for five and a half years. Several months after he was sent back to live with us, he was killed in a single-car accident. When Mother called to tell my aunt he was dead, she told my aunt they didn't know how they were going to pay for his funeral. My aunt and uncle didn't hesitate to bring their boy back to be buried in the family cemetery nearby.

Not long after that, the older of my brothers and my stepfather had a severe altercation. It was agreed that the only person capable of handling my brother would be my uncle. He lived with them several years then went into the military.

Both my aunt and uncle were very loving toward me. After finding out about my childhood, I once asked my uncle why he never disciplined me the same as he had his own children. I was amazed by what he told me. He said he knew that, if he raised his voice, I would crumble into a heap. It was amazing that he was able to tell how fragile I was. He may have been a tough farmer, but when he needed a tender heart, he was more than capable of finding it.

Two other partial memories I have of them had to do with an accident my mother was in shortly after she remarried. I had been staying with my aunt and uncle for the weekend. When a phone call came telling them what had happened, they agreed to keep me until Mother was released from the hospital. I'm supposing they told me Mother had been in an accident—the same words that were probably used when my father was killed. I threw a fit. I'm thinking that in my eleven-year-old mind, the word *accident* meant she wouldn't be coming back.

In those days children weren't allowed in the hospital. Mother was in a coma in the intensive care unit. That was even more reason I wasn't allowed to see her. I cried and screamed for days. I probably didn't believe she was alive, but if she was, I was certainly determined I was going to see her to make sure. Finally they devised a plan so I would calm down. My aunt and uncle took me to the hospital parking lot and pointed to a window on one of the higher stories. They told me that, if I watched, I would be able to see my mother. My aunt left so she could tell the nurses to bring Mother to the window. Now think about this—Mother was in a coma and had severe head trauma. Would they have brought her to the window so she could wave? It was years before I could put the pieces together and decide it hadn't been Mother waving; instead, it was my aunt. I guess I was satisfied with what they had done, so I settled down. To this day I can still see the woman in the window waving, and me thinking it was Mother.

Their home was a wonderful haven for me. I cannot begin to tell you how grateful I have always been that they took time to help me manage part of my life. The only story I remember having to do with my cousins was how I would sit in a tree while they took naps. When they would wake up, they'd come looking for me. They loved it when I would visit, and I thought they were spectacular. The two girls would stand at the bottom of the tree I was perched in and beg me to come down and play. When I tell my cousins that story, it sounds as if I climbed the tree to get away from them. That wasn't true. I was sitting there waiting for them to come outside and find me. As for my boy cousin—what can I say—he peed on my new pajamas one Christmas morning. That's all I remember about him. They had another son, but he was also killed in an accident. When he was killed, it was almost as if they had lost two sons because my brother was as much of a son to them as their biological son.

My mother's other sister lived at her parent's house for only a short time after my dad was killed. She was soon married and moved away. Before she moved, she worked at a local department store. After my father died, our clothing had to be burned. My aunts decided to buy me something nice. This was to be my very first store-bought dress. Everything else had been hand-me-downs or sewn by Mother. Needless to say, I was thrilled. As I stepped down into the bargain basement of the store, I felt like a princess. I found three dresses that were perfect. Because my aunt worked at the store, she was given a discount. Both aunts had agreed beforehand that they would share the cost. I have no idea what happened after that, but by the time I arrived home, I hated the dresses. I always thought that was peculiar since only a few hours earlier I had loved them. Mother was extremely jealous of her sisters. I think between the buying of the dresses and the trip home Mother made it quite clear how undeserving I was. She never seemed to show any pride in whatever I might be able to do or win.

Mother's feeling of not being enough was one she probably carried throughout her own life. Her father was absent for long periods of time. Children have a way of deciding they are in some way responsible for fights, long absences, divorces, and deaths. That's just how it is. Can you see how the trickle down happens?

My Favorite Uncle

I am so grateful for my uncle. He's actually the only remaining living member of Mother's family. Even though he isn't an official blood relative, I always saw him that way. As I said earlier, he was a farmer, and my father was too.

When my aunt became ill, he was spectacular. He was there for her as much as anyone could be. After she died, I wasn't at all sure he would still come to see Mother and me, but he did. I know it was out of respect for my aunt because he wasn't that fond of Mother's behavior toward her sister—his wife.

My uncle remarried a spectacular woman. Her husband passed close to the same time as my aunt. They had known each other in the past, so when their daughters set them up, they found they not only didn't want to remain alone, but had a lot in common. At that point I again became unsure if he would continue to keep up with me, but he did. He shocked me when he said after Mother remarried that he and his wife had been cut out of my life. I find that sad because my uncle had in some ways become a surrogate father, and that separation was like losing my father all over again.

Mother

Without Mother

Without you I could live my life
Without any pain—without any strife.
But without you it's all plain to see
Without any you—there's not any me.

Spring

When I was just a seedling
Within my mother's womb
They said the day that I was born
That spring would come quite soon.

So I waited and I prayed
That life would take me in
And make me feel I'm welcomed
So I could grow to win.

Life I knew would be
Quite difficult for all,
But on the day that I sprang forth
I sprang into my fall.

The trees were bright with colored leaves,
Wind whipped them all about,
But spring it wasn't and I cried
Then heard all nature shout.

"You'll take what we give you
And be glad that you're here.
Now shut up your mouth.
Don't shed any tear."

So I put forth my chin
And walked into the wind,
Hoping that God
Would find me and send …

Spring

The days were all dreary
With torture and pain.
I tried to escape
Again and again.

But life has its way
Of keeping you here,
Of making you stronger
Even though you have fear.

Fear of most all,
Or so it did seem,
I couldn't take life
So I made it a dream.

I'd pause in my slumber
And then I'd begin
To think I heard Robins
And I'd wonder when …

Spring

Fall lasted forever
Or so I did feel
I wondered if
I'd ever feel …

Spring

All of a sudden
The seasons made change.
I was hoping for sunshine
And maybe some rain.

But in came my winter;
I fell to my knees,
But now there was snow
Where once there were leaves.

The wind blew like ice
And froze through my soul.
I felt I would never
Be able or whole.

"Where are my flowers?"
I screamed out in pain.
"I want my life over.
I don't want to remain!"

I kept hoping the ice
Would trickle and melt

So I could live life,
Or so I had felt.

"No more!" I cried.
Your promise you broke!
"You've let all my life
Go up in smoke.

Am I not important?
Don't you really care?
I'm not sure about spring
Can it really be there?"

Then all of a sudden
Birds broke forth in song,
And I found myself growing
Ever so strong.

Then I turned on my heel
And spun myself round,
But you'll never guess
What it was that I found ...

Summer!

Mothers are always the toughest members of the family any child or adult can deal with. Mother's life was complicated multiple times over. Her father was gone for extended periods of time, and therefore she was her mother's entire world. That's a big responsibility for any child.

Because of this, Mother was spoiled and allowed to have her way in almost every situation. When her sisters came along, she wasn't happy. They were only six and eight when my parents decided to get married. By the time I came along they were twelve and fourteen.

My father and mother were eighteen when he told her he was leaving the area. Her choices were to let him go or get married. It was against her mother's wishes, but she had raised her daughter to get her own way, so my parents were married, and now Mother was the ruler of her own home, or at least a want-to-be ruler. My dad had been raised in a staunch German family. There was going to be only one ruler in their home, and it wasn't going to be Mother.

In that day and age, many young people were married far younger than my parents were when they wed. The problem was that Mother had no idea how to be a wife and caretaker of her own home. Thankfully they didn't start a family right away. She was twenty before the older of my brothers was born. He was two and a half when my second brother was born, and I came along a year and a half after that. Dad's name for me was "Tootsie."

Mother hadn't been given homemaking skills because Grandmother did everything. Mother never helped with cooking, cleaning, laundry, or anything else. I'm thinking she may have been asked to do some things, but there was always her old standby behavior she used with her parents and that was to whine, scream, or pout when she wanted her way. That didn't work with my father. It only made him mad.

About a year and a half after I was born, Mother became pregnant for the fourth time. She and my father were having severe marital problems, and the last thing they needed was another child. Even before I found out about my childhood, I knew about the pregnancy, but had been told she lost the baby. You're not going to believe what happened to the baby. Mother said she buried him under a fruit tree in the backyard of the home where we lived when I was two. I'm not sure if Mother named him, but I did—I called him Lucky.

Another story my father's sister told me happened when she went to the hospital to see Mother. She found Mother crying. When she asked what was wrong, Mother told her my father and a friend had been to visit, and he told her they couldn't stay because they had dates. My aunt sent a letter to her parents telling them what Mother had said. Not long after that there was a knock at the door, and when my father answered it, there stood his father.

As soon as the letter reached Dad's parents, his father bought a bus ticket and set out to have a father-to-son talk. It was decided during that conversation that my father and his family had lived in the city long enough, and it was time for him to return to the farm. When Mother was released from the hospital, my father gave her another ultimatum. He was moving back to the country and taking all three children. She could come with us or stay with her parents. Mother agreed to move.

Just because our family moved from the city didn't mean the marriage became better. We moved into a run-down farmhouse near where my paternal grandparents lived. By then Mother was finally on her own when it came to taking care of the house and children. Even though my parents were doing better, the fighting never stopped. Finally Mother told her parents the violence was getting worse. Rather than our family going back to the city, my grandparents and aunts moved to where we were. Shortly after that my parents had another knock-down, drag-out fight, and as soon as my dad went to work, she hightailed it to her parents' house. When my father came to get us, he was greeted at the front gate with a shotgun. I vaguely remember watching from the attic as the standoff took place. After things calmed down, Mother bundled us up and took us back to the home she continued to share with my father.

Not long after things settled down, Mother's family moved back to the city and bought a corner grocery store. Why did they return? My grandmother's sister lived there, and she and her husband were running a small neighborhood grocery store about six blocks away. When another store became available, my grandparents took advantage of the opportunity and bought it. We still lived on the farm, but I remember packages coming in the mail that contained candy and gum. I'm sure there were other things, but I didn't care about that. For a while after my grandparents moved, things in our household became quiet. I don't know if it was because their interference no longer influenced her behavior or if Mother had just given in to the situation.

I remember a game I played with Mother. When she took a nap, she'd tell me she hoped a fairy would sneak in to sweep the floor and wash dishes. I was seven. That was my cue. As soon as I thought she was asleep, I'd rush around doing what I could to prove to mother a fairy had indeed been there. Mother once told me she would wake up before I finished and pretend to be asleep. I still remember pulling a chair to the kitchen sink and washing dishes. I loved doing things that offered me the opportunity to pretend.

The weather was strange the day my father was killed. He had taken my brothers and me to school then dropped Mother off at a neighbors' house. By that time, Mother's cleaning skills had improved, and she found it was a way she could earn money. After dropping everyone off, he drove to town. On the way home, he wasn't paying attention as he approached the railroad crossing. Two men watching from inside the country store saw the whole thing. One said to the other that he didn't think my father saw the train. There was a controversy over whether the train whistle had blown or not as the train approached the crossing.

As soon as he died, the sheriff came to our house and padlocked the doors. Since my father hadn't left a will, Mother wasn't going to inherit anything. The only possessions she was allowed to keep were things my father had mentioned on greeting cards. He wrote things like: "Don't sew me out with your sewing machine" so that was hers. "Don't freeze me out with your freezer." That was hers as well. The only other property she was allowed to keep were a television, a fur coat, and a chaise lounge. Everything else was sold at auction.

I vaguely remember the auction, but only because someone bought my doll's cradle, and I wanted it. I followed the man to his truck and watched as he put my dolly's bed inside. Later I came to realize the state would more than likely have let us to keep our toys. It was Mother who told them it was okay to put our toys in the sale. Our clothes may have been old, ragged, and ill fitting, but, as you will have noticed, our family had a sewing machine, a freezer, a television, a fur coat, and a chaise lounge.

The funeral was held at a church other than the one we attended because our little church wasn't big enough to hold everyone who would be attending. I don't know who delivered his eulogy, but at one point he said my father had gone to hell. That's all took for Mother to run to the front of the church and attempt to climb into the casket. Her family wasn't far behind. They pulled her back again and again. Finally she collapsed. Where were my brothers and I? We were sitting alone in the pew watching the show. I don't remember the funeral. I was told they rushed her to the hospital. As I waited outside the emergency room, I found a long container I suppose was used for flowers. I vaguely remember looking in to see if there was someone inside.

Climb Out, Climb In

Climb out of that casket.
Can't you see
I want you to stay
Here with me?

It's different for him.
His life is gone.
Stay here with me;
We must go on.

But if you do
The things he did,
Go on—climb in
I'll close the lid.

Later I found that, when Mother purchased a gravesite for my father, she purchased six. One was for my father, one was for her, and three were for my brothers and me. Later I thought it might have been appropriate to have buried my baby brother in the last one instead of leaving him in the backyard. It felt creepy to know about the five empty graves next to my father.

Empty Graves

Five empty graves
Open wide
Waiting to take me
Deep inside.

What do you think
It will take
For me to feel
I'm not a mistake?

That I might be
Whole inside,
Perhaps it's only
When I've died.

My father's family tried to take us from Mother because she had no way to support us. Her parents signed papers telling the court they would take full financial responsibility for us, and so it was settled.

My brothers were immediately sent home with Mother's family after the funeral, and I remained behind. The only thing I remember is that, one evening after I had been put to bed, I began coughing and vomited all over the sheets. I can still see Mother bent over the bathtub rinsing out the sheets, scolding me for what I had done. This wasn't an unusual occurrence; since the day I was born I had cried, thrown up, and coughed my way in and out of the hospital.

Even when I was a newborn, Mother would tell me how she hated me, wished I was dead, and that I never should have been born. I think it was partly because I was so sick. I wish I could find a way to excuse what she said. Even if I couldn't understand her words, I still felt her body's tension and filed everything deeply inside to use against myself as I grew up. As you will soon see, her words trickled down into me.

Mother was more or less childfree for the next few years after my father's death. Everyone and no one took turns being in charge.

A little over two years after my father's death, Mother remarried. I was eleven and had been allowed free reign over my life for several years. Having someone not related to me come in and begin to tell me how I was going to live didn't go over well. Worse was the impact it had on my brothers.

Not long after Mother remarried, she was in the accident. As terrible as it sounds, after she was released from the hospital, she could no longer scream, switch, or slap. If she raised her voice or moved too quickly, it made her head ache. Now her techniques of dealing with me changed from screaming to heavier but softer tones of shame, guilt, and fear. Let me remind you this wasn't an unusual way to punish children in the midfifties. Children's memories of these events still hadn't been addressed and wouldn't be for years to come. These forms of discipline I'm sure trickled down into all our lives, not just mine.

After my stepfather finished chiropractic college, our family moved. The younger of my brothers stayed behind. I don't know how long we were there before my stepfather became ill and we had to move back to the area we had just left. This move happened without warning. I came home from school, and Mother told me to pack my clothes because we were leaving. She gave me just enough time to run to the school, leave my books, and empty my locker. There were no good-byes to classmates or friends. One day we lived there, and the next day we were gone. Sometimes I wonder what my schoolmates thought when I simply disappeared. We were back for only three months before we moved again. During one school year we moved three times, and with each move I studied fractions and how to diagram a sentence. This definitely put me behind in the classroom.

I liked the next place we lived. I quickly adapted, hoping to make a life for myself. Mother worked a block away at a corner grocery store. My stepfather and I more or less tolerated each other, and when she was gone, I'd stay away. Things were going smoothly until the younger of my brothers returned to live with us. Shortly after that, he was killed.

When the call came informing us of his death, I answered the phone. Since they wanted to speak to an adult, I gave the phone to my stepfather. His office was in the home, and the rule was that all calls went through him. Within a few minutes after he hung up, I heard Mother screaming. When I ran to see what was happening, I found Mother on the bed with my stepfather holding her down. At first I thought he was hurting her, so I began screaming for him to let go. She finally stopped struggling and asked which son had died. I wasn't used to having this brother around, so his absence basically meant nothing.

This brother had been widely accepted and loved in school, so there was a memorial. I refused to sit with family, but instead sat with the students. I identified more with them than with our family. It was hard to understand why kids were crying. I wanted to tell them it was okay; it was just my brother.

After the memorial the body was transported by hearse. As the vehicle traveled to where the funeral was to be held, my brother's face became distorted because of the lack of active muscles holding his face in a recognizable way. Now his face had to be repaired. The only way this could be done was to put a slight smile on his lips. I followed behind Mother as she lifted the tulle netting to kiss him good-bye, and I saw the smile on his face. That image still remains with me even today.

We stayed put for two more years before we moved again. By now I was used to pulling up stakes and leaving. Moving day was only another day in my life. Again Mother worked full time, and my stepfather stayed home waiting for patients. I still avoided spending time in the home if Mother wasn't there. We long ago had become nothing more than people who happened to live in the same house.

When I was married and moved with my new husband to California, my mother and stepfather were finally rid of me. Even though I would be gone for only three years, Mother gave me an ultimatum regarding my possessions: If I didn't take it with me, it was to be thrown away. I didn't have much, but I guess she needed to wipe out all traces of me. I felt upset and because of this I tossed things I should have kept. One was a letter I had received from President Eisenhower. When I was ten I had written to ask him to settle an argument between a classmate and me as to whether he was a five-star or a forty-five-star general. I think my classmate, when he heard people call Eisenhower a four- or five-star general mistakenly thought they were saying forty-five. He argued with me, and that was all it had taken. When it came time to write a letter to someone as a project in English class, mine was to the president.

President Eisenhower's answer to me was, "Forty-five stars would be a great many stars array indeed." I read his answer to my letter in class. I can only imagine how embarrassed the other student had been. The terrible thing is that Mother sorted through what I had thrown away, found the letter, and kept it. What happened to it? Who knows? I hoped to find the letter when I moved her into our house because it meant quite a lot to me and I'd loved to have shared it with our children, but I highly suspect someone else in the family snagged it.

After my husband was discharged from the military, we moved back to the area so he could continue college. I had already arranged for my mother-in-law to watch our sons when I started back to work. Under no circumstances had I ever expected Mother to babysit or watch our children if we wanted to go somewhere. I hoped she was going to be allowed to enjoy her grandchildren. Instead my stepfather intervened and kept them apart. Every spare moment Mother had, he insisted she spend it with him. Mother and I never chatted on the phone or shopped together; neither did she ever come for a random visit. The only time I saw her was if I went to her house or invited them to mine for a family holiday. I had been issued out of Mother's life when I was eleven, so this didn't seem unusual. She was never really allowed to be the grandmother I hoped she could be, and I missed that for all of us. This was nothing more than another trickle down.

We moved out of the area at one time for three years then decided to move back to our home base. Only a month before we were to return, my stepfather suddenly died. I flew back in order to drive Mother to the place where he was to be buried. After that I took the bus back so I could continue to pack for what I was hoping would be our final move.

After the death of my stepfather, I hoped Mother and I would have the opportunity to form a close relationship. She hadn't ever been in charge of her own life, and she more or less expected me to take over. Instead we taught her what she needed to know so she could take care of herself. If she needed help, we were there, but for the first time in her life she was the ruler of her own destiny.

Please remember that by now the losses in her life were huge. I never saw her grieve after the death of my brother in 1957. She didn't grieve in 2001 when the older of my brothers passed or in 2002 when her sister died. After that came the death of both her dogs and the sale of her house. It wasn't just the death of the home she had shared with her husband, but the death of her independence. Maybe if we could have moved her directly into the apartment, things might have been different. Instead she had to live in the house with us for a year and a half, and that didn't go well.

Did we ever bond or become close? No! After his death in 1982, she replaced my stepfather with painting china and becoming deeply involved in religion. She was a loner thanks to my stepfather, so we were like ships passing in the night. She began writing a book about God after that, and since we didn't really agree on that subject, the distance between us became even wider.

We never did discuss my childhood. Occasionally she asked how things were going, but that was more to be polite rather than to find out how I was doing. I took into consideration her childhood issues and left it at that. At this point things had become distant but stable, but the complications surrounding her move felt almost insurmountable.

I cooked, cleaned, washed laundry, and took her to town and to church. Between being there for our grandson and taking care of Mother, my life disappeared. Did I feel upset? Wouldn't you? What did that do? Without my awareness, my circumstances began bringing childhood issues back into my life. My mother's look, a tone of voice, a behavior toward her grandchildren, or screaming at her dog suddenly became intolerable to me. It took everything within my power to attempt to manage my behavior. Even with all this happening, I still didn't blame her for my childhood, but I was disappointed our relationship never became what I'd hoped it could have been.

After moving mother into her apartment, I eventually hired someone to assist her in taking showers or to take her to the senior center for lunch so I could breathe. I tried taking her with me on trips to town, but she wouldn't leave the car. This meant, if it was too hot or too cold, she needed to stay home. I wanted to be a good daughter and take loving care of her, but that was hard. Who was I upset with? Myself!

After she had been in her apartment for several years, one day while I was gone, Mother sat on her bed, slid down, and ended up on the floor. The phone was nearby, so she dialed the operator and was connected with 911. Paramedics came to get her and took her to the hospital. As soon as we heard what had happened, we headed home. From a distance we saw the ambulance as it pulled away. We drove to the hospital where she was evaluated and then sent home. It was clear that she needed more help than I could provide. After that she lived in a care facility for her final three years. That is a decision I never regretted making. She was close to where we lived, so it was easy for me to visit, help her eat, and bring snacks.

In the care center she became a favorite. She sang and told everyone she was praying for them. Once when they asked her to tell them about her favorite Christmas, she told them that the only gift she received was a potato. They said she told them how hungry she was and how much she loved her gift. I had to smile and tell them she had never been quite that poor when she was a girl. She did tell funny stories that didn't have anything to do with the truth, but that's sometimes true for someone her age. I eventually began to see her age as something that allowed me the grace to filter through my childhood, see her for the damaged child she had been, and put our past behind us.

Stepfather

Mother was the one who brought him into our lives. He was living over my grandparents' store and attending the nearby chiropractic college when they met. He had served in the war and was going to school on the GI Bill. He was thirty-eight and had never married. He may have had it in mind that, since he was an adult male, making himself the head of our family was going to be easy. Our entire family was damaged and broken before he came into the picture, and for him to feel as if he was going to be in charge didn't go over well.

My stepfather was stubborn and bullheaded. Mother was easy to manage because others had been in charge of her entire life. First it was her father, next her mother, then my father, and now it was my stepfather's turn. Mother stepped right into line and tried handing over the reins to her family so he could be in charge. The problem was, they weren't her reins to hand over. The older of my brothers had an explosive anger issue, and my other brother was under the protection of my aunt and uncle. Now as for me, what can I say?

One of the things I heard about him was how he was going to "get us in line." I'm not exactly sure what he meant by "us," but when it came to the boys, I think he bit off more than he could chew. The younger of my brothers had been living with my aunt and uncle and had a great attitude. He came back to live with us for a few weeks, but before long my brothers were fighting, and he went back to live with my aunt and uncle. My stepfather might have fought in the war, but he was about to encounter a completely different kind of enemy.

My stepfather talked about getting us in line, but I was the only one he could discipline. It didn't take long for me to understand that I needed to keep quiet, out of sight, and fly beneath the radar. I was really good at becoming invisible while still in plain sight, but then an abused child finds this tactic quite useful.

At eleven I was whipped by someone, but I don't recall who did it. All I remember is how I looked afterwards. I remember going to school and running into the bathroom stall to look at my injuries. I'd been afraid to do it at home for fear someone would catch me and I'd pay for that too. My backside was black and blue from the bottom of my spine to just above the knees. In 1989 I asked my brother about it, and he said he remembered an argument between Mother and my stepfather about who would discipline me. Thankfully, I think Mother may have tried to stand up for me by telling him I was off limits. At least it put him on notice even though it didn't stop him.

I know if he was home and Mother wasn't I wouldn't go inside. I remember once when Mother was at work and an argument ensued, he grabbed his belt and began to chase me. I ran out the front door with him in hot pursuit. As he followed me with his belt swinging in the air, the minister of their church happened to be in his yard and saw him. As soon as my stepfather saw the minister, he lowered his belt and went back inside the house. I have no idea what might have happened to cause him to be so mad, but he wasn't able to take his frustration out on me that day.

My stepfather was in charge where Mother was concerned. She did as she was told, so most of her free time was spent with him. Later, after his mother passed and I was married and out of the house, he was able to take the money from his mother's estate and build an office. Mother became his office secretary as well as his assistant.

Something I found disappointing was that, after Mother remarried, the visits to see my father's family stopped. The first summer after their marriage, I was allowed to visit my grandmother, but when they came to pick me up, I was told to wait in the car. I didn't know then, but he and Mother were inside telling my grandmother I wouldn't be back and no one in the family was to contact us again. I'm sure he felt that cutting my father's family out of my life meant he was going to take his place. That never happened. This trickle down isn't unusual in a lot of families, especially today. When I was a girl there weren't as many divorces as there are today. Children now have several sets of parents, possibly even on both sides. At least I had to contend with only one stepparent, but he was a doozy.

Brothers

As I mentioned, I had two older brothers. I really don't remember much about them when we were children. When we were small we lived in the city. Shortly after I turned two we moved to the country. We had only each other to play with. Needless to say, since I was small and sickly, I was good entertainment for my brothers.

One of the incidents I remember had to do with my brothers playing cowboys. Their horse was a large fuel tank my father used to fill his truck and farm equipment. The boys were sitting straddled across the fuel tank, and—you guessed it—the nozzle was their gun. As I came out of the house to see what they were doing, I became their target. As soon as I came close enough, they pulled the trigger and fired. Fuel shot out and covered me from head to toe. Needless to say, I began screaming. I remember Mother running out the door of the farmhouse, grabbing a washtub, putting me in it, and filling it with ice-cold water from the well. She quickly began trying to get the fuel out of my eyes and hair. I don't know what happened to the boys when my father came home, but I doubt it was pleasant. As most people of my age remember, belts came off, and whippings were applied.

If I tried to follow the older of my brothers, he would turn around and punch me in the stomach. After I bent over he would take off. The other brother liked to tickle me until I threw up. One hit me on top of my head with a hand-held grass sickle. I have a scar. I don't think it was very deep, but who hits another person on the head with something sharp? Another thing they liked to do was destroy toys. They threw my trike down the hill by the road and wrecked it, took my dolls, and destroyed them. Once they took my favorite rag doll and put her in the lard press so she came out looking like a greasy waffle. Needless to say my dolly went into the garbage.

After my father died, we moved in with my mother's parents. I recall seeing the older of my brothers in the attic crying. I tried to cry, but nothing happened. I don't think I understood what my father should have meant to me. I just went on living my life as if he had never existed.

Since we now lived in the city, there wasn't any way for my brothers to rid themselves of pent-up energy. On the farm there had always been activities to take care of this. Between chores, play, and picking on me, at the end of the day they were ready to settle down. In the city there wasn't anything to do other than to fight. The older of my brothers had a lot of displaced anger—another trickle down.

At one point when the boys were eleven and thirteen, my aunt came to deliver eggs, and she heard the boys fighting. As she ran toward the house to see what happening, both boys ran into the yard. The older of my brothers was holding a loaded rifle. About the same time, the postman was delivering mail. He quickly grabbed the gun from my brother, pulled out the firing pin, and handed both things to my aunt. I don't know how the conversation went between the family members, but it was decided that, if the younger of my brothers wasn't removed, he might be killed. After that my aunt gathered my brother's things and took him home with her. One of the questions I asked my aunt in 1988 was why my bother lived with them and for how long. My aunt and uncle kept my brother with them for five and a half years.

At one point, after Mother remarried, it was decided that, since there was now a father figure in the home, my bother should return to live with us. That didn't last. I don't know how long he was there, but since my stepfather was going to school and working nights cleaning offices, he wasn't there much. Mother was helping at the grocery store during the day and helping clean offices at night, so there wasn't any supervision. I was eleven, one brother was thirteen, and my other brother was fifteen. Needless to say, it didn't take long before they fought. As quickly as he had returned to live with us, he was again sent back to live with my aunt and uncle.

We moved three times after he was sent away. Finally, when my brother was almost sixteen, my mother wanted him to live with us. He lived with us for a short period of time before he was killed in the car accident. My aunt and uncle had instilled in him a good work ethic, so after his return he found a job working at a nearby orchard. He was on his way to pick up his check when the accident happened. Since my brother had a learner's permit and the boy with him had his license, it was legal for my brother to drive. As they drove toward the orchard, they began to follow a farmer in his pickup truck. As my bother began to pass the truck, the farmer, without turning on his signal, began to turn onto a side road. My brother tried to avoid hitting the truck, and instead the car he was driving hit a cement culvert, and the car went into the ditch. My bother cracked his skull on the steering wheel and died instantly.

Funerals

I've seen the face of sorrow.
I've touched the hand of death.
I know that come tomorrow
I'll do what I do best.

I'll find my place and go away
Just like I do.
But funerals aren't just play pretend
They take a part of you.

They take that part and leave you less
But now it is my goal
To fill those voids and heal my wounds
Until I feel quite whole.

In 1989 my father's sister told me that she and my grandmother had attended the memorial for my brother, which was held in 1967. They hadn't come to the house afterwards because they had been told to stay away. My paternal aunt had taken a picture of my bother lying in his casket. The picture she had taken shocked me to the core. Remember how I saw his smiling face as Mother lifted the tulle netting to kiss him good-bye? That smile, to me, told me he was happy to be dead. In the picture my aunt showed me, my brother's smile was missing. His face seemed somber and cold. I immediately went to mother's sister for the explanation. To me, if the smile wasn't there, then maybe he wasn't as happy to be dead.

After my brother was buried and we were home, things became even stormier than before. The older of my brothers and my stepfather were continually having knock-down-drag-out fights, and it was decided my brother would live with my aunt and uncle until he finished high school. I know I must have at least seen injuries, but I don't remember. I didn't know why he was sent away, but by then I didn't care.

At one point after this, Mother and I had a terrible fight. I can't tell you what it was about, but what else is new? The only thing I can think of is that perhaps I asked to live with my aunt. All I remember is as I ran down the stairs, looked up, and she screamed, "I hate you!" I asked my aunt if she knew anything about the argument. At the mention of Mother's words, my aunt paused then asked if she had said anything else. When I told her no she told me that, from the time I was born and for years afterward, my mother's go-to words to me when she felt upset were, "I hate you. I wish you were dead. I wish you were never born." A friend told me my aunt had no right to tell me that, but I was thankful because, from the time I was fourteen until I was forty-eight, those had been the exact words I used to myself when I became upset. I would go to the bathroom mirror and tell the girl in the mirror how I hated her, wished she was dead, and that she never should have been born. It wasn't until my aunt told me what Mother had said that I realized I had been repeating her exact words to myself all those years. See the trickle-down process? Hoping my aunt had heard this only a few times, I asked how often this happened. My aunt said, "If I heard her say it once, I heard her say it hundreds of times." Evidently hearing Mother say "I hate you" triggered something in my subconscious mind that allowed the entire phrase to escape, and I began using her words against myself.

Mind Rape

The words she spoke are locked in my mind
And through it all I often find

The power they have within my brain
Gives me cause to worry because they still remain.

Echoes of words—unkind 'tis true
They were spoken to me—shall I speak them to you?

And now I feel sadness—for you see
Her words became a part of me.

So when you're speaking to your child,
Make your words loving and make them mild,

For words can get all out of shape
And to that child you've caused mind rape.

You rape good feelings and dreams from the mind
When it's too late you might find

That words of anger and words of fear
Remain very close—they always stay near.

As I grew up, when I felt upset, I'd always head for the bathroom to have a face-to-face with the girl in the mirror. My goal was to spew those vicious words at her until I was able to crush her. After I'd use those words, I'd continue by telling her what a stupid, ugly, worthless person she was. I'd stay in front of the mirror and continue degrading her until I could see the girl break. Suddenly there would be this deeply sad look come across her face, and I would know I'd won. I wanted her broken. With my victory, I'd give one last huff, give her an icy-cold stare, turn, and then leave so the girl could think about what I had said.

After the argument that night, I began to pray that God would let me trade places with my dead brother. I reasoned that, because the Bible told the story of Jesus bringing Lazarus back from the dead, it seemed my brother could be brought back too. I asked God to wipe out the memories of my brother's death and take me instead. I told God everyone loved him and no one loved me, so it made sense to bring him back. From 1957 until 1990, I don't think a day went by without me wishing I could be dead like my brother. He seemed happy sporting that smile. I thought he and Lucky (my name for Mother's unborn child) definitely had gotten the best end of the deal, and surely being dead couldn't be as bad as being alive.

Now let me tell you what I know about the older of my brothers. There really isn't much. I do recall one thing that was sexual in nature. It couldn't be classified as childish exploration because my brother was too old for that.

What else do I remember about him when we were children? Nothing! I lived in the same houses as he did from the time I was born until he left in 1957.

One thing that bothers me when I try to remember my family in any of the homes we lived in is that I can't picture them. I see myself doing things, but other than myself, the houses are always empty. You'd think I would remember something that wasn't traumatic, but I didn't. If something wasn't connected to something to do with abuse, it never registered. I'm sure there must have been happiness now and again, but I haven't been able to recall any.

Another thing my brother and I talked about as adults was the dead baby. He was positive he had been sent to bury him. This was something he saw as part of his abuse. I suspected Mother hadn't just lost the baby, but may have aborted it. I asked him where we lived at the time and how old he'd been. Without hesitation he told me it had taken place on the farm, and he was ten. I told him he was mistaken. The baby died before I was two, and my brother was only six. I doubted anyone would have been so callous as to send a child that at age to do that. I told him that, after Mother had been sent to the hospital, the only way to save her life was to perform a hysterectomy. I mentioned he might have buried a pet at ten, but not a baby. He agreed but seemed disappointed.

My brother almost seemed to celebrate all the ugly things that happened in our childhood. It wasn't until I wrote the book *Slow Train Coming* (yet unpublished) that he realized he hadn't been the only one traumatized in the family.

One of the things I told myself I would never do was fill in the blanks with what I thought might have happened. When I began going through my process, I was determined that each piece had to connect to the next. If it didn't, I refused to make up what might have happened between the spaces. If I didn't remember and wanted to find out, I talked to others who might have had a more accurate picture of how things fit. Since my aunts hadn't seen each other for over forty years, they couldn't have concocted something to say. If one aunt told me something, it seemed the other had the same story or the missing pieces. Because of this I was able to build bridges between what happened. I am still in awe at how seamless everything was.

In a four-year period of time, my brother died of leukemia, my mother's sister died of an inoperable tumor, my brother-in-law passed, and then my paternal aunt died and my husband's sister was killed on the way home from visiting us. I hadn't even thought about dealing with one death before the next one was thrust on me.

After my brother's death, when I found out my aunt was dying, my blood pressure bottomed out, and I must have gone into a state of shock. My mind was awhirl with one loss after another, and it took years before I could admit to myself they truly were gone.

Paternal Family

Grandfather

I have only one memory of my paternal grandfather. Once before he died, I was sitting on his lap, and he was drawing butterflies a small blackboard. He died of stomach cancer three months before my father was killed.

I do, however, love the story about him coming to our house after Dad told my hospitalized mother that he and his friend had dates. The idea of this staunch, hard-working farmer getting on the bus and traveling to give his son a "talking to" tickles me even today. Evidently Dad knew my grandfather meant business because it wasn't long afterward that we moved, and I became a little farm girl.

Grandmother

I can't say I really have memories of my paternal grandmother. When I was little and we went to her house, she always gave me a graham cracker with marshmallow crème. On one of my visits after my father's death I can almost see her peering out the window watching me play. For some reason, I was afraid of her. I really wish I knew why. Later I found her to be one of the nicest people you could ever meet. How do I know that? She came to see me when I was pregnant with our third son. She brought our new baby a blanket, and our boys small rubber balls. I hoped to see her after our son was born, but she died before I had a chance. Thoughts of my grandmother and how she had been cheated out of her right to be in our lives saddens me. Just before mother and my stepfather sent me to the car to wait while they talked to her on our last visit, she gave me a small heart necklace with my birthstone. I still have it.

When I graduated from high school, she sent me a handmade quilt. I could see how, over the years, she hadn't forgotten me. One of the things I found as an adult was that my mother continued to keep in contact with her. My question is—if it was okay for her to be in contact with my grandmother, why couldn't I? When I needed my father's family's addresses, who had them? Mother!

Father

Father

Weep not for me for I am gone.
You are my child; you must go on.

For though I die please stay awake.
You are my child for goodness sake.

Miss me not for you will find
I'll live in your heart and in your mind.

I couldn't tell you for sure, but I think I loved my father a lot! When I was born he immediately looked at me and said, "Oh, look. It's a little tootsie." That's what he called me—"Tootsie." I used to sit on his foot while he walked around. When he came back from town with a sack of candy, he'd hold it in the air under a vent, and the boys would run upstairs and grab it. He'd pretend to be mad.

The Christmas before he was killed, he took us to church for the Christmas program. Guess how we got there? He hitched the tractor up to our farm wagon, and off we went. I'm sure we were as excited as any children would be under those circumstances. Instead of coming inside the church he stayed outside, climbed on the roof, stomped around and said, "Ho-ho-ho" while he shook jingle bells. All the children inside thought Santa had arrived, including me. While we delighted in all the happy feelings, we were each given a gift from under a tree. I received a pretty handkerchief and an orange. That may not sound like much, but I thought it was wonderful.

After that we went home where our family loaded into our farm truck and set off for a Christmas with Mother's family. They put blankets in the back of the open truck, which had tall sides, so the boys could sleep. I sat up front where it was warm. While we were driving, I saw a car in front of us with one taillight. I asked my father what it was, and I remember him telling me it was Rudolph. I don't know why Rudolph would have been flying backwards. I was eight, so I'm sure I must have laughed.

When we arrived at my maternal grandparent's house, there was excitement in the air. That night the entire family on mother's side had been invited to one of her cousin's houses for a party.

I hadn't ever been in such a grand house. The floors were carpeted, the furniture was expensive, and all the guests were dressed in their finest. I'm thinking my family members stood out like sore thumbs. Everyone was sent into the basement where the party was to be held. This wasn't anything like any dirt basement I had ever seen. It was every bit as nice as the upstairs. I saw a Christmas tree with presents piled high. I was sure that, among all those gifts, there must be something for my brothers and me.

The tradition was that the first gift was chosen by the hostess. A chair sat near the tree, and the person receiving the gift was supposed to sit in the chair, open his or her gift, and hold it up for everyone to see. After that he or she was to choose another gift, call the name on the tag, and hand it to the recipient. I have to tell you, there were hundreds of gifts to be opened. Each time a present was chosen, I shivered with excitement hoping it might be for me. I felt a sense of disappointment as the pile of gifts began to dwindle.

Finally my name was called, and someone pointed toward me. You can only imagine how excited I was. I'm sure I was smiling from ear to ear as I made my way forward in front of over sixty people and reached for my gift. I sat in the special chair and began to open the present. After the paper came off, I opened the box. Inside I found a huge white pair of women's underpants. Of course someone in the group yelled, "Hold it up! Let's see what you got!" I don't know what I did. I probably just quickly chose a present and called someone else to come open the next gift.

Over and over names were called, and my brothers and I watched as all our cousins played with the multiple things they had received. My mother's cousin made her way to where the children were playing and then left the room. Finally, with only a few things left, my name was called again. I was less excited this time as I went toward the head of the room, sat in the chair and received my present. This time it wasn't a pair of women's panties, but a colored pencil color-by-number set. The thing is, I had seen someone take the gift from one of the other children and then leave the room. When she came back, she was carrying the gift they said was meant for me. I'm not sure if my brothers received anything or not. You would have thought when they realized we would be there that someone would have remembered to put something under the tree. I was eight. My brothers were ten and twelve. I have grandchildren that age now, and I can only imagine how they might feel if something like that happened. Even now when I recount the story I feel bad for that little girl.

When I began writing psychological stories, I wrote one titled "They Never Called Me Mary." You see, I wasn't the only one with that name because I was named after my maternal grandmother. No one in the family ever called me Mary; instead, I was known only as Mary

Ann. I firmly believe it had been my grandfather who put the first gift under the tree intending it as a joke on my grandmother. I believe that, instead of calling her name, he felt it would be funnier if the panties were given to me. The reason I think it was him is that he was more than capable of pulling that kind of meanness. I wonder how my parents felt when that happened. My father was probably not in the room, but I'm sure Mother was. Isn't that a mean thing to do? My grandfather was a pedophile, so doing something like that wouldn't have bothered him at all.

That was our last Christmas with my father. It was also the last year Santa was part of my fantasy. Before Christmas, Mother caught me playing with a doll and the clothes she had sewn before Santa had a chance to deliver them. Oh, well, we all had to find out somehow, didn't we?

My father had visions of doing well in life. That's why we had the television in 1950, and mother had a fur coat. He was hard working. Besides farming for himself, he farmed for his parents and for a neighbor known as the squire. He also worked grading roads and welding. I remember going into the area where he was working and being told not to look at the light from the welder.

Shortly before he was killed, he and one of my uncles slaughtered pigs. Someone called me over and put a pig's eye in my hand. I thought it was funny. I remember it looking at me as I rolled it around in my hand.

I told you earlier about my father taking us to school and Mother to work for someone while he drove to town. One thing I haven't told you is that he had a bad habit. He loved to race trains. When he saw one coming, he would step on the gas so he could cross the tracks before the train arrived. I'm not sure he was racing the train the day he was killed or not. Someone in the feed store nearby remarked they didn't think he'd seen it. My aunt told me a story about how he had taken her on a motorcycle ride when she was in her teens and he'd pulled that stunt. She said they could feel the wind from the train as it whizzed behind them, blaring its horn.

Evidently, according to my father's sister, shortly before he was killed, he told them he was planning to divorce Mother. His plan was to take Mother to visit her family, and while she was there, pick up the woman he had told Mother about and leave. His plan was to take my brothers and me. Before he had a chance to carry out his plan, he was killed.

Now I'll tell you why I think I might have heard gunshots once I started to examine my childhood, because they connect to my father.

Story one: It was nighttime, and my brothers were upstairs trying to sleep when they heard a rat gnawing in the attic. They complained to my father, and he came upstairs with his shotgun. He aimed the gun and shot through the ceiling. Not only did he kill the rat, but he blew a hole through the roof. The next day he and his brother had to fix the holes left from the blast.

Story two: The next story has to do with me trying to bring home the cows when I was seven. My parents had all our family over for a meal. Dad was well known for making homemade ice cream. As he watched over the freezer, I decided it was time to bring in the cows. To do this I had to drive them across a little creek a short way from our house. I made it across the water one way fine, but when I started driving the cows across, they disturbed a nest of water moccasins. By the time I was ready to cross, there were six or seven poisonous snakes swimming around. I could see the house, so I began to scream. I don't know how long it took them to hear me, but before long my father came on the tractor to get me. It didn't take him long to see why I was upset. The next day he went to the creek and began shooting snakes until there weren't any left.

Story three: I am also thinking that, when it came time to butcher hogs, my father probably shot them. I don't know for sure if he did, but it makes sense.

All I can tell you is that, after I realized my childhood was less than perfect, I began to have dreams involving gunshots. I'd wake up counting them. I don't know if it was one of the incidents I've mentioned so far or if there had been something else.

Another remnant of a story I remember about my father and me has to do with me going with him when he went to chop wood for our stoves. I remember standing in the wagon, seeing his axe lying on the bed of the wagon, picking it up, and trying to hand it to him. I can still see my father's hand reaching out to take it from me. The wagon was moving, so as I tried to hand him the axe, it came down on my right leg—not once, but twice. It hit once on the front of my leg and then again on the side. As I grew up, I felt embarrassed by the scars when I went to the pool or wore shorts. I wasn't taken to the hospital to have my leg sewn up; that's why I have scars. I have another big one on the back at the top of my left leg, but I have no idea how it happened.

When my father died, he didn't leave a will. I guess he was of the mind he would live forever. When it comes to the slips of stories that I carried with me, you can see most of them were traumatic, and I was screaming. There were gaps in some of them, but I was able to find someone that knew just how things fit together. It was amazing to watch as the abusive and traumatic things continued to trickle into every part of my life and mind.

Uncles, Aunts, and Cousins

I have only one childhood memory of my favorite aunt on my father's side. It was my seventh birthday, and Mother had a group of women from church at our house. I was sitting in a small tree looking at clouds. My aunt drove up, stepped out of her car, and said, "Happy birthday!" I didn't know it was my birthday. Mother had forgotten. When I took my present inside and opened it, I found a doll. All the ladies wished me happy birthday, and then I held my skirt open, and they gave me money. That's the only birthday I remember.

I still ask myself, "Where did the nicer memories of my childhood go?" Was it really necessary that I forget everything that happened in my life? I wish I could remember something that wasn't attached to something traumatic. And when I do remember something traumatic, why do I have only tiny pieces? I would have thought I wouldn't have retained any of it. Then again, if I hadn't kept those small random slips, I never would have known what questions to ask my aunts.

The last time I remember seeing this aunt had to do with my birthday in 1949, so when I first wrote to her in 1989, I wasn't sure how she would react. I actually wrote to all of Dad's siblings who were still living. Who had their addresses? Mother! She had continued to correspond with them after Dad's death but never once shared any of it with me. I feel I had a right to have been given the opportunity to know my father's family.

I wrote to two aunts and two uncles. One by one I began hearing from all but one aunt. Usually the letters started out with how happy they were to hear from me. When my husband and I visited, we stayed with the aunt who had taken care of me when mother was in the hospital. When we met her, she had the biggest smile on her face. I felt I had loved her as a child, and now as an adult I instantly fell in love with her all over again. She was a spectacular woman.

One of the questions I wanted to ask her had to do with a thought I had as a child shortly before my father was killed. I had casually mentioned this thought to Mother, and without missing a beat she told me something that shocked me to the core. I told her, "I was standing at the top of the stairs, and someone was there. I hated that person and wanted that person to go home and never come back. Instead, my father died and we moved away." All of a sudden Mother told me, "Oh, I know what you're talking about." That really surprised me because Mother hadn't ever tried to help with my memories. For her to volunteer information caught me off guard. What she told me was more shocking than I could ever have imagined.

What Mother said went screaming around in my skull as if the children in me had been scalded with hot water. I had no recognition of the actual event, but the puzzle piece fit exactly into what I remembered thinking and feeling about wanting this person to go away and never come back.

It seems a man and his son had come for a visit. My brothers and I were upstairs with the son who was near our age. Mother thought we were being too quiet so she opened the door leading up the stairs and saw that the boy was ready to do something sexual to my brother. Mother looked at them and said, "You'd better stop that right now."

As I said, I was shocked. I tried to stay calm because I knew if I overreacted Mother would shut down. "What did you do?" I asked. To me, what she did was unimaginable. She closed the door, leaving the four of us behind. I could only imagine what I might have done if something like that happened to one of our sons. I'd have been in the middle of that situation at the drop of a hat. Instead, she walked away.

Again, without wanting to shut her down, I asked, "How often did these people come to our house?"

"Oh", she told me, "they came all the time."

I'm sure the boy was more than likely attempting to do something he had experienced himself. I've read that, when children do something like that at a young age, it is their way of trying to let someone know there's something wrong in their world. It made me wonder if this had been happening before. Even viewing something like this can be classified as sexually abusive. My question would be, did he target only the boys, or was I involved at some point? I was seven.

Since my aunt knew these people, I ask if the man or the boy could have been sexually abusive. Her face turned beet red, and she nodded her head yes. It was important that I had been able to recall my thoughts because it led to a conversation I could never have imagined. Not only did she tell me the truth, but from that point on I knew she was going to be as honest as possible when she answered my questions.

I went to see her quite often over the next few years. She knew where all the bodies were buried—literally! She knew the location of every out-of-the-way country and family cemetery. It was because of her that I was able to find my great-great-great maternal grandparents. They were all nestled closely together in a cemetery down a back country lane known only by the local residents.

Before I went to see her the first time, I had already started writing psychological stories. I mentioned one to her I had titled "The Infant and the Bath." Again, as in the case with Mother, when I told her about this strange story, she began to recount something that had happened to me when I was a baby.

When Mother was in the hospital, my aunt was sent to take care of us. When it came time for me to take a bath, she said I screamed and refused to sit in the tub. Finally she saw a small wooden chair in the bathroom. She put it in the bathtub and then sat me on it. She said I was okay with taking a bath, but wouldn't sit in the water. She carefully soaped me then poured a glass of clean water over me. In my story, the infant was being sexually molested while being given a bath. That, along with the fact that I wouldn't sit in the bathtub as a child, makes me wonder if the psychological story hadn't been about me. It's one of those things I'll never know. What I thought I was expressing in the story was how easy it can be to molest a child in what should be a perfectly innocent circumstance. I don't know I that I ever wrote a psychological story that didn't have a seed of truth in it for me.

I never knew what part was about me until something would catch in my breath as I read it out loud. The catch was my truth.

One of the neat things about meeting this aunt was how much we were alike. I always had a very different way of behaving than anyone in the family. Now it was apparent there was more of my father's family in me than I had ever imagined. I liked that!

When families break up, children too many times are treated like pawns. They don't have any say about who they are and aren't going to be allowed to visit. Instead of sharing the children, family members begin using them like bargaining chips: if you want to see them, you have to do this or that. I'm a child from the past telling you that children need to know their roots. I remember telling Mother how what she had done was akin to cutting me in pieces and then asking me to live without the missing parts. This trickles down as well. Sometimes generation after generation of people use children in order to maintain the upper hand. After my father was killed, his family petitioned to take care of us so we could be kept in the area. As I said, Mother's family signed papers stating they would be responsible for our financial well-being. I think we would have been better off living with someone in my father's family. I know the family I would have been sent to live with. The husband and wife were fun, loving, and warm. They had two children. Their girl was a few years older than I, and their son a few years older than my older brother.

I have another snake memory. Once, before my father was killed, I stuck my hand in a chicken's nest to gather eggs, but instead I grabbed a blacksnake. When I screamed, someone came to my rescue and stabbed the snake with a pitchfork. It was the older boy. It would have been a wonderful family to have grown up in. I wouldn't have been moved around and probably would have lived in the same place from the time I was eight until I was old enough to go to college or get married. This was the aunt and uncle who brought my grandmother to see me. They stayed for only a few hours and then headed home. It must have been exhausting for my grandmother to have ridden that far at eighty-one, but she told them she wanted to see me one last time before she died. Within a year she was gone.

I met lots of cousins when I went back to visit in 1990. I actually remembered them from when I had been allowed to visit during the summer. They were warm and welcoming. I don't think I met a single person in my father's family I didn't like.

That's all I can tell you about my father and his family. They were quiet, hard-working Christian people and truly seemed to want only what was best for us. So many times families are separated by death, divorce, or family drama, and the ones paying the price are the children.

My Chosen Family

My Husband

Before I write about myself, let me explain the dynamics of my husband's trickle-down past. I'm doing this because of the way he compared his mother and me.

His mother was married twice, so when my husband was born, he had a half-sister who was thirteen years older. Both his sister and his mother doted on him. They told me a story about him. He was three and hadn't yet started to talk. If he wanted something, he merely tapped his finger on something solid then pointed his finger. That was meant to show them he wanted something. He would point, and they'd ask about various things in the area he indicated. When they came to what he wanted, he'd tap his finger again and that meant they'd found the correct item.

One day he was playing on the porch while his mother was doing laundry. Because he wasn't paying attention, he got too close to the edge of the porch and began to fall. His mother reached over to grab his arm, and instead grabbed him by the hair. After she pulled him back onto the porch, he indignantly looked at her and said, "Let go of that. It's attached to my head." She said she could hardly keep from laughing. "I thought you couldn't talk," she said to him. Without missing a beat he looked at her and said, "I didn't have anything to say."

Four years after his birth, his younger sister was born. My husband's mother thought the sun, moon, and stars circled around her children. No one was ever good enough for either of them, and that was especially true for me.

My husband's dad adored him. He hadn't been married before, so having a son meant everything to him. He was one hard-working man. One of the things his family would do was buy a run-down house, live in it while they remodeled, sell it, and move on to the next run-down house.

During my husband's teen years, his father was in a work-related accident and was put on disability. I met his father for the first time several years after this happened. Even disabled his father could work the pants of most able-bodied men. He once told me that the minute he stopped working he'd stove up and die. (That meant his joints and body would become stiff and sore).

Because my husband's mother was taking care of not only her daughter, but several grandchildren, it was next to impossible for her to work. Instead, at the age of sixteen, my husband started working a man's job at a man's salary. He would go to school during the day and then head to his full-time job. When he was paid, he would hand his check to his mother so she could pay bills. After bills were paid, she would give him money for personal expenses.

As I said before, we started going together a short time after graduation from high school. He started college and then decided to join the military. We were engaged for a month before he left. I tried everything I knew to get his mother to like me. Her hands were still full raising her daughter and grandchildren, so she wasn't interested. When we were married, I'm not even sure she came to the wedding. His dad gave us twenty dollars, which to them was more like a hundred.

I turned twenty a month and a half after we were married. My husband's mother sent a card but cut out the birthday wishes. Shortly after that she sent me a letter telling me how terrible it was that I was keeping her son from writing. My husband caught the letter before I saw it and told her he was a big boy, and I wasn't the one keeping him from writing. I found out later that she was upset because, until we were married, he had been sending his checks to her. Once we were married, we needed his earnings for our own expenses. I had no idea what I had done to upset her.

Now you can see my husband's own trickle-down problems with his mother. She had always been in charge of his life, and she saw me as a threat. Once we were married and he started going to college, he wanted to do all those things his mother never let him do. The only person standing in his way was me. Even though I wasn't demanding, in his mind, his mother and I were the same. For twenty years he hadn't been able to let go of trying to defy the woman who had originally ruled his life—his mother.

Unknowingly, I had taken the place of his mother in his mind, and that explained a lot about how his behavior changed toward me after we came to recognize my childhood issues. In many ways, the trauma from my childhood followed me into our marriage, and after seven years of a somewhat good marriage, things became every bit as traumatic as my childhood. It was plain to see how the destructiveness of my childhood continued as it began to trickle down into the next generation.

Our Sons

We raised four sons. They are grown now and have their own families. Personality wise they are spectacular. Yes, they have had their issues growing up, and some of them are still working to change any trickle down left from their childhoods. The main thing is that they never stopped growing and changing. My husband and I tried to set a good example, especially after we learned about my childhood. We held ourselves together both individually and as a married couple. Even when there was an obstacle to overcome, ever since 1988 we met the challenges head on and used our own past behaviors to point out not only where we went off the tracks but also how we were able to regain balance. We both love our sons and have faith that, even though we haven't been able to achieve the perfect family example, we set our own. Ours is far more realistic.

I'm not going to go into detail about our sons' problems but only into how my trickle down played into their lives. From the beginning they never saw me as different. I was the only mother they knew, and when I would change behaviors or go from one reality to another, they never paid attention.

Our oldest was able to read my moods wonderfully and sometimes gathered his brothers and pointed out how they needed to help more and not be so rambunctious. When I first became aware of my childhood, I told them about it, and they've been supportive in the way I've handled things. They all assured me they knew I'd never do anything to hurt them and told me I have been a great mother. Sometimes they tell me things about their past antics, and if I don't remember what they might be talking about, I shake my head. I tell them that, if they survived, I'm not interested to hear about their mischief. All four of our sons love us and aren't about to change their minds no matter what I might say in this book. Writing about what happened has come to be something they expect of me. I've shared many of my healing tactics with them as I've changed. I taught them coping techniques before I even knew I had any. They do the same cutting apart of their situations in order to understand what is happening the same way I always did, and they are quite good at it. It seems funny to me that, even though my realities were rather unique, my children are all able to come in and play in both my worlds as if it was their choice.

Yes, they had issues directly connected to what happened to me, but my husband and I have never stopped helping them in any reasonable way possible. I think of what we do as an investment in who they are and who they are still becoming. I have all the confidence in the world that in years to come the negative things I've learned about my childhood are going to have a positive impact in all their lives.

I promise myself that, if I'm able to make a success of this book, I will help reconstruct their lives. I'm not talking about handing them cash as if I'm ashamed of what happened and I owe them something. I'm talking about helping them enlarge their futures in whatever way might suit them best. This means going back to school, opening their own businesses, or whatever else they feel might benefit their lives. Since we have been able to clear out the rubble of my trickle-down past, we have all seen what a strong foundation my husband and I placed there. What a joy it has been to see that, even if I failed myself, I was always trying to make sure I didn't fail them.

Grandchildren

As for our grandchildren, there isn't one that hasn't heard about my past. I've worked on my childhood issues from the time our oldest granddaughters were two and three. Along with the other four, they accepted me as I am and seem to be proud to be part of our family. I've tried to teach them what I've learned so they have the tools for the best futures possible, which is exactly what any parent or grandparent wants.

My husband and I were privileged to raise our oldest grandson. When his father temporarily lost his way, we stepped in. We even went so far as to buy a mobile home and place it on the property so his dad could be part of his life on a daily basis. The investment we made in our son and grandson paid off.

Our youngest son still struggles to reconstruct his foundation. Since he was the youngest, his was less solid. When he was a newborn, his dad was both working full time and finishing college. He worked tirelessly to make sure I could be home for the boys. My husband and I were young, poor, and ill equipped to handle the stress this placed on us. Our youngest was four when his father started medical school. When we moved, my own foundation became less solid, which wasn't good for any of our children. I was working full time and being both mother and father to four rambunctious but fantastic young boys. My support system disappeared along with the safety of my junky house in the country. I no longer had family, friends, or a church willing to help hold me up, so I began to lose my strength, and sometimes, I think, my mind.

The effect of my husband's medical school experience on our sons is the one thing my husband says he regrets. We survived, and since he found out about my childhood, he stepped up and became a leader for not only me but for all of our sons. He has worked tirelessly with them to help each one find his center. Every day our sons gain strength and are thankful to have his help.

As for our grandson, who is now twenty-five, in many ways we see him as our fifth son. He is fantastic and has been a good example for his two younger brothers, who are now eighteen and twelve and who both work hard at emulating him. Our oldest granddaughter has already started working on past issues. Since she and her sister were two and three when I started finding out about my childhood, I wasn't able to help when they were little the way I could help now, but over the past few years she has stepped up to the plate and taken a swing at her own childhood past due to her dad's trickle down and is knocking it out of the ballpark. I'm really hoping that, when the time comes for me to help my family regroup, she will finish college and become a psychologist. Her ability to help others, including her own father, is astounding. My youngest granddaughter, at seventeen, refers to me as her rare edition—a well-worn, treasured, one-of-a-kind book. Since we both love reading, I find this to be the highest compliment anyone could ever pay me.

Friends

Being my friend, I'm sure, can be both off-putting and interesting. I always tell people, "I'm a big pill to swallow." By that I mean that all my childhood coping skills, along with my openness about my childhood, can be intimidating. When I change the subjects, they roll with it. When I talk about my childhood, they honor my right to do so.

I have found I need to be careful about those I allow to be close to me. I have the tendency to be over inclusive and at times say more than I need to. It is a pain in the neck to constantly have to monitor myself, so I maintain both my balance and my boundaries.

My personality is such that I come across to most people in a reasonable way. It is important to me to maintain a sense of both truth and honor about my story. It isn't about "Hey! Look at me! Look at all the terrible things I've endured. Don't you feel sorry for me? Look at these terrible people and what they've done to destroy my life."

Hopefully my story has a higher sense of honor than that. Many of the people who changed my life did so without knowing how devastating their behavior would be. One of the things I dislike is telling my story and seeing a look of sympathy. I want to tell them it's okay—I'm okay. I survived. And, besides, I don't remember what happened. I'm not upset with people from my past, but I do find it upsetting to know similar things are still happening to other children, and they are still being hurt. My friends understand my message and support it. Those who have a problem with my behavior drift away, which is fine with me because I'm not going to stop until I succeed in getting my information to the reading public.

I have found it is necessary to constantly examine friendships. I find there seem to be four types: 1) Business: They are cool and cordial. It is your responsibility to resist overreaching and remember how you connect and why. There are some with whom you have a professional relationship who eventually turn into friends. 2) Casual: Those who are friendly but may not be actual friends. In this area there can be pretenders. These people seek information and drama and might like to find a way into your life so they can poke around. That doesn't mean a relationship can't develop into a friendship; it just means you should remain cautious. 3) Internet: I don't worry about this because I'm not into that. I've been told that Internet relationships can be dangerous simply because there can be not only pretenders but predators. Proceed with caution. 4) True friends: They stand by no matter what and tell you the truth as they see it in a loving and honorable way. They are as valuable as gold, so invest!

I once had a relationship with someone I felt was a treasured part of my life. I believed in our friendship and loved her with all my heart. It is bad enough if someone in your family betrays you, but to be betrayed by someone you truly love and care about is devastating. Believe it or not, I actually went to see a therapist so I could understand what happened. Since this therapist was new to my story, it didn't work out the way I hoped. I did the next best thing. I went to talk to the man who was doing my therapeutic bodywork. To me he represents the role of a true friend. He had been with me from the very start and knew not only my story, but how I thought and felt. I paid him for a full session, not to work on my body but on my mind. There is a strong correlation between the two, and since we shared the same sense of honor and trust, I believed him to be a better fit.

What happened was funny because we had our own temporary miscommunication, and it turned out to be the answer I needed. We were talking about my progress when he mentioned an author he felt I might want to check out. He said it was "wobble" or something like that. I later found the man's name was Wallace D. Wattles. Anyway, I went home to think about our conversation, and suddenly I was mysteriously drawn into writing a poem which seemed to mysteriously answer my question.

The Bicycle

I was riding my bike down the path of life
Piled high with the stress that I feel,
Peddling fast to try to catch up,
Watching the spokes of my wheel.

Around and around and around they go
Moving me forward in time,
But alas it seems I can never put down
The burden I claimed as mine.

When I was small—my bike was too.
I loved to go out and ride.
Back then it was easy and fast I would go
Never once breaking my stride.

I started on four wheels—the extras were small.
They kept me steady and straight.
"I'm flying," I'd scream as I went faster than fast.
The wind felt warm on my face.

Over the years I struggled with life
Just waiting my turn to go.
Training wheels which once were a must
Were making me move too slow.

So I made the leap into the unknown
As all good travelers do.
I took off the spares and went on my way
Under me now there were two.

Now with two where four once held me fast
Again I felt my life filled with glee.
Travel it seemed went quite well for a while
I was fast on my way to be free.

This change felt good. I knew I was right
In changing my mode of success.
I was pumping through life as fast as I could
Until I hit the hole of distress.

I stood on the pedals and forced my way forward
Even though I felt heavy and slow.
I was riding the bike as well as I could
But now it would no longer go.

It wasn't 'till then that I spoke to a friend
And told him my pain and distress
"I've come so far," I heard myself say
"I've really given my best,

But I can peddle no more, can you open a door
And show me the way out of here?
I've done everything, I've gone everywhere
I even learned how to change gear.

I can ride no farther. I'm tired and I'm sore.
I'd like to give up if I may."
"No you can't," he proclaimed. "You've traveled so far.
Now I have something to say.

When you first started riding you wobbled.
You fell now and then I would guess.
Why would you quit? Why would you stop?
When you're finally so close to success?"

A light flickered on in my brain
With a thought I hadn't thought of at all.
"I know what's the matter, and you won't believe,
All that's wrong is my bike is too small!"

In my mind I traded that bike
For one that was shiny and new.
I got on that bike and started to ride
And behold on that bike I just flew.

I'd been working too hard to change my life
Still carrying my troubles and woes,
But look at me now after leaving it all.
Watch how fast I can go.

I'd been pumping too hard with burdens piled high.
Now I'm coasting and enjoying the view.
I'll never again ride a bike that's too small.
If you want it, I'll give it to you.

My hope for this life is to clear the way
Down a path that is happy and free.
Now let me ask one simple thing,
"Do you want to go riding with me?"

Can you see how I was in both worlds at one time? I didn't want to give up what I felt was a perfect relationship, but at the same time, I knew our dynamics had changed in such a way I needed to grieve for what I thought I lost and leave it behind. The following poem describes that journey. One of the things I will forever emphasize is the need to grieve. Dying isn't the only thing we need to grieve over. The death of a relationship, behavior, or idea also might need to be recognized and grieved for when change occurs. This was hard for me to do, but after I did, my ride became much smoother.

Good-bye

Once we were friends,
Or so I did feel.
It was an illusion,
Not really real.

Like the bird in the poem
I set your soul free,
And it didn't come back
Ever to me.

Then I thought,
Maybe we could relate,
But that too was wrong.
It was a debate.

I'll miss you forever.
To me it was true.
For all those long years
Our relationship grew.

But now I feel empty,
So what should I do?
I'll love you in spite
Of whatever you do.

Now I know
Since we've grown apart,
I'll treasure the memory
You left in my heart.

This poem is about someone I met later who threw me temporarily off balance. Once I realized how I was being tested, I moved on.

Life's Test

When someone comes into my life
I do my very best
And try and remind myself
That everyone's a test.

Some come into our lives
To spread joy and peace,
And when that miracle happens,
I feel a great relief.

I know with all our differences
We may not all agree,
But that's how I continue
To remain true to me.

People in my life
Can sometimes come and go,
But I try to remember
No one is my foe.

I'll always continue on in life
No matter who you are,
But when someone breaks my heart
It leaves a tiny scar.

That's when I remind myself
That they are just a test.
I'll let them remain a while,
But they are just my guest.

I must complete my journey
Or live through it again,
For those are the rules in life
If ever I'm to win.

It seems your presence in my life
Is not for my better good.
Instead I'd like to run away.
I really wish I could.

The trouble with that plan
We all could agree:
The only way to do it
Is to run away from me.

I live within this life
Every single day,
But when some people come along
I just don't want to play.

So I will spend time with you,
But do your very best
Not to muddle up my life
So I can pass life's test.

CHAPTER THREE

Taking a Personal Look into My Life

Who was I?

The Happy Girl

When I look at the Happy Girl
What am I to say?
To me she always seemed
To follow her own way.

The Insane Girl didn't like
What was in her mind,
So she did what she could do
her peace within to find.

The Psychologist Girl
Tried hard to obtain
A quality of life
In helping her feel sane.

The Curious Girl knew
Deep in her heart
She should have had happiness
Right from the start.

The Sad Girl disappeared.
I don't know where she went.
I hope she never finds a way
Since off with her I sent.

The Hopeful Girl never stopped
Pushing into life.
She never saw her ending
No matter what her strife.

The Determined Girl couldn't quit.
It wasn't in her core.
It wasn't in her nature
Not to open every door.

The Friendly Girl was sure
That she could convince
Others to open up their lives.
It really made good sense.

The Spiritual Girl found her way
By listening to herself,
By questioning every answer,
Reading books on every shelf.

The Chameleon Girl no longer hid
What was lurking in her brain.
She had nothing more to lose
And everything to gain.

The Smiling Girl feels content
Every single day.
And now I am quite positive
I'll always be this way!

Word Salad

I recently came across words I hadn't considered might be associated with childhood behaviors, but they definitely were able to show how and why I became the person I am now.

The word *independent* refers to someone free from authority, control, or influence of others. That person might be described as self-governing. Whereas the word *indifferent* is about being impartial or neutral and showing no response. Both describe me.

Even on the farm, before my father was killed, I was a loner. My brothers had each other and weren't interested in me. Mother was doing "mother things," so I found my own forms of entertainment. Remember earlier how I explained that I began to talk about something known to me as my "internal family"? I wonder if they were part of my earlier years or if they came later. I don't think they fit into that category of invisible friends; neither did they fit into the category of split personalities. Later I'll explain how I may have enlarged their importance so they could slip through the cracks and into various places in my mind so I could remain safe. Maybe I did it so I wouldn't be alone. I do know I forced them to carry each abuse as it happened.

I was an extremely *independent* child. I made my boundaries appear soft so I could slide into the world of others without being noticed. I never met a stranger I wasn't willing to temporarily allow into my circle. At the same time, something in me was like a prickly porcupine ready to throw quills if I sensed danger. My best defense was a method through which I could leave my body, go into my mind, and disappear. My body became vulnerable, but my mind—let's just say it was beyond not only the reach of others, but mine as well.

In today's world, I stop thoughts before they become behavior. I still easily drop myself into random conversations with strangers, but this enables me to meet interesting people. This behavior not only has a name but a diagnosis. It is called *overinclusiveness*.

Independence was good because it made me strong. I was also a curious child and felt frightened of nothing and everything all at once. As an adult I recognize that there have multiple times when this behavior could have caused serious problems.

The same seems to apply to the word *indifferent*. I cared, but I didn't care. This isn't an unusual behavior for an abused child. I had an entire circus of things I was attempting to do without caring about what kind of consequence I might encounter.

When it came to people dying, I was indifferent. That's another behavior used by abused or neglected children. Another word is *disengaged*. This is how I viewed people who were causing harm to my psyche. I distanced my emotions so I didn't feel anything about them or what they were doing. The problem with this behavior is that I cut myself away from others. Is it hard to live this way? Yes and no. Yes because I had to be constantly be on guard, and that takes energy. No because I not only cut myself away, but off.

My mother is a prime example of someone caught in her own world. She never allowed herself to grieve for anyone or anything after the death of my brother in 1956. I'm thinking she provided me with a prime example of how to behave. The only difference is that she lived in only one world, and I lived in two. She never experienced an internal family because she had her mother and I didn't have mine.

When it comes to being *defiant*, I wasn't about to remain frozen in place once I found out about my childhood. Even as a young child, I was defiant but in a good way. As for *determined*, I had more than a sufficient supply of determination. It almost seemed to be cemented into my brain that I had to change no matter how hard it might be. This is also something I did as a child. I recognized early in my process how *driven* I was to find my truth. It felt like a fury in my brain. In many ways I saw this as a bad thing because I was so unrelenting. I was thankful when I was able to see it change into a softer, easier way. Finally I began to feel more *directed*, as if I was following a GPS system rather than an outdated roadmap. At this point, I was able to lean back and trust in whatever message I was being given. It was a satellite view. By this time I taught myself to change the word *control* to *manage*. This not only worked great but it felt better too.

Original Pain

There are no tears inside of me
As I bow my head and cry.
I am so glad I'm living,
Yet deep inside I die.

When someone says, "I hate you"
I assume that I am bad.
Then I think of what's been said
And become instead quite sad.

I tell myself that I am good.
I am so nice you see.
But when you tell me I am bad,
It makes a dichotomy.

Bad/Good—Hate/Love—Death/Life
So what! They're all the same
It doesn't matter just what's right.
It's how you play the game.

Games are fine if you're a child
And there is no loss or gain,
But when you're grown and play again,
It can drive the mind insane.

I'm not insane—I just forgot
Those things they called my life.
Now tell my body to be still
Or we'll have to live it twice.

It was hard enough the first time.
What would I have to gain?
They tell me I have to remember
But only the original pain!

"Original Pain? My God!" I cried.
"It sounds terrible to my ears!
I won't! I can't! I'll die!" I say.
"Touch those original fears!"

If there was another way—I would,
But I must go down to be well
So I comfort my child and take her hand
Into a journey through hell.

I'm not quite sure what we'll find in there
In this thing I call my mind.
The answers I hope will be there,
What I'm searching for to find.

"What are you searching for?" they ask.
You won't have to ask me twice.
It doesn't matter—the memory
I'm searching for peace in life.

I know that it won't be perfect.
Other problems will take their place,
But it will feel so good to feel quiet inside,
To know I have courage in place.

In place of what? A way of life.
A life that I've claimed as mine.
And when problems arise within my space
I know I'll handle them fine.

Myself as a Baby

All I was told about myself as a baby was that I was sickly. From the time I was born I had problems. I was constantly throwing up, crying, and coughing. No one knew what was wrong. When I was nine months old, the doctors decided to remove my tonsils thinking that was the problem. No such luck! When I was six, I remember being in the hospital. The nurses pulled my metal crib close to the window so I could watch for my father's truck. The doctors had no idea what was the matter. Colic and other things were ruled out. Eventually they told Mother that, if things didn't change, I would die, and they left it at that.

At home my crib was always placed in an area where I could remain warm. Sometimes it was in the same room as the potbelly stove, and other times I slept in a closet connected to my parent's room. I was still sleeping in a crib when I was eight. In many ways my world never grew much larger than that crib until I began to address my childhood. That was when my trickle turned from a puddle to a pond and then to a lake before it became a river. The trick was going to be stopping what was happening before I was swept into the ocean.

I vaguely remember the bed in the kitchen where Mother could keep an eye on me as she worked. Playing outside was too strenuous, so on days when my health was bad, Mother gave me a knife and a bar of Ivory soap. I'd carve the soap into shapes, and then Mother would use the shavings in the laundry.

Myself as a Child

When I think about myself as a child, I wish someone had been there to see how I was struggling. All it would have taken would have been an adult who cared, or even noticed how I was living—or not living—my life. There were plenty of signs, but I guess no one then knew how to read them.

I've already told you that the memories I owned before Dad was killed had screaming in them. Other than that, everyone who knew me said I was a sweet little girl. I have a picture of myself with my family when I was two. I was wearing a dress. My hair was blond—almost white—and slightly curly. My head was tipped to one side, and I looked precocious. I have a picture of my cousin and I when I was four sitting outside on a wooden table with a washtub of freshly picked flowers. In that picture, my hair was straight, and my bangs came nearly to my eyebrows. I wore an ugly dress and a puzzled look on my face. I have a picture of myself, along with my brothers, taken a short time before my father was killed. We look like we lived on Tobacco Road. My brothers were wearing high-water overalls without shirts, and neither was wearing shoes. I wore a skirt that was too short, and my hair looked as if it had been styled with an eggbeater. We were standing in front of a dead, naked tree, devoid of anything that might make it look anything other than creepy. There wasn't a blade of grass to be seen.

The next pictures I have are of my brothers and me a few months after my father was killed. We were standing in front of my grandparent's house. My brothers were both wearing long coats along with Frank Sinatra–type hats perched on their heads. I'm wearing a dress of a proper length, patent leather shoes, and a straw hat. We had come a long way in only a few months. My hair was cut straight with bangs, and I wore it that way for years to come. Later I remember, if my bangs grew long, I would look from beneath them as if they were someplace safe where I could hide. By the time I was fourteen, I began chopping my bangs until they were an inch long and sweeping them to the side.

When we moved in with my grandparents, we all slept in the attic. I couldn't tell you much about the house other than the two buckeye trees that grew in the front yard. The house was across the street from my grandparent's store. Sometimes they let me fill the candy or pop machines and wait on children as they sorted through the wooden penny candy box. I liked bubble gum and usually could be found with several pieces in my mouth. I hated spitting it out—so I swallowed it.

School was a block away from where we lived. That was the school I attended when I wrote the letter to Eisenhower. By now I must have been feeling better because I became more active. I have scars on my knees from falling while wearing metal roller skates and tumbling down a gravely hill near where we lived. I always seemed to be nicked and scraped, but that's something abused children do. I've heard it said that bruises, cuts, broken appendages, and accidents can be considered outward signs of an inward problem. Abused children also take risks that create injuries to draw attention to how they feel. I hardly ever used caution. I was almost impervious to pain because, without it, I felt nothing.

When I was eight, a girl who lived close to my grandparents asked if I could go shopping. Our town was built around a square and, when my father was alive, I was never allowed to go there alone. After his death, my grandmother not only approved of my shopping expeditions, but would give me a dollar to spend. With them I was living in a metropolis on the banks of the Mississippi River. I can't imagine why they allowed me to go into the city with a girl who was only two years older. What fascinated me about her was that she had a glass eye. I joke about Grandmother letting me go by saying the girl promised she would keep an eye on me.

The first place she took me was an F. W. Woolworth five-and-dime store. It was huge! It even had a basement. Once we arrived, she immediately lost track of me. I looked everywhere, but she was nowhere to be found. I didn't know my grandparent's address or phone number. The only thing I remembered was the name of the grocery store. I hadn't talked on a phone before, so someone must have helped me. When someone answered the phone, I told them what happened. They knew where the dime store was located and told me to wait on the corner and someone would come get me. Before long, I was safely home. I never saw the girl after that because her family moved. Since the whispers were that my grandfather was a pedophile, I wonder if she had been one of his victims, and this was her way of getting even.

After that I became what I call a "girl about town." Now I was on my own. I'd ask permission to go for the day, and as I said earlier, Grandmother would open the cash drawer and say, "Here's a dollar, honey." I was nine.

By now I didn't just walk around town. Before long I had a list of places I would go. One of the first places was the swimming pool. Another thing I loved to do was go to one of the two movie theaters. I'd go inside, buy a box of Boston Baked Beans (candy-coated peanuts), find a seat, and wait for the movie to begin. I'd watch the previews, the movie, the intermission, the cartoons, the news, and then I'd start over. I knew exactly when I should leave so I could abide by the one rule at home: be home in time for supper. Until then I was as free as a bird.

Sometimes I'd pay a nickel and ride the ferry across the Mississippi River from Iowa to Illinois. Instead of riding the ferry back I always chose to walk back across the busy bridge back to where I started. If I was lucky, a barge would come along, and I'd wait as the bridge lifted to let it through. Doing this I'd feel an adrenalin rush that made me feel alive.

There was one other place that gave me the same feeling of danger and exhilaration. To go there, I had to go to the rail yard. There were wooden steps going up from the ground to a walkway over the track that ended up connecting to the street almost half a block above where the bottom of the stairs began. It made me feel sick to do this, so I'd practically crawl up the steps to get to the walkway. Then I'd hang desperately onto the wooden handrail until I reached the street

There was also a museum where I would look for hours at mummies, Native American relics, and a plane that hung from the ceiling. In the same area was the local television station. More than once I'd show up as one of the kid's shows was about to air. I'd sit on the cowboy fence like a bird on a wire and smile as if I belonged. Several times a customer would come into the store to tell Mother, "Mary Ann is on television again." She'd go to the house, turn on the television, and sure enough there I was. My hair was a tangled mess, and of course I had a mouth full of bubble gum.

There were other places farther away. One was the roller skating rink. Just a short time ago I asked my uncle how far I had walked to get there. He told me it was a little more than thirty blocks from where we lived. I'd walk to the rink, skate, and then walk the thirty blocks back home. Now the world was of my own making, and no one ever seemed to care or know where I was except me, and I loved it that way. I knew where I was, and that was all that mattered after the dime store fiasco. I was ten.

After Mother remarried, we moved across town. Now in order to get to the places I had gone to before, I took the bus. Sometimes, instead of doing that, I'd ride my bike through the city and up the steep hills to my grandmother's house. Why? I needed money. "Here's a dollar, honey," my grandmother always said, and off I'd go to begin my day's journey.

One summer day when I was twelve I rode my bike across the city to grandma's house. Two girls I knew from school stopped me. It was summer, and somehow our conversation turned to swimming. Since I knew my way around the city, I told them I knew how to get to the pool. I only had one problem: I didn't have my swimming suit. I left my bicycle at grandmother's, and we hurried to catch the bus. There was only one other obstacle: I would need to get off the bus, run to my house, grab my towel and suit, and get back to the bus stop before the bus circled back.

The girls pleaded to come with me. I tried to get them to stay on the bus, but they insisted they wanted to see where I lived. I told them we had to hurry so we hopped off the bus, ran two blocks to my house, picked up my things, and headed back to catch the bus. Just as we got to the four-lane highway, we saw the bus in the distance. One of the girls became excited and, instead of stopping to look, she ran out into the busy road. *Pow!* Halfway across the road, she was hit by a car. I felt upset. Why? I missed my bus!

I watched by the side of the road as the ambulance arrived, picked the girl up, and drove away. I don't remember seeing the police. In the distance I saw another bus coming, so I talked the second girl into getting on the bus so we could go swimming. I mean, so what if the other girl couldn't go? We boarded the bus, but by the time we got to the pool, the girl was crying. She wanted her mother. I stayed with her as she called home and waited until her mother arrived. I'm sure her mother offered to take me to my grandmother's house, but I declined. After all, I was on a mission to go swimming.

I gave my money to the person at the window, rushed inside, skipped the shower, put on my suit, and jumped into the water. I felt disappointed I wasn't going to be able to stay long, but at least I had completed my mission. Since I was running late, I caught the bus to my grandmother's because I still had to pick up my bicycle and ride home.

Once I arrived, I went in to tell my grandmother good-bye, and she told me the injured girl's mother called to let me know the girl's arm was broken. My grandmother told me to get a soda from the pop machine and candy from the penny box and to take it to her. I did as I was told, but my mind wasn't on the girl being hit—it was on getting home before I was in trouble.

Within a short period of time, I was on my bike peddling toward home. When I was halfway there, a policeman stopped me and asked if I had seen the accident. I told him yes and then probably told him it had been her fault for running out into the street. Satisfied with what I'd said, he left, and I was back on my bike peddling even faster toward home.

Here's the thing about that story—if the girl's mother hadn't called, and if anyone had asked what I'd done that day, I would have said, "I went swimming." The girl being hit was a non-event to me.

It wasn't that I was callous. I just forgot whatever was happening to or around me as quickly as it possible. This story was one the director of the rape crisis center noted because it was a prime example of abused children can become.

Another adventure happened when Mother sent me to overnight Bible camp. I'm not at all sure I wanted to go, but Mother told me I could go for a week and come home if I wanted to. I may have tried to tell someone I was coming home; I'm not sure. I rode the church bus back from camp to the parking lot where I was to be picked up. When I arrived, my family wasn't there. Someone offered me a ride, but I told them no. I knew they weren't coming, but I wasn't about to admit that to anyone. As soon as the last child was gone, I grabbed my camping gear and set out for my grandmother's house. It was about three miles.

After some time, I arrived at my grandmother's house. No one was home. I grabbed my stuff and walked two blocks uphill to catch the bus. When I arrived home, no one was there. I was exhausted, so I sat down and waited. Several hours later, they pulled up and were surprised to see me.

No matter what, I always knew what to do. Instead of leisurely walking wherever I went, I marched with my shoulders pulled back and my head high, seeming to transmit that everyone should get out of my way because I was coming through.

Myself as a Child and Religion

This part of my personality may surprise you. Remember earlier when I told you I attended my aunt's Sunbeams class at her church shortly after moving to the city and how I began to see God as the only Father I knew? Well, that was only part of the story.

Wrapping myself in religion kept me from the consequences my childhood might have held in store for me. It gave me a father after mine had disappeared, and I was content. This father figure became locked into my mind and held my life together until I was able to claim it. It was my breath when I wanted to stop breathing. It was my eyes when I no longer wanted to see. It became my feet when I could no longer walk into the future. It became my loving heart when all I could feel was pain.

Before Mother remarried we attended a Baptist church, and I loved it. I was eight. I'd sit up front with Mother and listen to everything being said. When the alter call went out or the pastor asked if anyone needed prayer, I'd lift my hand. It wasn't that I was such a bad person; I just wanted them to pray for me. I continued doing this until Mother took me to a Billy Graham revival. I raised my hand when he asked if anyone needed prayer. Soon someone came to usher me into a room to talk to me about accepting Jesus. I had already done that, and this particular person scared me half out of my mind; I refused to go with him.

I was eleven when mother remarried. When I was thirteen, our newly formed family moved from the city to a town a little bigger than the farm community we'd lived in when my father was alive. Mother dutifully began attending the Methodist church across the street, which was where my stepfather wanted to go. When I voiced my disfavor, because I firmly believed I was a Baptist, I was allowed to attend the Baptist church directly cater-corner from where we lived.

So now I was attending church alone. Before she married, church was the only thing Mother and I shared. When she changed denominations and started attending the other church with my stepfather, it was as if I had been ushered out of her life and I was now an outsider.

In the Baptist church, no one was interested in me because I had nothing to offer but the nickels and dimes I put into the collection plate. I'd show up for Sunday school and then stay for church. After services, the families that attended church together went home to eat. I'd go home and eat, but after that I'd wait for evening services.

Late Sunday afternoon the Christian church a block away held teen services. Since it was earlier than my church's service, I'd head down the block and take my seat in their building. As soon as services were over, I had just enough time to go back to the Baptist church where I would attend a second teen service. After that I'd go to church and take my regular spot, second row center. I sat there, happy as a lark, with a church family that truthfully didn't know I existed. I'd sing and quite literally immerse myself in the presence of "my Father" for the entire day. If there happened to be a revival, I'd be there every night. I was more at home in church than I was in our house.

Come Monday evening, there was another teen service at the Methodist church. This was the church my mother and stepfather attended, so I went there as well.

On Wednesday I was back at my church for Bible study and prayer meeting. I loved being in my Father's house, no matter which one it was. I felt accepted and comforted in those places more than anywhere else. It was a strange ritual, going from church to church, but one that gave me a sense of stability I had never been able to find since my biological father's death.

It was my childhood beliefs that kept me going throughout my progress. I had closeness with God the way a child has, or should have, with a parent. I was constantly aware of any inward directions my Father might have. God and I were constantly conversing with each other the same way a parent would with his child. This was one of the few things I was grateful for as I probed into my past.

As strange as it may sound, I really never thought about having a flesh-and-blood father until I was almost fifty. My own form of belief about my Father as a child kept me alive and was the only close relationship I had. I lived in a house with my family, but we weren't really a family. We were just people living in the same house. When they weren't there for me emotionally, God was. I think that's part of the reason I did so many things alone. I not only had God but also my dissociative internal family. I didn't really need anyone or anything else in my life.

As an adult, it took a lot of courage for me to change the relationship I had with God, and I've never regretted it. I made the mental and emotional changes in increments. Because of that, I was able to keep my spiritual oneness intact. Through it all, I followed a path that almost seemed to be laid out for me. I still listen to that inner guidance on a daily basis because it was my life's foundation.

I never felt as if my Father was condemning. That only seems to be something attached to religion. To me, God was simply a loving parent who wanted only what was best for me. Even now, as I continue to journey through life, I still feel a sense of comfort and oneness trickling into me from my past life with my Father.

Myself Today and Religion

I never question my idea from childhood that God adopted me after my father's death. He was a viable force in directing my life. I continue to use the word God, but what I mean is something bigger than myself and greater than I know. I don't see why doing away with God would make any sense. As I said, I equate the words *God*, *Spiritually*, and *Universal Oneness* with my own internal guide, intuition, or knowing.

Changing my opinion about God, religion, and spirituality was what finally began to open a new world for me. I allowed myself the grace I required to find peace. I realized I needed to find my own way. I've never felt as though I have gone outside the boundaries of what I can comfortably believe.

My own form of belief kept me alive so when others weren't there for me emotionally, God was. With God I never felt alone. I not only had God but also my internal family. I didn't need anyone else. It took a lot of courage for me to change the relationship I had with God, and I've never regretted doing it.

Today I am thankful to be religion free. As I've said, this doesn't mean I don't honor a higher power; I just have my own sense of what it means to me. I am grateful for the role religion and God played in my life when I was a child. I found what little solace I could in God. That was the path I followed as I worked my way through my life's maze. As my new journey presented itself in 1988, I was already on my way to relating to God differently. My sense of a higher power has never let me down.

Religion had done its job in my life. As a child I marched to the song religion played at the same time I made up my own rules and followed them as if they were the law of the land. I was a brave little soul. I was *in* this world, but I wasn't *of* this world. The world within me was safe. As the adult I am today I sometimes I wish I had stayed more into reality. My world was too real and full of too many real things happening to me and around me. I wasn't able to understand or tolerate it, so I went away. Now my reality is sometimes too real. I can see why it was necessary for me to numb myself and hide in religion and God just so I could remain alive. But now I have to ask myself: Was this all really necessary?

I Heard the Drummer Drumming

I heard the drummer drumming
But I didn't know the song.
Instead I seemed to go through life
Just muddling along.

For me there was another sound
No matter how He bid.
I wasn't giving in to life
That wasn't what I did.

I never really realized
I didn't truly live
Until I found a key to life
I had no more to give.

The key they say has power
To open every door.
Until I found the answer
My life was filled with war.

A battleground that ravages
And never stays confined;
Instead it seems to make me feel
I'd lose my very mind.

The drummer pounded harder
Just hoping I would hear,
Trying desperately to change my beat
Saying I had naught to fear.

Avoiding all the music
I could not afford to care,
I let the marching force my way
It was all that I could bear.

It wasn't until my life grew dark
And I couldn't find my way;
No matter how I shouted out,
Life had nothing more to say.

Soon I began to realize
My life was pure despair.
I was trying just to live a life
That truly wasn't there.

Mary Davenport

I never really trusted life
What more was there to say?
Until I heard the whispering
"There is another way."

As the drumming faded
I tried to find my song,
And soon to my amazement
I was following along.

Faintly I began to hear
The thumping of my heart
Asking me to "Join the dance.
It's not too late to start."

I tightly closed my eyes
So nothing would distract.
I finally let life lead the way,
And soon I was on track.

With each step I took
I came closer to my goal.
I didn't try to stop myself
Instead I let it roll.

When I finally stopped my movement
And focused on that song,
I ended marching into life
And began to dance along.

Today the Singer leads the way.
I'm now in tune with all.
It wasn't 'till I opened life
I was welcomed to the ball.

So if you hear a drumming,
You must take a chance.
Because His song is in your heart
Just lift your feet and dance.

One thing I want to say is that my views are mine and mine alone. I worked to change my thinking, and I can tell you I'll never go back to the way it was in the beginning. Before 1988, religion was a very important part of my life. I went to church and did all the things I felt God expected me to do, without questioning why I might be doing them. However, I was soon to get a major lesson on the difference between believing in organized religion and believing in something higher than and bigger than myself. The lessons I learned erased my need for a lead-lined boundary and enabled me to enjoy the spirituality I could feel in not trying to confine God to a building, denomination, or to a series of rituals or controls.

In 2010 I found that what I was doing was probably quite normal for me. I may have a condition known as temporal lobe epilepsy (TLE). Some people who have TLE also have Geschwind syndrome). One of the aspects of this condition has to do with hyper-religious behavior. I definitely feel my dedication to organized religion in my youth fits the bill.

Without God

Without God
I don't have a prayer.
When I make a call
No one will be there.

All days would be empty,
Leaving naught but despair.
If I don't believe in something
Nothing will be there.

So I believe in something.
I'm not sure just what it is.
But when I come a calling
It is just what it is.

They say you can only pray
Above into the heaven,
But that's like throwing dice.
Seven-come-eleven.

Is gambling on the unknown wise?
That question is profound.
I'm not sure what you're looking for,
But my answer is quite sound.

There is this place inside of me
Which speaks with wise intent.
And with the answers I receive
I really am content.

I don't know what to call that voice.
It could be I'm unwell.
But when I heed the answers
I really feel quite swell.

The church preaches God is out there
While science argues loud.
I'm thinking God is everywhere
Within our Universe quite proud.

Proud we have the questions
And seek the answers wise,
Not just looking toward the heaven
Expecting magic answers from the sky.

Going Quantum

You wouldn't think someone graduating from high school with a C average would want to delve into quantum physics, but I did. I'm not sure how it got started. It was probably a random piece of information included in one of the books I was reading. All it did was whet my appetite, so I wanted more. I'm not going to tell you I understood what I read, but something in it felt familiar. After that I began to delving into information about the quantum world like a starving child. When I read about the quantum world, my mind spread out into the Universe in such a way that I felt I could touch its heart. This delicate balance is set up so that even one tiny fraction of difference can change or destroy the entire Universe in one fell swoop. I read about the quantum world to see if I could understand how I fit into the scheme of things. This is where I get my emotions. In other words, the Universe needed me here to help in any way possible.

I always wished I could feel this same oneness as I deal with people. I've found as I incorporate universal entanglement into my life that I feel hopeful as I touch and understand more about humanity. When I do this, I feel as if I am part of something, everything, and nothing all at once. It takes my breath away.

I depend daily on this delicate balance to sustain our planet. Today too many times society treats the Earth as if it's disposable, as if we can take without giving back. If this is done, an unnatural balance—a vacuum of sorts—happens that could easily suck the life out of everything and everyone we love.

I often thank the Universe for showing itself to me. Even the tiniest peek into this greatness gives me hope.

Going to School

What if I had applied the same drive and determination into going to college? I might have gotten through college but would I have had the same amount of wellness as I have now? Would I have had the ability to work my way into a successful career carrying all my baggage? I doubt that would have been possible.

Another thing I learned is that I'd always felt stupid. Mother gave me the message and convinced me that what I had to offer didn't have value. The few awards I won didn't mean anything to her, so they didn't mean anything to me.

In school I was a good student even though the best I could earn was a C. I managed to get by in classes by doing extra-credit work. It played into my hypergraphia, which has to do with the need to write, write, and write some more. I didn't realize at the time about its possible connection to temporal lobe epilepsy, which I was unaware of at the time. I'd study into the night and try to force my mind to absorb and retain the information I needed or do extra-credit work so I could stay even.

The problem was that the forgetfulness I placed in my life when I felt stress worked against me. I could memorize facts and information and recall them when I was alone, but when I was put on the spot to answer a question, the amnesia kicked into gear. It would wipe out everything I had learned and cause me to relearn everything again and again just to forget it again and again. When I was stressed to the point of sheer panic, I would dissociate and go into my magical place where I was safe. It didn't matter that school should have been a safe place where I could display my intelligence, because for me, nowhere was safe. I had a few teachers who noticed how distressed I seemed and allowed me a bit of room. Even though I wasn't doing well on paper, I excelled by using hypergraphic behavior to earn extra credit.

In junior high I had a teacher who encouraged me to excel. He made a game out of class by allowing one of us to teach on certain days. He would start by asking a question about our assignment pages. Whoever answered his initial question came to the head of the class and was allowed to ask a question of his or her own. Guess who taught the class on those days. I did!

Somehow I was able to memorize everything anyone might even think of making into a question. When it was my turn, I'd pick out the most obscure piece of information possible. Occasionally someone knew my answer and took my place, but only until they asked a question. The game proved to me that my success had to do with my stubborn unwillingness to be trumped by classmates. The teacher had taken the stress out of the class and plugged into my competitiveness. Because of my personal home situation, I was extremely unwilling to be wrong, and that evidently overrode my fear.

In high school I lived in an elusive and invisible world. In many ways I liked it because it enabled me to individualize myself. If most people liked one thing, I'd like the other. When kids my age were dancing rock and roll, I was doing the polka. If they liked listening to Elvis, I liked listening to Night Train, which played only the blues. They liked riding in cars, and I liked long walks. They were day, and I was night. I was different, and I liked it that way.

I did have an English teacher who allowed me to step outside the required reading list and make my own. I tried it her way and then complained about the list she had given. When asked what I wanted to read, I whipped out a 600-page novel and told her I wanted to do my report on it. She asked what it was about, and I told her. After that she gave me permission to read whatever I wanted. I can't tell you the number of times I blessed her for allowing me to feel as if I wasn't a failure in school.

Later, as an adult, try as I might, I couldn't memorize Bible verses or learn how to do signing for the deaf. Even though I spent hours trying to learn, my brain light would switch off leaving me in the dark.

Now let me explain part of the reason I had problems in school. The instant something felt threatening, something in my body and mind would panic, and my mind would scan for a problem that had nothing to do with school. At that point my body would go on high alert and into a fight, flight, or freeze stance because of the release of adrenalin and cortisol into my system.

According to Dharma Singh Khalsa, M.D. with Cortisol is a hormone secreted by the adrenal glands and is prevalent in stressful situations. This hormone can rob the brain of glucose, which is part of our brain's fuel. The cortisol dumped into my system played havoc on my neurotransmitters, which were supposed to be allowing my thoughts to be carried from one brain cell to the next. When this function changed, my glucose level lessened, and it became more difficult to concentrate or remember.

Dharma Singh Khalsa, M.D. with Cameron Stauth in the book Brain Longevity noted my problem with Cortisol was that my high level of cortisol due to stress created by trauma and abuse set me up for failure long before I learned about my childhood. If my brain system was preoccupied with stressful conditions, it produced a type of "static" that interfered directly with memory. Finally I realized my memory loss, or amnesia, could have developed because my brain never created the right neurological pathways to keep them.

Cortisol is part of the system that prepares the body for high-energy physical effort. When the threat passed, my body was supposed to go back to its normal way of functioning. Because I was always stressed, I stayed locked into fight, flight, or freeze. My body and mind were on constant alert and ready for action. It is supposed to be a protective measure, but in me it was more harmful than helpful. It may have been a contributing factor into why I created my "internal family." I could assign each of them the responsibility for what I need to flee, fight, or freeze from and go on my merry way without the problem I assigned to them.

There's only so much room in my mind to carry around all these beings. My internal family wasn't interested in math, dictation, typing, history, and such. They just wanted to be left alone in their misery. As for the out-in-the-open me, forgetting was my way to continue living. If my education was put at risk because of it, so what? I could live without the history dates and other facts, but if I wanted to stay alive I had to choose—forget it or die. At the time I didn't realize TLE might possibly have been the magician behind the curtain pulling the strings. I can't help but shake my head at the level of determination I had as I tried to understand what happened mentally and emotionally and why I handled myself the way I did.

I Lived and Slept Where?

I'm telling this just because I find it funny. Normally I didn't have a room when I was growing up. I know I'm not the only one who dealt with odd sleeping arrangements.

When I was a baby, the house we lived in could easily have been called a tarpaper shack. In a cubbyhole upstairs logs were visible where the plaster had fallen off. The outside was covered with tar shingles. I was two, and my parents put my crib where I could be nearby in case I needed help. At times it was in a closet along with my parents' clothes. If it was winter, they pulled it close to the potbelly stove so I could stay warm. In the summer it was in the kitchen where it was cooler.

After my father was killed, we slept in our grandparents' attic.

I don't know if Mother shared our space or not. I was eight and have only one vague image of the attic. When Mother remarried, I had my first room. We lived there for two years before we moved. I was eleven.

Once my stepfather graduated from chiropractic college, we moved to a small town. The house we lived in was nice, but we had to share the space with my stepfather's office. My stepfather was always given the prime rooms, so I did the best I could with what was left.

I have no idea where the older of my brothers slept. I think he was with us, but I can't find him in my memory. My other brother was living with my aunt and uncle. As for me, I became quite adventuresome in carving out a space for myself. At first I slept on the couch in the living room, which was actually a small space meant to be a dining room. The kitchen was used for cooking and eating.

I don't know how I came up with the idea of using part of a wraparound screened porch for my bedroom. I was too young to set it up, so I know I had help. A big piece of furniture called a chifforobe, which was like a wardrobe with a chest of drawers, was put across part of the porch to separate out a space about ten by twelve feet. Plastic was put behind the chifforobe and over the screen, making my walls mostly plastic. That was my bedroom. I loved it. The problem was that, as the weather grew cold, I had to sleep under a pile of blankets to stay warm. The other issue was that I didn't have a door. There wasn't a way into my room except through a window. It might have been embarrassing for friends to see my room, but I didn't have friends, so my secret was safe.

The reason we moved was that my stepfather became ill. In the next house, we didn't have to make room for his office, so I had a room, but it was creepy, cold, and dark. It was like something you'd see in a scary movie. Thankfully, we were only there for three months, so I didn't have to check under the bed for monsters for very long. The location of that house was at the top of a steep hill. It was in a northern state, and we lived there in the dead of winter. I walked to the school, which was two miles away. It's hard to describe how hard it was to go up and down that hill to and from school. There were times I'd grab a bush or tree so I wouldn't fall. At times I walked in the road because it was too steep and slick for cars. I'd jump from bare patch to bare patch where I could find a dry spot. It was miserable, so I was thankful not to live there long.

My next space was almost as funny as the one I accessed by crawling through the window. My stepfather was feeling better, so we moved. Once again we had to parcel the house so he could have part of it for his office. His space took most of the downstairs, so we lived upstairs. Okay—now use your imagination.

Upstairs there was one large master bedroom, a hall, the bathroom, and a small bedroom. There were four of us who needed to find places to sleep. The large bedroom was turned into a bedroom for my mother and stepfather, and a living room. I slept on a chaise lounge in the cramped bedroom, which had been turned into a kitchen/dining room, complete with the stove and refrigerator. In other words I didn't need to go far for a midnight snack because I was sleeping in the kitchen!

Since there wasn't a sink in our make-do kitchen, we got water from the bathroom. This included water for cooking. In order to wash dishes, we put two dishpans in the bathtub along with a dish drainer. I would get on my knees and bend over the tub to wash dishes. After I was finished, I had to dry the dishes and put them away so the tub could be cleaned and used for bathing. Then there was the matter of what to do with the dishwater. Well, what do you suppose we did? We poured it down the toilet.

When the younger of my brothers came back to live with us, there were five people had to fit into an already cramped space. Don't ask me where either of my brothers slept. I think they slept in the real kitchen my stepfather used as a lab.

After the younger of my brothers died, and my other brother was sent away, so his space in the kitchen/lab was up for grabs. I claimed his bed. The problem was that, if my stepfather had patients and I needed to use the bathroom, I'd have to put on my coat, go out the back door, go around to the front, and then go upstairs to the bathroom. Okay, now both brothers were gone. One moved and the other died. By now Mother was beginning to feel sorry for me. They took what should have been the living room from my stepfather's office and put that old chifforobe between what was going to be my bedroom and his smaller office, which was actually the dining room. If he had patients, I had to stay quiet so they wouldn't know I was there. I could easily do that since no one knew I was around anyway.

We moved again, but in this house I claimed all sorts of spots. The office occupied only the living room and entry. We used the kitchen as a living room/dining room. There was a tiny bedroom downstairs, which I claimed for a while before I moved into the basement. Finally I settled into a small area upstairs. We all shared one closet. It was a tight fit, but I didn't care because I liked the strangeness of how I lived.

Sometimes Mother would wake in the night to a racket coming from whatever space I claimed. I often did that as I cleaned every single inch by straightening, scrubbing, and rearranging.

Psychologically speaking, I was out of it. Nothing fazed me. I taught myself to do the best I could with what I had and not complain.

When my husband was in medical school, I was able to fit all six of us into a small two-bedroom, two-bathroom trailer. When I ran out of room, I'd stack things. Once, since we had two bathrooms, I put our youngest son's bed in the tub. That didn't last because, when one of his brothers came to use the bathroom, he yelled at him to get out of his room. I knew what was going to happen. One of his brothers was going to turn on the faucet. I could see myself trying to dry the blankets and pillow from his makeshift bed.

Do I still do things like this? Absolutely! You should see my office space. I love it! It is stacked floor to ceiling, and everything seem so cozy.

Going to Work

As a teenager I worked various jobs. Like most girls, I babysat. I also cleaned an apartment over a funeral home. The woman who lived there was in a wheel chair and followed me around, making sure I was doing a good job. She needn't have worried since I loved cleaning. There was never a spot in my room that didn't get my attention. She paid me fifty cents an hour. On the way home, I'd buy something for my mother. I also ironed for ten cents a garment. It wasn't that I liked ironing; it just helped me get rid of nervous energy.

After high school, I had an opportunity to become a dental assistant. I'm not sure how I would have done, but before I had a chance to find out someone suggested cosmetology college. I foolishly decided that was for me. I got my license but I hated doing that type of work. When you are filled with fear and self-doubt, trying to please people by cutting and styling hair is a bad idea. I worked for a while, but once I was married we moved to California. I didn't have enough hours to qualify for a license there, so instead of going back to cosmetology college I began working as a bank teller.

This was another disaster, especially after I cashed a bad check. I enjoyed dealing with people, but when it was time to count my drawer, I panicked. About that time I became pregnant with our first son, so I was able quit and stay home with him. After my husband was discharged from the military, we moved home, and my husband became a full-time college student. This time I took another job in a bank, but instead of being a teller, I ran a check-sorting machine. I was able to do that, but my sense of panic was still rampant. I was able again to quit when I became pregnant with our third son.

I took on my next job after my husband started medical school. I worked for an insurance company. I used an old-fashioned computer and limped along as best I could. I hardly knew what I was doing because my mind was befuddled. If I handled your claim and botched it up—sorry.

Nothing I ever did when it came to working was easy. I was filled to the brim with pure panic all the time. I wasn't aware I had a mountain of coping mechanisms set up in my childhood that constantly interfered with my ability to work outside the home.

I was finally able to land a job in the school system. It was in the media center, and the job wasn't difficult. I worked alone, so that was great. I'd fill orders and occasionally answer the phone. When there wasn't anything to do, I'd invent something I thought would make the job easier for the next person. The people in my area were professionals and extremely nice. I must admit that, more than once, I'd get to work and run to the bathroom and cry a bit before I could start my day. I felt numb trying to work, take care of our sons, and at the same time, attempt to live a somewhat normal life—which it wasn't.

When it was time for my husband to do internship, we moved, and I was able to pick up a part-time job in the school system as a substitute secretary. Eek! Next I found work clerking in a hardware store. I was friendly, and all I had to do was work the register and stock shelves. It was then I came to realize I loved selling things. I was energetic and exuberant and perfect for the job.

One evening I was standing behind the register and someone wearing a black motorcycle helmet came in. He knew where the button was to open the register, and he hit it. The instant the drawer popped open, I slammed it with my hip and closed it. I notified the office I needed assistance. As people came to the front to see what I wanted, the guy took off with me hot on his tail. I was furious! I can still picture myself running across the parking lot. When I returned, the manager was standing there with a what-the-hell look on his face. I took a deep breath and explained the robbery attempt. I don't think what I had done had registered with me, but the would-be thief didn't have a weapon, so why not chase him?

I'm not sure I told anyone other than the manager and the police. It was another one of the stories like the girl being hit by the car. All I remember is how mad I felt. It was probably nervous energy that propelled me after the thief. I never once thought how dangerous it might have been.

An Overview of Reality

How could anyone ever begin to answer questions about reality? I had no reason to believe I was looking at the world differently than others.

My world seems, and has always seemed, real enough. I touch things and they seem solid even though quantum physics says that isn't so. I never had any reason to question my "truth."

I thought everything was exactly the same for everyone. That is why, if truth is questioned, there are so many disagreements about and versions of the same event.

Why didn't I question how I viewed life? A mind is a world within itself. Outside, my world appeared to be a reflection of what I saw, felt, and heard within my own personal sense of reality. Even if it wasn't real, it seemed real enough to me, so I never thought about questioning myself.

Today there are other ways to look into alternate realities. One is virtual reality, which lets us look into a different type of world, which could easily be just outside our own dimension. Since I'm overly attuned to different realities, it's probably better I don't go there because I do this naturally.

My Internal Family

This is probably part of what you've wanted to hear since I mentioned them. I don't talk about this aspect of my personality very much, so listen up because I don't plan to repeat myself. Talking about this is not only complicated, it is also uncomfortable because it is difficult to talk about it without sounding crazy. There isn't any need to completely explain this phenomenon. It was a behavior I used so I could remain alive before, during, and after what might have been happening to me.

From the beginning, talking about me as an individual was another glitch in my view of the world. At that time, I didn't realize anything was unusual, and I saw no reason to change my behavior. Instead I did something akin to manifesting a separate personality to deal with each situation.

Believe it or not, using other personalities seemed to make perfect sense. They were and still are my family. Even after all this time, they can be an intricate part of my behavior. They are like the close-knit family I never had. I'd miss them if I cut this behavior out of my life.

This is only one of the things I was able to do as a child to stay alive. I was fortunate that, when my flesh-and-blood family ignored me, I had a family of my own who were always there. This behavior helped protect me throughout not only my childhood but also my adult life. One of these events had to do with the problems I experienced in our marriage and was the reason my husband and I are still married after fifty-four years.

Today, even though it isn't as active as it was before, the thoughts attached to this behavior circle the rim of my mind waiting to make sure they can protect me. They seem to stay like guardian angels in the recesses of my mind, watching and waiting so they can protect me.

When I began trying to retrieve my past, part of my psyche wouldn't have anything to do with retrieval. They offered no cooperation with therapy as I tried to shake out memory. The strength of this phenomenon astounds me. Was it an involuntary act, or did I do it on purpose? I don't think there is any way to answer this since, even though I've tried to find the core of its beginning, it eludes me.

The phenomenon of going away in my mind enabled me to leave when my body or mind was being assaulted. When the event taking place around me was finished, I was able to take what happened and leave it behind with the member whose age was most suitable for carrying my mental and emotional burden.

What is a phenomenon? It is something known by sense perception rather than by thought. Everything about it is connected to senses. I don't verbally talk to these entities; rather, I have an internal knowing of what I need. I can't see them, but I sense their forms and stance and know how they are feeling and which burdens they are carrying. We are separate but also the same. I am aware they aren't real, but I appreciate the part this behavior played throughout my life.

Just the other day someone came to visit, and her conversation turned into one about this behavior. I realized it was about trying to understand something almost beyond comprehension. It is my normal, and I never think twice when something like this happens. In my world today I barely sense their presence. This happens only when I bring them to mind in a purposeful way. If others seem curious about them, they in turn become curious as well. That part of me seems to wake up and look out of my eyes so they can see if they're needed. As soon as I refocus my attention, they go back into a recessive part of my mind.

In 1989 and 1990 I was dealing quite a lot with my internal family. When the therapist asked to be introduced to them, it seemed silly. Why would he want or need to meet these figments of my imagination? A better question might be, why didn't I seem willing to dive fully into exposing the behavior? To me it was nothing. I found out years earlier that talking about what happens seems to increase the strength of the behavior. It is almost as if I'm fine tuning it, which in turn means, if I focus too much on it, the behavior begins to take over more than I'm willing to allow.

Names

Give them names? Never!
That would not show logic.
That would show them disrespect
And be quite pathologic!

Catch Me If You Can

If you think you can catch me,
Try if you can,
But you'll never quite know
Who I am.

I'm this and the other.
I go this way and that.
And you'll never know
Where I'm at.

I don't care
If you can't see.
Strange maybe to you,
But not to me.

Tears

The child curled up.
Tears she shed.
Not real you say?
Within my head?

"Then why?" I asked
"Do you see?
Those tears slide down
Outside of me?"

Please understand these aren't trick ponies I plan to trot around to entertain people. This is a serious behavior that I don't fully understand, so this is your only look-see into this part of my psyche.

Away

In this place I cannot stay
When my mind goes far away.

It hurts ever more to be
This person that I shall call me.

I'll gather up with all my might
And drop my guard and start to fight

My way back into the world to find
I'll chase this fear far from my mind.

My world with joy I soon shall fill.
I'll gather strength and climb that hill.

I know that peace will never be
Another place but inside of me.

So majestic words in an aching heart
Left crying in shame shall be

A saddened child, left untouched
Deep down inside of me.

The introduction to my internal family started as I began telling my husband about a new family member. He looked at me and asked if I had told the therapist. Glibly, I looked at him and said, "No. Should I?" It was my normal, and they had been with me for so many years I had never given them a second thought. By that time, my husband and I had been married for twenty-seven years. Boy, was he surprised!

When it came time for my next appointment, I tried to explain the process to the psychologist. I'm not sure what he thought. Since I started the conversation in such a casual way, I think it threw him off guard. The next time I came, he wanted to talk about the behavior again, and I told him no because to me these entities weren't a problem. He said, "I promise I won't kill your babies." I found that funny. I'm fortunate that he wasn't interested in divulging my behavior to others by exposing them as split personalities. I've read about therapists doing that, and the patient becomes a windfall. Exposing this behavior could have made quite a splash. In the meantime I would have been left looking as if I should be taken to the loony bin, and my therapist might have come across as a hero for discovering an oddity no one else recognized.

Babies

I showed my babies to someone,
And they came back scared and crying.
"It is of life I speak," I cried,
"Not of death and dying."

In silence did they fall?
Did they make a sound?
I might ask with questioning heart,
Or was no one around?

Unsaid words, left unheard.
Silent sounds left screaming,
Tormented soul; living un-whole
Left to the world of dreaming.

Me/Myself/and I

Please don't kill my babies.
Don't make them go away.
Please don't hurt my children.
I want them all to stay.

Ring around the rosy
A pocket full of rye.
No one else is playing,
Just me, myself, and I.

We cry and laugh together,
A whole new family.
They're mine, and I adore them,
Just I, myself, and me.

Someday I'll make them go away
And put them on a shelf.
But right for now I'll tend to them,
Just me and I myself.

I know that you can't see them.
There is no need I know.
But when the proper time has come,
I'll let you watch them go.

They'll all hold hands and turn around
And walk away—you'll see.
But you will always know they're there.
We're confident, you see,

That life will never pass us by.
We'll live and love and laugh.
We'll be complete in all we do,
For we'll be one at last.

One behavior I recognize is that the more attention placed on this behavior, the more puffed up it becomes. It's almost as if there is an excitement that seems to be created when I see how people respond. It's as if my trick ponies begin stomping their hoofs ready to begin their performance. At that point I stop what I'm doing and begin to change my behavior before it goes out of control. I can't begin to tell you how grateful I feel about not wanting to display this behavior. Instead I keep it quietly within my mind. That doesn't mean I'm not doing it; it just means I'm not going to display it. I am going to share them with you one time. I would like for you to notice that the ages of my internal children match the age I was when certain traumatic things happened.

The first thing to notice is that I call this phenomenon of my internal family a behavior. I prefer to avoid calling them splits, even though they are similar. They are like hiding places for abuses. One thing is, if I am talking about it, there's part of me that wakes up and wants to participate. It's kind of like a child showing off when company comes. I may use different pronouns occasionally. I've always done this. I used to put quotation marks around the words to show my awareness, but after a while I stopped because there were too many.

This behavior is one I have used for as long as I can remember. I can't say when it started, since my first is called the infant. Maybe it started that early. Remember, a child's sense of self isn't supposed to start at age as young as my infant seems to be. I wasn't quite two. I realize a psychologist might disagree with the things I say, but I don't care. I'm talking about a personal experience, and for anyone to discount what I say was happening is not helpful. My internal family is not a problem, so for someone to make it into one is nonsense.

The Infant: She is about two years of age. In my mind she can be found sitting in a crib that is pushed against a wall. Her back is pressed against the wall. Her behavior is fearful as well as angry and dangerous. She is opposed to anyone touching her. Mistrust can be seen in her eyes and in her actions. Several months after I started therapy, she began coming in dreams with a big smile on her face. I wrote this poem so she would go away and leave me alone.

Teeth

A smiling infant mild and meek,
Behind the smile, infant teeth.
Even though meek and mild,
This definitely was an angry child.

One of the problems I encountered with these entities is that I've never been able to clearly see their faces; neither can I tell you how they are dressed. Because I needed to understand the situation better, I did find pictures of how I looked at various ages, and I tried to acquaint myself with how the entities might look accordingly.

The Child: She is the second in the family and appears to be about eight, which is the age I was when my father was killed. I've also noticed there seem to be duplicates. One is extremely morose (sad) and troubled, and the other seems confident and defiant. The troubled child is sitting on the floor with her knees drawn up and her arms wrapped around them. Her head is lying on her knees. She doesn't appear to know I'm looking at her until I think about her, and then she seems to have an awareness of me. It seems to be hard for her to raise her head to look at me because it seems her head feels so heavy she has a difficult time holding it up. Almost as quickly as she looks at me, she puts her head down. She seems tired, sad, and overwhelmed. My opinion is that she is the same age I was when a lot of things seemed to be happening, so it isn't just one traumatic, detrimental issue I've dumped on her, but piles and piles. No wonder she has such a problem. She was my go-to when I needed to drop something off before I walked away clean, wiping it completely from my mind so I could pretend it never happened. I felt especially bad when I was attempting to do inner child work and she thought I had come to see her and instead I stepped over her in order to work with the infant. I almost felt as if I needed to apologize to her—but how can you do that to something that isn't anything but an illusion or a mirage?

The Girl: Next we come to one known to me as the girl. She seems to be about fourteen, and I never really see her unless there's trouble brewing. If I were to label her, I'd call her the protector. If either of the other two is in trouble, she comes to help. Until she is needed, she stands in deep doorways and around corners. As soon as she has tended to one of the others, she disappears again.

The Dancer: This seems rather odd. I think she is more of a psychological figure. She represents several different things that really don't have anything to do with me personally. This is not a child, but a grown-up. I have no idea what her age might be. All I can say is she is dancing. She's dressed like a ballerina. Sometimes she is wearing a pink tutu, and at other times a knee-length flowing skirt. Her hair is dark, pulled back into a bun, and is circled by a ring of flowers. There must be some type of music, but I can't hear it. When I hear actual music, her clothes change into the appropriate style she might wear if personally dancing to that piece of music. If it's Western, she's wearing Western clothing and boots. If it modern or jazz, her clothes are transformed again. As soon as the music I'm listening to stops, her clothing changes back into the tutu or the flowing pink skirt, and she begins twirling again. If I happen to think of her or place my attention on that part of my psyche, she stops, walks to what appears to be a small, old television screen. She tips her head to the side, gets her face close to the screen, and asks, "What do you want? Can't you see I'm dancing?" As quickly as she finishes saying that, she walks away and begins twirling again. I am of the opinion she could be one of several things:

1) She could represent my mother, since her hair is dark and my mother's was too. Mother was always too busy to bother with me, so this could represent her irritability with my desire for her attention. She might have asked what I wanted, but I seriously doubt she wanted to wait for my answer; rather, she wanted to go back into her own world instead of bothering with mine.

2) I once heard about an optical illusion known as the "spinning dancer." I'm not sure what is meant by that description, but it does seem to fit.

3) She could be a representation of my own mind. I have always been rather impatient when it comes to dealing with me. I've taken on a lot of demands I couldn't meet if I had a thousand years to finish them. The spinning could show how busy I always kept both my hands and my mind. One of my sons described me as going fast, faster, faster—pause and then repeat.

The Chair Girl: Now for the one I discovered in 1989. I was watching a talk show on television. A psychologist was going to show people how to do visualization with an inner child. I'd already done this, and I knew it could be complicated, upsetting, and somewhat dangerous. Instead of switching channels, I participated. *Wow!* As the psychologist took the members of the viewing audience on their journey, my mind split away (dissociated). The session was mind blowing. As much as I'd like to share it with you, describing this event would leave you thinking I'm crazy. This isn't a game, and it can leave a wake of damage. It should be done only in person by someone with a very high level of qualification.

First the psychologist wanted me to go to a house where I had lived in as a child. I vaguely remembered how the house looked when I was eight, so I decided to use the child as my subject. A few weeks earlier, I had been taken past the house where I lived when I was two. I decided to use that house instead. The instant my hand touched the "virtual" doorknob, I felt the house was alive and waiting for my return.

Once inside, on my way to find the infant, I found the child. She believed I was coming to her house and felt disappointed. In order to reach the infant, I had to step over the child. As I did this, she disappeared.

The worst part was that the psychologist told me to touch the infant. Eek! At one point after I was finally able to retrieve the infant from her crib, we encountered a part of the visualization in which I was to take her to confront her parents. I had no memories of my family, so instead I envisioned a picture on a table. The infant wasn't happy.

Next I was to leave the house with the infant. Wow! What she did at that point gave me a terrible sense of panic. Her arms and legs wrapped around me like coiled snakes. All I wanted to do was rip her off and sling her against the nearest wall. It was terrifying. The instant my hand touched the doorknob, the infant disappeared. I drew a sigh of relief for being given permission to get the hell out of that house. I knew the infant had returned to the safety of her crib.

Now the psychologist told me to leave. All of a sudden, as I walked down the sidewalk, I saw an open grave. As I approached it, I could see a girl inside who appeared to be about fourteen years old. She was sitting inside the open grave on a straight-backed chair. It was positioned at the head of the grave, and she was staring at the far side. At first I felt alarmed and wanted to get her out. I lay on the ground and extended my hand. She didn't notice me. I noted a blank, peaceful look on her face. It was pure contentment. I knew at that point that she was in her mind, and there wasn't any way to reach her. At that point I stood up, and the entire process ended.

Looking at what I have just written, I considered how, throughout my entire life, I have buried my feelings, experiences, and personal self in a way no one could reach me—not even my current self. Later, after the therapist promised not to kill my babies, I began to somewhat integrate my internal family so I could lessen the impact they were having on me. Even today they linger in my mind waiting to see if I need them. I don't feel this is something I need to mess with; neither will I allow anyone to deal them out of my life.

In my last book, I asked myself if I would ever miss them if they were gone. My answer was to ask if I'd miss my leg or arm if someone chopped it off. Hell yes, I'd miss them. As nonsensical as it may sound, I love them. I have far more love for them than I ever had for my original family.

Fragments

I've let these children play with me,
But now I've come to set them free.

To let them know their fate
I need them all to integrate.

To turn them loose. To let them run
Beneath the sky, beneath the sun,

Half hidden images locked deep inside,
A part of me that never died.

Free to dream of an abandoned past
Free to be—Me—at last.

Whoever That Is.

Mary Davenport

Integration

My babies smiled and waved good-bye.
They blew a kiss to an upward sky.

At last—no fear—we've come to rest
Upon this place we feel is best.

I opened my heart and in they ran.
I hugged them all and held their hands.

I touched their faces and wiped their tears
And bid them melt within me here.

My babe was the first to sigh,
As if I'd sung a lullaby.

New safeness within her heart had crept.
She laid her head and went to rest.

The child came next, her eyes turned bright
As if she'd seen an angel's flight.

She laughed out loud for all to see,
Then went deep into the heart of me.

The girl, relieved of her eternal task,
Silent of children took off her mask.

She wasn't a mom—just a little girl,
Hidden no more her life unfurled.

She took her spot within me there,
Glad at last without a care.

She had tended my children—it was her way.
"I'll do it now," she heard me say.

The dancer started to turn about.
She leapt into me and gave a shout.

"It's up to you now, our lives to live.
We've given you all we've had to give."

Their gift of life lay at my feet.
Their challenge left, I now could meet.

New life within these feet were shod,
Walking on pathways leading to God.

God smiled at me and said, "At last
You've begun to deal with that dreadful past.

And now within your heart to cheer,
Keep your babies close and near.

They all were wise and took their part.
Now they'll stay within your heart."

I love them all, for I could see
That they were all just parts of me.

I awoke from a dream I thought I'd had,
A dream that made me feel quite sad.

Then a tickle inside made me smile and say,
"I do praise God for this brand new way."

Far away they must go, yet near enough that I might see
They were all just parts of me.

Through colored eyes no tears were shed.
I glanced their way; they bowed their heads.

They knew their fates, their destiny
Was just to be a part of me.

I smiled at them, reached out my hand.
We all agreed, upon command.

I filled my lungs and sucked them in
And held them close and near within.

We hugged at first. No sad good-byes.
No tiny tears in frightened eyes.

I love them all and thanked them for
Becoming me—forever more.

Quiet

Now they are resting.
It is quiet you see.
I'm not them.
I'm just me.

As you can see, this is an odd behavior. I don't need judgment as to what I did to survive; neither can I tell you how, why, or when this happened. Enough said!

A Message for Me From?

Now let me share something that happened in 1977. At the time, my husband and I were having a lot of marital issues.

I'm not going to try to convince anyone to take me seriously. I'm just going to believe it was a series of random thoughts, or was it? Things sometimes happen that can't be explained.

One evening I began to talk to my Father the way I always had. All I wanted to do was to find a way to deal with marital issues. As I talked (prayed), I told my Father I had always tried to be a good person. I begged my Father to help me understand why so many things kept happening. I looked toward the heavens hoping I might find an answer. Suddenly I began hearing a conversation in my mind.

"What am I doing wrong that's making all this happen?" I asked. Call it God or whatever else you want, but it was like someone speaking into my brain.

The message sounded as if a friend was talking to me. "It isn't what you are doing; it is what others are doing. You aren't causing it."

"Why are they doing these things?" I expected my friend to give me wisdom that would make sense, but instead I was met with silence.

Then suddenly I heard, "How can you tell others if you don't know?"

"What?" I said. "Tell others what? I don't have any idea what to tell anyone. All I need are answers. Tell me what I don't know and who I'm supposed to talk to, and I'll do it."

I never sensed an answer, but that challenge never left my mind. Over the years I've felt I might have an idea what the message meant, but it wasn't until 1988 that things began to fall into place. I often think about my journey and how things came together in such an odd, unexplainable way. Is there a message? Has it always been my destiny to tell others about what I've learned and how I've changed? I cringe when I'm around adults who treat children like property. My skin crawls when I hear children enduring terrible things because of adults who should be protecting them. I want to scream out and warn people how damaged these children are apt to become. What is said to children or around children counts! So does what is done to them and around them. Since I am still damaged, the only way I can do this is by writing this book and telling my story and hoping I'm being heard and understood. I want others to stop letting their own detrimental childhoods trickle down into the lives of others.

My Sense of Reality (More Word Salad)

Since I've exposed my mental misbehavior, now I may need to explain why it isn't as bad as it seems.

This is the reason my husband and best friend wanted me to write this book. Later I'm going to explain a style of writing called hypergraphia. I have been warned that under no circumstances was I to go into even the slightest state of dissociation as I wrote. As far as I'm concerned, that is like telling a zebra to change its stripes into polka dots.

When I got to the place where emotions needed to become implemented into my reality, I wasn't willing to do it. Why? Because feeling intense emotions throw me off balance, and I end up feeling only panic. So it wasn't about my handle on reality; it was the amount of reality I was willing to handle. Notice the word *willing*. I didn't say *able*. I've proven to myself and others that I'm able to handle a lot and still go on.

Generally, when I'm researching something, I break a word or phrase down into word association. When I took the word *dissociation* and put it with the emotional value I should have, I came up with the word *disengagement*. This seemed to fit my situation better than simple dissociation.

What happens when you become disengaged?

To be engaged in something, you have to participate, and I didn't participate if I had to become emotionally involved. I know how I should behave, but since I avoid it I do what needs to be done by *purposeful intent*. I pretend to know what I'm feeling, but I'm not really feeling it. I act it out.

It isn't that I don't feel something. Instead I feel a coldness inside that insulates me from the heat of an emotion I should be feeling. Mother not only modeled the behavior, but also had no true warmth for me. If she had, it might have kept my own coldness away.

It took quite a while for me to understand I had always been living in a dual, fractured sense of reality. It sounded farfetched. Either that meant I was highly intelligent or certifiable. How can anyone ever be able to answer the question about a secondary reality without it sounding strange?

This has been a long and drawn-out process. I've questioned every thought, every feeling, and ever distraction in order to keep thoughts in check. You've heard the line about herding cats? Well, just call my mind Fluffy.

Much of what I encountered during this period of self-examination had labels. By that time I not only knew my labels, I also knew how I fit into their descriptions. Every time I encountered a label, I would quickly expose it, examine it, and then decide if I could keep it or if it needed to be changed. By that time, I had taught myself how to look at my behaviors in a neurological way.

Let me try to explain the adaption I put into my style of thinking in a way you might begin to understand.

In the beginning of my journey, we were enemies, my mind and I. Now I call it a friend. A friend is willing to tell you the truth, but not in a way that's meant to harm you. I really felt the way my mind processed information in the past was normal. When I told my husband I felt normal, he laughed at me. When I told my friend, she laughed too. They both reminded me that what I did was *my* normal, but that didn't make it wrong. I developed my ways of behaving in order to live. What was wrong with that?

I asked both of them the same question: "How can there be so many versions of normal? I know it has to do with personal experience and the way we filter things, but come on."

My best friend was especially verbal when it came to correcting my thoughts about normal. Here is what she told me: "No, it wasn't normal. I promise you it wasn't normal. That's why we want you to tell your story. I wish I could write it for you," she continued, "because I know what I want you to write. I don't want you to dissociate the story or make it fictional. Just tell the story as it happened. At least tell what you found out about your story and what you did to change yourself and your life. Everyone should know how much you've changed. The story is amazing. Forget about normal because you're probably one of the most abnormal people I know. At least the story is abnormal, and that's what I want you to write about."

My friend, you see, lives in the world of reality. She seems to appreciate visiting my world occasionally when I tell her something that's not too far-fetched for her to comprehend. Even when I told her about the train in the church she never blinked an eye. All she said was, "Of course you did!"

After telling her about something, I'd go on to explain how it had come about in a neurological way. There were always solid explanations for almost every trick my mind played.

Let me explain some of this in a way I hope you can understand better, but so you also won't find what I'm saying about other people's reality as offensive.

Make a picture of reality as if it were the ocean. There are people happily playing in the water, taking chances with what may be under the water. By doing this they are enjoying life and taking what pleasure they can from reality. To me, in that way, I can see where reality might be a little more enjoyable.

Now, picture me standing on the shore watching others having fun and all the while wishing I could join them. Eventually, the pleasure watching isn't enough so I begin to wade into the unknown. Ankle deep, I feel confident. I can begin enjoying life alongside all my reality companions. "You see," I tell myself, "you can do this. It won't be quite so bad to be part of the game of life." I wade out further, maybe to my knees. My excitement at being able to join in with the truth lovers almost begins to become a reality. Suddenly I feel a breeze, and the waves begin to lap harder onto the shore—and I panic. The reality people don't see it as a risk; they just ride the waves with jubilance. I can see they don't feel threatened, and I envy them, but not enough for me to go out any further. Soon one of the reality people thinks of a joke to play and pretends he is having a problem. Some of the reality people know it is a game and join the fun. A few think, momentarily, that there may be an issue, but quickly recognize it's a game. They live in reality, so they know when it's time to get out of the water. I don't have that information. Even though I like the water licking my knees, I begin to imagine all sorts of problems. Suddenly there's that panic inside of me, and I hurry back to shore where I'm sure I'll be safe. The reality people remain out there having fun, living in the real world, and I'm on shore fighting my thoughts.

Think about this though: maybe they are in the water up to their necks playing and having fun, and I'm on the shore thinking I'm safe, but at the same time there's a rabid dog loose and running toward me. What am I to do? Take my chances with the dog or run back into the water where I may or may not be safe?

This is how I live my life. I live it cautiously, easing myself into the water up to my ankles, then up to my knees, but running out again as fast as I can at the slightest inkling of trouble. This is the game I have played every day of my life. The nice part now is that now I know what is happening and why, so I can allow myself to feel a bit safer and occasionally enjoy what life might bring my way.

As I examined books on psychology, I found myself nicely wedged inside under the guise of a multitude of labels. In other words, I wasn't just one label; rather, I was labels layered within more labels. To find the actual source of my "out there" behavior would be almost impossible. I think the psychologist said it best when he told me it was a good thing I never got into LSD or any other mind-altering drugs because I do naturally what others take drugs to accomplish. I admit I found that funny, but also regrettably true. After he told me that, I asked what he thought might have happened if I had taken psychedelics. Without missing a beat he told me I probably would have been lost in the hippie generation with no way out.

Getting Married

Now I am going to show you another trickle down from my childhood into my adulthood as a married woman. You will also understand how my husband's trickle down with his mother entered into our marriage.

I've talked to my husband to make sure it is okay for me to share. I reserve the right to hold back if I don't think something is relevant in showing how my trickle-down survival methods worked to help keep us together. I have great respect for my husband and for our marriage. Yes, at times it was difficult to stay together, but the dynamics of marriage is complicated. It isn't about what happened as much as it is about how I handled what happened.

First I will tell you that my husband had a lot of other women in his life for a while. Without excusing his behavior, I want to explain. We were both almost twenty when we were married. He was in the military. By the time he was discharged, we were twenty-three and had two sons aged one and two.

When we first moved back to the town where we graduated from high school, our goal was for him to go back to college. I mentioned earlier that his plan was to become a teacher. I worked full time, and he went to college full time and worked part time. After a year, I became pregnant with our third son. Up until then things were still going great in our marriage.

I worked a few more months and then became a stay-at-home mother. He found a full-time job and started going to college nights. Two years after our third son was born, I became pregnant with our fourth and last child. Now we were parents of four boys ages newborn thru five and a half. Now here's where the trouble began. My husband was working with a single guy who liked to party. This person didn't respect women, so to him I was an anchor weighing his friend down. I'm sure my husband could see his point. Me? I was obliviously living in a busy world full of children, church, and stay-at-home chores.

Both of us by then were twenty-seven. This may sound tough, but remember this was 1969, and couples married young, immediately began having children, and the average family size was four. In other words, we were normal—except he was still in college. Even that was manageable. His parents sold us a few acres of land on which there was a dumpy little house, which I absolutely loved. It was our original plan for him to become a teacher, find a job nearby, build a new house near family, friends, and church, and live happily ever after. To me, life was ideal. It was hard, but it was also wonderfully worth it as far as I was concerned.

Every time I offered to work, he told me the minute I did he'd quit college. It was a wonderful gesture, but not practical. By now he was going to school full time and working full time. The other students in the classes he was taking were at least ten years younger. None were married, and no one had children. Now, can you see what lies ahead?

We were making ends meet, but at the same time we were as poor as church mice. Both of us had grown up poor, so it isn't that we felt we were missing out. That is unless you count on the fact he was living in one world with one group of people and I was living in another with our sons.

At this point, I was very religious and a prude. Now don't forget, I had been sexually abused as a child, but had no memory other than the incident with my brother and the partial memory of the man by the river. I had no idea how deeply damaged I had been as a child.

He was seldom home, and I was always at home or at church. Occasionally a couple he knew from college might visit, but that was as close as I was allowed to get when it came to his world. Years later, I heard from a fellow student of his that the first time she met me it blew her mind. She said she couldn't imagine me as the person my husband had been describing.

It is well known that, when something else is going on within the marriage, the wife is happy to wear blinders so she doesn't have to confront the truth. I didn't have to wear blinders because all I had to do was go inside and be with my "family." This allowed me to do what I needed to do without confronting him. There were phone calls and hang-ups, but I ignored them even though I knew it was a women.

Now here's where it becomes more complicated. Shortly before his last semester in college, he told me he had been taking premed classes and applied to several medical schools. One sent a letter requesting he come for an interview. I was devastated. By now our sons were three, five, seven, and eight. I couldn't believe what he was saying.

Now there wasn't going to be a teaching degree, a new house, or a family-oriented, stay-in-the area aspect to our lives. My snug little world had been invaded by moths and was now full of holes.

In 1972 the only way someone was able to go to medical school was if he or she had money or knew someone of influence. We didn't have either, so in some ways I felt confident this wasn't going to happen. I begged God not to let this happen—but it did.

After he received a letter from the college for an interview, we piled into our VW van and headed for the interview. The boys saw it as a fun adventure, but I saw it as possibly the beginning of the end. I couldn't imagine how we could ever accomplish such a crazy thing.

He told me all his interviews went fine until his last one. The man asked why he wanted to become a doctor, and my husband went into detail about what this meant to him. More time was spent talking, and then, just before the interview ended, the man again asked why he wanted to become a physician. That did it! My husband stood up, told the man he had explained all of that once, and if he hadn't heard him, or didn't believe him, then the interview was over because they both had better things to do. When my husband came out and told me what happened, I was ecstatic.

Shortly after the interview fiasco, the first letter came, and my husband was told his application had been placed on hold, and was still under consideration. Soon after that, another letter came saying the same thing. Finally there was one last letter; he was in. It had taken three months from the time he told me his plans. The person turning the tide on the board's decision had been none other than the man who had given him the hardest time.

Here's what happened. The university had implemented a program to accept applicants/students who were willing to become family physicians and then go into rural areas where the need for doctors was desperate. He fit the bill. If he had been two years older, his application would have been rejected because of his age.

Let me briefly tell you about the number of students applying for his spot. There were 112 openings with 115 students applying for each "slot." That meant there was a total of 12,880 students trying to get what my husband had just received—a spot in the upcoming class.

The divorce rate for married medical students, even without children, was 97 percent. We were in for a rough ride. The night we left for medical school there was a storm with heavy rain and wind. Just before I closed and locked the door to my wonderful junky house, one entire wall of windows fell out. It seemed the entire Universe was crying for me. The house was falling apart, and so was I.

For medical students, jobs weren't an option. If you took one, you were out. The pressure in medical school was tremendous, but the hours were worse. He had all sorts of people he could identify with since they were all going through the same things he was. Then there was me trying to balance a job, cram us into a two-bedroom trailer, and take care of four little boys.

I finally found a full-time job with some of the nicest people on earth. When I left work, I went home to what was known to me as second shift. At home I'd wait until the boys went out to play or went to bed, then I'd go into the closet, close the door, and cry. This type of life was, in some ways, exactly what was keeping our marriage together. I was numb, but I tried desperately to be both mother and father to our sons and still maintain a life that wasn't totally insane. Fortunately one of the women I worked with owned a three-bedroom house on the edge of town with a small, shallow creek at the edge of the yard. She rented it to us, and it was almost as if it was a sign from God. It was perfect.

Living in a city with multiple colleges was not the best place for me. I love college towns, don't get me wrong, but the people living there don't always have much to do with the students because they'd be moving. Students were all in the same position, so they had each other to lean on and talk to. The churches catered to the young, first-time-away-from-home students without much baggage. Needless to say, I had baggage, and a lot of it. The church the boys and I chose was huge and filled with students. Attending put me in an odd situation because I didn't fit in with the singles, but at the same time I also didn't fit in with the marrieds because my husband wasn't there.

If my husband had any time to do something fun, it wasn't with us—it was with his classmates. Besides, we didn't have enough money to go out as a family or alone as a couple. Now you know why the divorce rate was so high.

As for me, I had my trickle-down coping behaviors, and they were serving me well. I couldn't keep anything disturbing straight in my mind. Before graduation, my husband had to do a preceptorship in the area where he would be doing residency. To do this he would be gone a month. Believe it or not, while he was gone, I had a tubal ligation so we no longer needed to worry about more children. I waited until Friday so I would have the weekend to recuperate, and the boys would be at home if I needed help. I took a taxi to the hospital to have the surgery, and then I took another one home. Why didn't I wait until my husband was home? I didn't want to inconvenience him.

Thank goodness I not only had God to keep me company while he was gone, but also four lively boys who kept me busy.

I was hoping things would be better once he graduated from medical school and began working on his residency, but that was a long way from the truth.

Since we were going to be in the area for three years, we decided to buy a house in a subdivision away from the hospital. We hoped this would help stabilize the boys so they didn't have to deal with even more upset.

At long last we were able to find what I felt was the perfect church, and things began to settle down. That was until one night when the phone rang and a woman on the other end of the line said, "He'll never love you." She hung up. The next evening she called and said, "He'll never love you in a million years." This was one of many calls I received from her. The instant I'd answer, I'd hear a click on the other end of the line. If the boys answered, she would ask to speak to me. They'd call me to the phone and say, "That woman's on the phone again." I'd answer and—click—she'd hang up.

I had thought medical school required long hours. That's was nothing compared to residency. My husband was still hardly ever home, and when he was, we weren't getting along. Gee, I wonder why? My childhood coping skills were still firmly entrenched, so I did what I had always done in the past—I just went inside, ignored even the most blatant things that might happen, and tried my best to stay alive.

We did go our separate ways for a few months. He stayed at the hospital in one of the apartments, and I stayed home. Since I was involved in church, I decided to talk to our minister. That ended up being a big mistake as well as the end of my blind relationship with not only church, but, temporarily, with God.

When I went in to counsel with the minister, he asked the most insane question ever: "What's the worst thing that could happen to you?"

Without hesitation I said, "I could die."

"No", he said, "you could get a divorce, find someone new, get married, and live happily ever after."

I thought, "What? Didn't you hear what I said? I could die!"

That answer seemed to go unheard by him. Did we seek any other counsel? Yes! We went to someone my husband knew from the hospital. He was a psychologists/marriage counselor and was sure he could help us with our marital issues.

It was the type of therapy in which you go in together, then separately, then together again. After our first appointment as a couple, we discussed our issues. Next my husband and I each went for individual sessions. We had one more session as a couple, and then my husband had another appointment alone. After that it was my turn. When I went to see the therapist, he told me that my husband and I should get a divorce. He went one step further and told me that, if I decided I wanted to do that, he would see me through the process, but he wanted nothing more to do with my husband. He said there were only three psychologists in the area capable of handling our in-depth problems. He was one, and his wife was another, but he didn't share with me the name of the third.

I immediately went home and decided I knew a fourth option, and that was to let God direct me. I had taught myself to listen to God throughout my entire life, so this wasn't anything new. When I heard something inside telling me what to say, I said it. If I was midsentence and sensed the words *shut up* I'd stop.

Meanwhile I decided to go to work. We were living separately, and I hadn't decided what I wanted to do. I was still getting phone calls, and he was talking to other women about our problems. (Bad idea!)

The minister's question was still circling in my mind, so I did something stupid. I decided I needed a second opinion about my attractiveness. My boss happened to be single and was only going to be in the area long enough to sell his parents' business. After hearing what both the psychologist and the minister said, I began wondering how anyone would ever find me attractive. Surely I was flawed or I wouldn't be having problems. By now you can more-or-less color me insane.

Okay! Now I'm going to show you how insane I was at the time. At that point I decided to ask my single boss if he would go out with me. I felt surely he could give me a better idea of how others might view me and tell me if the sexual world was so different than what I knew. We went out only a few times, but it didn't take long for me to decide I'd had enough of "dating" and either needed to mend the marriage or end it. By now I knew I would be fine if we decided to go our separate ways. One last incident happened with me, and I decided I was going down the wrong path and ended any ideas of needing to know how others viewed me.

For a short period of time, things seemed to change, and we began to get along better, or so I thought. We had one last move to make so my husband could finally open his own office. It was our hope this would be the last time we were going to uproot our family. By now the boys were growing older, and our problems were becoming more difficult by the day.

I moved a month before he was able to finish his internship. This would give me time to set up our house before he arrived. I thought he was staying with a friend while we were apart. Shortly after we moved, his female friend did as well.

Originally, when we first opened the office, I took the position of receptionist. Once our business began to pick up, we decided I could stay home. After a year, the amount of cash coming into the office dropped, but we didn't know why. I went back to work as a bank teller to help pay bills. Not long after that, we found the reason the office income was slipping. The person who had replaced me had been pilfering money and not filing insurance. She was fired, and I went back to work.

Thankfully, our neighbor was able to come in and help in the office. Without her we would really have been in trouble. I was trying so hard to do everything right, but still everything kept going wrong. I won't even begin to try and explain the trouble our sons were having.

We lost almost all of the money from the unfiled claims because too much time had lapsed. What had been done was destroying our family, and we were about to go down for the count. This was when I started having trouble with alcohol and sometimes prescription drugs.

I was trying my best to keep my head above water, but no matter how hard I tried, I was always drowning. Through it all, my coping techniques were in high gear, and every time things became too much, I'd shut down. After being in the area for three years, we decided he would take a position back in the area where our families lived.

We stayed in that area for three years then moved to where we live now. By now he was working both in emergency rooms and filling in at private offices where he was needed. Finally one of the offices where he was working made him an offer, and he took them up on it. By now our marital issues were a bit better, but we were still considering divorce. One last woman finagled her way into our lives, but after I confronted her she was gone, and he never strayed again. By now we were tired, and our love for each other was wearing thin. That was about the same time I found out about my childhood issues.

Remember how I talked to him after finding out about my childhood issues? From that point on, I began telling people our years of marital issues were due to misperception.

That was the end of that! Once I began working on my childhood issues, the strength and support he gave me was absolutely outstanding. We originally had seven really great years. They were followed by twenty years of pure hell, but since then, everything has been great.

My Experience with Alcohol, Medications, and Cigarettes

After I confessed all those things about our marriage, you may be wondering if I ever did anything detrimental to deal with what was happening. Yes I did! These are things some people do if they have been abused or are dealing with extremely stressful issues. I've always recognized I do everything with all my might, so I was grateful I wasn't willing to allow myself to be trapped into any of these on a long-term basis.

I never took anything stronger than an aspirin or antibiotic before I was twenty-nine. When my husband's older sister took us out for our anniversary, I drank one glass of champagne, and it knocked me on my ass. Later my husband would occasionally give me a swallow of alcohol so I would relax when we did the deed. My tolerance was low, so that was all it took for me to be able to be less tense.

When he was in his last year of medical school, my primary physician gave me a very low dose of medicine to relax. Why? Because when he asked how long it had been since my husband and I had been anywhere to relax and enjoy ourselves, I took too long to answer.

After medical school, when my husband was beginning to start his residency and internship, I accidently did something which could have easily ended my life had he not been home. I had taken our sons to the store. One of them stuck a Hot Wheel car into his sock, and we had to go to manager's office. At the time, I was as strict a mother as I could possibly be, and I was wound tighter than an eight-day clock. I was mortified. As soon as we got home, I took a pill to calm myself. I fed our boys, but failed to eat anything. About then my husband came home and ate his supper. I told him what had happened, and then he lay down for a bit before he was to go back to work. Even after telling him what happened, I still felt upset. Now, remember, I had a low tolerance for drugs and alcohol, so it wasn't going to take much for me to be in trouble. Hoping a swallow of alcohol would help, I did that without remembering I had taken a pill earlier and hadn't eaten. My husband woke an hour later and was about to walk out the door when I told him I didn't feel good. I promptly passed out. We were on our way to the emergency room when I began waking to the brightest, whitest light I'd ever seen. I told him I was okay and wanted to go home.

When we were going through the worst of our problems, my tolerance built enough so that occasionally I might have a glass of the gagiest, sweetest, ickiest wine on the market. No money, no taste. What can I say? Later I switched to something cheap but far stronger so it would work faster.

As our problems grew, so did my consumption of alcohol. I didn't drink often, mind you, but it could have easily become a problem because, for a short period of time, it helped me let myself down and relax. When the stress built up and I was nearly ready to explode, I'd drink to the point where I could talk about how I felt. I was still taking medication for nerves, but fortunately hardly ever did so along with alcohol. Except once! Enough said! I survived that one too. After that I learned my lesson about mixing the two.

All together, I had issues with alcohol off and on for seven years, and then it all just stopped. For one thing, I became allergic and was having to increase the amount I drank because, by then, I had a high tolerance. The last time I had any issues with either of these substances was over fifteen years ago. I just stopped!

I thought seriously about not telling you this, but as we all know, issues like mine fuel the fire when it comes to substance abuse.

As for cigarettes—well my neighbor made it look as if smoking might relax me. I went to the store, bought a pack, and tried to light up. No such luck. The end that was supposed to be lit kept falling off. I thought it seemed like more work than it was worth, and besides it not only tasted horrible, but we hardly had money for a soda let alone a smoking habit.

Myself as a Mother

Now let's travel into my life as a mother. Sometimes I feel maybe I should never have become a mother so I wouldn't have passed on my pain. One thing I have loved in life is being a mother. With our first son, I did feel resistance to motherhood. I had spent my entire life alone allowing only bits and pieces of others close. As a mother, things were going to need to change. I was going to be with this child 24/7. My breaths were going to be his, and regretfully my pains were going to be his as well. Now I was about to begin allowing my own trickle down to drain into another generation. Even now as I think about what I'll be saying my heart aches for them.

I've been able to understand so much about what was happening now. I loved our sons, and we did have fun doing things that didn't cost much money. I made up stories, sang, joked, hiked, and did a ton of other things to normalize their childhoods as much as possible. Not one of our sons ever blamed me for their mistakes, mostly I think because I've always tried to help in a healthy, loving balanced way.

A Mother's Pain

They didn't know their mom was hurt.
Sensing only pain
They tried so hard to comfort her
And make things whole again.

When it comes to broken souls,
Children aren't well equipped.
They have no way of knowing how
To get back all they'd missed.

So onward go those broken lives.
And surely as the dawn
Those holes in her—those empty holes—
Will surely be passed on.

As time went by and they grew up.
No matter how she tried
Her hurts and aches and tears would touch
Every passerby.

I'm sorry for the lives I've hurt.
For that's my only shame,
That those I love have had to feel
The deepness of my pain.

But now I know that I will heal
And help them all to find
That none of us could be to blame
For the pain within my mind.

It may take years to mend us all,
But this promise I hold true:
I'll do whatever it may take;
That's all that I can do.

So I started stretching out my mind
To find the hidden parts.
But the sorrow that had crossed my path
Was filled with poison darts.

I looked at me most every way
Assured that I could know
What happened to me as a child
So very long ago.

And as it started to unfold
As every story will,
I found a pile of empty dreams
On a great and giant hill.

Mary Davenport

So I began my journey home
With patience, tears, and shame,
To gather up our broken hearts
And make them whole again.

One by one and day by day
I spread my wings to fly,
And yet my strength had gathered not
No matter how I'd try.

But one day I'll find my place,
Those wings I will unfold,
And turn my saddened notes to songs
Of silver and purest gold.

Broken though we all may be
It's up to us in the end
To dance our dance and change our lives
If we our souls would mend.

So take your heart within your hand,
Be brave as knights of old,
Mount that steed and fight that fight,
Since peace is for the bold.

Forget the past and look to now.
That's all that there is left.
A treasured child—a woman now—
Doing her very best.

I think it's grand what God has given
For peace of mind has been my task.
My life I am living now
And I can fly at last.

Our first son wasn't the easiest child for me as I tried my hand at motherhood. He was as lively as any child could be. He was up with the sun and never stopped. He was an extremely sweet child, and before long we clicked. My only regret was following church rules as well as trying to heed the new advice about raising children. I let him cry when I should have picked him up and held him close. He could manage his way out of his crib when he was seven months old, and he was walking by the time he was nine months old, if you can call running learning to walk. And climb? Our first encounter with his monkey business was when he opened the refrigerator shortly before he turned one and tossed eggs onto the floor. The next morning he was sitting on the counter ready to mix my sugar and flour. The third day he was attempting to climb on top of the refrigerator to snag a cookie. A few days later, at five in the morning, he woke up, pushed a chair to the front door, unlatched a night latch, unlocked the door, and took his tyke-bike out for a spin. Our neighbor brought him back after finding him heading toward the highway. Thank goodness our neighbor knew where he belonged!

That day I put foil over his windows in an attempt to convince him it was dark. Next my husband put a night latch on the outside of his bedroom door. I removed everything from his room that might be dangerous until his room was child proofed. Before my husband went to work, he would put a bottle and a cookie in our son's room, latch the night latch, but leave the door ajar. I'd wake up shortly after he left and hear our son happily playing. It was the only way we could keep him safe. Shortly after that, when I was pregnant with our second son, I took my eyes off him for a minute, and he unlatched the gate to our backyard and ran to climb the chain-link schoolyard fence. He was seven feet up off the ground when I caught him.

As our other sons were born, our first son taught them everything he knew. They were a lively bunch, but also the sweetest boys you would ever want to meet. I dearly loved our boys. One of the best things about being a mother was how busy they kept me. Managing them kept my mind and hands occupied so I wasn't able to pay attention to my internal feelings of confusion and panic.

When I found out about my childhood issues, all four were grown. Our youngest was almost twenty, and our oldest was twenty-five and had two daughters of his own.

None of our sons or our grandchildren ever noticed that I behaved differently from other people. To them I seemed normal. To anyone outside of our family, my behavior seemed the same as it did to my husband—controlling. Everything I tried to do came across not as helpful, but as an intrusion. This caused a great deal of grief over the years. Even though my motives were pure, they came across as evil. Now we had taken my trickle down one more generation as it began filtering into the lives of our grandchildren.

For a while I felt guilty after finding out about my childhood. I scoured my mind to try to find anything I might have passed on to our sons. The worst thing I did was over explain situations. I made our sons into confidants when they were at an age when they had no control or understanding about what was happening. Finally I decided the only thing I could do to try to make amends was to teach them what I had learned and hope they could find a way to apply it to their own lives. Other than that I vowed to demonstrate my newly implanted thoughts, behaviors, and language into action and allow them to observe what I was doing.

One thing that did stick out in my mind had to do with bathing the boys. When they were very small, I still remember the thought passing through my mind, "Don't linger, and don't avoid." I always thought that was a strange, but my goal was to give them a healthy sense of their bodies, and I was able to accomplish that. I had no idea at the time about my own possible bathing abuse.

Doing something positive for our sons is the one thing I would like to accomplish if I am able to profit from this book. My husband and I left our sons shortchanged in some ways. When it came to college, even saying the word put visions of horror in their minds. From the time they were babies, we couldn't do this, we couldn't do that, we couldn't go here, we couldn't go there. It was a series of pack up, we have to move. Why? One reason and one reason only: because Dad's in college.

My husband started college after high school. After he joined the military he attended night classes. When he graduated from four-year college, our sons were three, five, seven, and eight. When he finished medical school, they were six, eight, ten, and eleven. After his internship, they were nine, eleven, thirteen, and fourteen.

I remember his medical school graduation. All the graduates' families were asked to stand up. I stood with our boys and someone proclaimed, "Oh, my God! They have four children!" I was proud, but I was also exhausted. Everyone was worn out from all the work it had taken for my husband—their father—to finish school. I still despise hearing the word *potential* after living with it for so many years.

In helping our sons in the future with profits from this book, I promised myself I would never hand over money in a way that even vaguely looked as if I owed them for their childhoods. I truly tried to make sure they had the best childhoods possible. Instead of allowing them to have a free ride, what I want to do is teach them to fish, so to speak. That way it will be up to them to find out what they want to do with what's left of their lives. I firmly believe mothers never intend for the lives of their children to be difficult. A lot of the time it happens because the mother has her own trickle down.

The same applies to our grandchildren. I want them to have a better future than their parents, and they are more than excited to tell me what they would like to do. One granddaughter would like to be a psychologist and another wants to be a teacher. Each one is acquainted with my story and has given me a tremendous amount of emotional support. With or without help from this book, I know they are all moving in the right direction and will be able to succeed in everything they do.

What I want is for each of them, from our sons to our great-grandchildren, to be able to do what would make them happy—get training for a better job, open a business, go to college. I want them all to have whatever will help them further themselves in life.

My greatest joy is seeing that our grandchildren have the information they need to make good choices. Yes, some have parental trickle-down damage in their lives, but they aren't blind to what happened the way I was. I've been able to both tell and show them how to change generational patterns into ones that will make their own children whole.

I have four great-grandchildren, and that too has brought me a great deal of joy. I'm thankful to see their parents shifting their lives in a healthier way even though they may have a little dust on them from their own parents dealing with their trickle down.

My Mother and I Trade Places

At some time in life it may become necessary to trade places with our parents. All of my original family passed, so I was up to me when it came time for mother to enter into the last phase of her life. Even if other family members were still alive, as her daughter I volunteered my support in meeting her needs. As in all good plans of mice and men, mine didn't exactly go the way I expected.

Originally my husband and sons were going to turn part of our garage into a nice apartment so when the time came she would have a small but comfortable place nearby to live. We thought we had more time and hadn't been prepared for how soon this needed to be done. We could see her dementia was happening faster than we expected, but we still thought we had time. Several things began to happen that seemed to speed up her lessening mental abilities.

The first thing was finding out that my brother had leukemia. Only one year went by from the time we were told about his condition to the time he passed. The fight was valiant but fruitless.

My grief for his passing didn't work the way it worked for others. I didn't cry. Instead, my stomach acid began to increase until my entire mouth felt like it was on fire. A headache of monumental proportions began to throb until it was hard for me to remain focused. When I was introduced to others by my niece, she would follow the introduction by saying, "And this is his sister. She doesn't cry."

What was I supposed to say? Maybe I wasn't crying, but then again I hadn't cried for anyone, so why would I start now? Instead drank several glasses of water, went into the bathroom, and threw up. I took several aspirins, went to my car, and slept for an hour. When I woke, up the burning had subsided and the headache was almost gone. That is normal for me when it comes to grieving. We each have our own ways of handling crises, and this was how I handled mine.

Recognizing how upset I felt internally has never been one of my patterns of behavior, so I never was able to show how I felt about my brother's passing. Consciously I felt as if I was fine with what happened, but subconsciously it was another story. I went through the same behavior when mother passed. I took care of business and moved on, or so I thought, until my husband pointed out how stressed I was.

Shortly after my brother's death, I was told that my aunt had an inoperable tumor, and her time was limited. I froze. I now regret that I didn't immediately get in my car and go see her, but that's something I've had to forgive myself for. After the call, my blood pressure dropped, and I knew I was in trouble.

Instead of seeing her right away, I waited until she was in her last days. I should have taken Mother earlier before my aunt was so near death, but I hadn't. By the time we arrived at the hospital, I found it difficult to recognize her as the once-vital person we had known. Mother wouldn't go near her, so I took her arm and led her forward telling her to say good-bye. I meant this to help her finish her business, probably because I never finished my own. In some ways I now know it might have been better to not take her at all.

When my aunt passed, my mind went to another place, just as it had during previous losses, and I was unable to face going to her funeral. My aunt and I had been close, and I knew she would have understood. After all, we had been working for years to deal with my past so I could move forward. Instead, I filed her death with all the others who had gone before. She loved me, and I loved her, so I kept that in mind knowing full well that, even though I hadn't been able to face my grief, I had been able to honor our love for each other, and that was going to have to be enough. Mother didn't grieve for my brother or my aunt. I hadn't done any grieving either and had no idea at the time that there were three more deaths to come. Both of us were trying our best in life, but by now the baggage we were dragging behind us could fill a boxcar. Before my husband and I moved Mother into her apartment, a brother-in-law passed. For a full year my husband had made multiple trips to help. After his death we were finally ready to move Mother. I hoped to make her transition as smooth as possible so her mental state would remain stable, but that didn't happen. Next our focus went to my husband's sister. Little did we know that, within a year, she too would be killed in an automobile accident. Before she died my other aunt passed. Now I was dealing with five deaths in four years, plus mother was living in our house. In addition, we were raising a grandchild. Each death was piled on the other like bodies on a funeral pyre waiting to be lit on fire.

Before we moved Mother to our property after my aunt's death, she had been living in her own home. One Sunday I called to see how she was doing, and she told me some family members were there cleaning her attic. It was hard to understand what she meant, so I told her I was on my way. It took an hour to make the drive, but when I arrived her attic was empty. That wasn't nearly as disturbing as the shocked look on Mother's face.

From what I was told, as each item was removed from the attic someone from the family presented various things to her and asked what she wanted done with it. Evidently, each time she told them they could have the item if they wanted it. No one noticed her state of mind. Immediately they told her that, if she wanted it back, they'd return it. By the time I arrived, everything from the attic was gone, and mother had no idea what was happening; neither could she remember what had been taken. I didn't know what had been taken because, to me, those things belonged to her, and I felt no one had a right to them until she passed.

On the living room floor was a small box set aside for me. Inside was the Future Farmers of America (FFA) jacket my brother was wearing the day he was killed, and his FFA T-shirt. It was shocking to see how small they were. He hadn't been quite sixteen when he died, and his frame had been strong but slender. The first thing to flash into my mind was something known to me as "a bucket of blood". Since Mother wanted to keep my brother's jacket they had to soak it in multiple buckets of clean water in order to remove my brother's blood. Each time I went into the basement I would see not only his jacket but the bloody water. I wonder if anyone cleaning her attic that day cared or knew the story about how desperately Mother grieved for her son or how she preserved his memory by keeping his jacket. Was it held it up for her to see? Had she told them to save it for me? After all, by now it meant nothing to anyone but Mother and me.

Other than the jacket, the only things in the box were my Girl Scout beanie and scarf. I was interested to see them because I remembered how I felt wearing them as I went from house to house selling cookies. It was a warm memory, but nothing over the moon like the memory brought on by my brother's jacket. What other memories had been in the attic? I wish I knew. I wonder if my letter from Eisenhower had been there or the necklace Mother was wearing when she had her picture taken when she was thirty-two. I still remember fingering the beads as I lay in mother's lap waiting for evening services at church to end.

The only thing that had been discussed was her piano. I think getting it was the reason someone came to the house. It was a large item and had been promised to someone after she passed. Earlier I talked to Mother and convinced her it was okay for the piano to be taken earlier than planned. I wish I had realized this wasn't the right time to let go of her piano. Instead, in my mind, I was thinking about convincing my husband we needed to move this large item to her apartment. Later I recognized it might have helped her to remain stable. I can't begin to tell you the countless times I heard Mother singing praises to God while she played that piano. I still picture it in the house where we lived when I was eleven, and in every house after that. I always feel terrible when I come across a "woulda, coulda, shoulda" event because, by the time you feel that way, the deed has already been done and the damage it created can't be repaired. Later I bought an electronic keyboard and even heard her playing it once or twice, but it wasn't the same. Her piano had been her friend at times when all the joy had been drained from her soul. She could always use it to recharge herself, and after it was gone, the void was so huge it could never be filled.

From that point on she was never the same. I could see the light fade from her eyes as she entered even deeper into dementia. About then, her house began to fall apart. The basement was being flooded with sewage, and her roof leaked when it rained. The apartment wasn't ready, but Mother was. To top things off, there were gnats coming from the basement. The final straw was when I found a box in which brown recluse spiders had taken residence. After that, we decided she could no longer remain in the house. Ready or not, the move was on. One day she was living in her house, and the next she was in mine. Neither of us was ready, but what else could we do?

My grandson, who was then fourteen, and I made countless trips in the heat of July to pack the house. With no air conditioning, we felt as if we were being cooked in an oven. At that point, my feeling of anger was beginning to rise right along with the temperature. We made trip after trip loading and unloading the trailer until every inch of our house, garage, and pole barn was filled to the brim.

I unknowingly put a box of dog biscuits in a room about as hot as her house, and before long my cabinets were infested with something known as weevils. Once they establish a stronghold, they infest anything that contains wheat. The only way to manage this is to put out traps, throw away anything that looks infested, and put the remainder of things containing wheat in the freezer or refrigerator. I kept busy smacking millers midair trying to put an end to their siege, but all I did was to make it appear as if I was losing my mind, which wasn't far from the truth.

I hadn't been around Mother 24/7 since I was married. I'm sure her mind was having a difficult time adjusting, but so was mine. All these years I'd envisioned her moving nearby so we could finally be able to establish a true mother/daughter relationship. Mostly all she did was sleep. This should have been a clear sign to me about her state of mind, but by that time I was blind to the fact that I was heading for trouble too. In some ways, we had traded places: I was the mother, and she was the child. I wasn't doing any better at protecting her child-like state of mind than she had protecting mine when I was the child.

I'd tell myself, "shame on you." Then I'd stop and remind myself we were both doing the best we could do under our difficult situations. It would have been easier if I hadn't been dealing with an abusive childhood. Since my subconscious mind knew things it wasn't sharing, more than once I had to remind myself to look at the bigger picture. I would never have allowed anyone to treat her with the disrespect I often found churning in me. This meant it wasn't okay for me to do it either, no matter what had happened to me as a child. I'm a big proponent of treating other people as well as I treat myself with love, honor, and respect. When I'd slip, I'd remind myself of her condition and pull myself together. Everyone kept trying to convince me I was doing better than they could under the same circumstances, but inside I was at war.

Mother lived in the house with us for a year and a half. By the time her apartment was ready, I was too. The day I was able to move her into her own place was a celebration. My husband and grandson were out of town, so I took that opportunity to move Mother and, at the same time, paint the inside of my entire house.

Once she was in her own house, things were better, but it was up to me to clean, make meals, do laundry, take her to church, and do anything else that needed to be done. At the same time, we were spending every weekend getting her home ready to sell. Wouldn't you know it that was when the housing disaster hit?

Since the roof on the porch had been leaking, we decided to have the roofing stripped and new shingles put on. The basement had to be drained several times until we finally replaced the sewer lines. Large items from her basement such as the washer, dryer, and freezer had to be tossed along with the contents. There had been two pieces of furniture I had planned to put in her apartment, but after sitting in sewage they had become so warped and fell apart. Her furnace also had to be replaced. This wasn't going as smoothly as I hoped.

When my husband and son began to repair an outer wall, they found termites. Since the wall was weak, it fell out, and they had to rebuild it. At the same time, a section in my stepfather's former office building was found to have termites. We had to have that section torn down and the outer part of the office back entrance fixed. Needless to say, we had to call the exterminator to spray both places before the house could be sold.

When the house was sold, we had the same amount of money in it that we could sell it for because of the housing situation.

Now all I had to do was concentrate on taking care of Mother. After several years, I hired someone to help clean her apartment and occasionally take her to the senior center to eat so she could socialize. I was finally getting a better handle on what I was doing. After spending the morning of Mother's Day with her, I left for a few hours, and while I was gone Mother tried to sit on her bed. Instead, she missed and slid down the side of the bed and onto the floor and was unable to get up. Since I had placed a phone by the bed, she was able to dial the operator, and an ambulance was sent to check on her. Someone called me to let me know what was happening, but as we got close to home, I saw the taillights of the ambulance pulling onto the highway. Immediately we headed for the hospital to check on her situation. Thankfully nothing was broken. She was checked over and, since she wasn't hurt, she was sent home with us.

I knew it was now time to check into different living arrangements. I was able to find a care center for her, but it was thirty miles away. I tried to make it there as often as I could to take her out for a drive and a meal. Going to see her was difficult. I kept reminding myself I needed to do the right thing, and I often beat myself up internally if I wasn't able to live up to what I felt was expected of me.

By then Mother's dementia had deepened, and when I wasn't there she wasn't aware of my absence. The people caring for her were extremely nice and loved her childish manner. By now even I was beginning to accept that the mother I'd known as a child no longer existed. In some ways this was good because it enabled me to separate her from the woman I had known as a child.

After a year, I was able to move her closer to where we lived, so now it only took a matter of minutes to see her. I continued to beat myself up for not going more often, but I finally realized she was content. The staff was fantastic. I can't begin to tell you how many times I was told by the people caring for her how much they loved her.

At ninety-seven her health was solid. Her blood pressure was normal, and her heart rate was perfect. She took no medication, and if she did it was administered in small doses. It was plain that she might easily live to be a hundred. The thing I wasn't aware of was that she was having nightmares and rambling on about how much she wanted to die. A few months before she passed, she told me "they" were trying to kill her. By that she didn't mean the staff, but someone from her childhood. I reassured her as best I could, but it never stopped being one of her greatest fears. About then it was noted on her chart that she had been sexually abused as a child. This had been one of the trickle-down issues I had also been confronting.

As with many people her age, her bones were soft, and at one point when she was being helped from bed, she suffered a vertebral fracture and was given morphine for pain. From that time on, her health and her mind began to slip even more. After hearing about how much she had been suffering mentally and emotionally, as terrible as it sounds, I was happy when her emotional and physical pain ended. Living another three years so she could become a hundred would have been torturous.

In some ways, I hate to admit how difficult our transition was. I'm sure it was every bit as difficult for her as it was for me. I tried so hard to do the right thing. Since then I've talked to countless others who have told me how hard their own transitions had been. It is difficult when it comes time to take responsibility for an aging parent. I knew I had done what I needed to do to be the best daughter possible. That's why it was important to make sure I honored her in the best way possible when I buried her ashes and put her to rest.

How am I choosing to remember Mother? One day when my granddaughter and I were cleaning Mother's apartment, we were being silly. I looked at Mother and saw the sweetest, brightest, most angelic smile on her face I had ever seen. She was enjoying our antics in a pure and loving way. It was that moment I have filed away in my mind so I can pull it up whenever I think of her.

A few months after Mother passed, I came across a picture of her taken at the care center, and I saw the same brightness radiating from her face. With each passing day, my love for her is finally settling into me. I only wish I could have felt this way when she was still here. Her passing seemingly has freed me from the lesser loving incidents we shared. I no longer need to protect her from anyone, and now my life no longer has to be lived in the shadows of our past. Yes, Mother loved me, and I loved her. Maybe it wasn't the kind of love I had worked so hard to achieve, but it was there nonetheless. We are now both at peace with what happened when our trickle downs bumped into each other and created a gap between us as wide as the Mississippi River. I have forever been thankful, however, that I bridged that gap between myself and my family and was able to shower them with not only the love they needed, but the love I needed as well.

CHAPTER FOUR

Noisy Mind, Noisy Body

The Places Where Trickle Down Goes

I wish I could begin the rest of my story starting with the day I started therapy in January of 1989, but for now I need to go back to February 1988 when I happened across a book by Jack Dreyfus titled A Remarkable Medicine Has Been Overlooked. This was nine months before I knew about my childhood. I had gotten to the point where living was more of a chore than a gift. I had no idea how or why I needed to begin changing or even what I needed to do. I just seemed to begin following an invisible path. I never knew what my next step was going to be, but something in me just kept pushing me blindly forward. Eventually there seemed to be an unbelievable sense of peace about following my path. Somehow life seemed to have filed a destination into my life, and even though I had no idea where I was going, I just followed directions.

I must admit some of the tactics I used as I worked my way toward wellness were things I hadn't heard of before. Even a few years earlier, I never would have attempted to try some of the things I did as I inched my way forward. Somehow I began to push organized religion ideas aside so I could try things that most people wouldn't necessarily have approved of at the time.

There was something that constantly seemed to be directing me in a very calm, reasonable, nonassertive way. I used to say I was slicing into myself like a surgeon. In many ways, I was cutting myself into paper-thin slices and then holding each piece to the light to see what I might discover. To tell you I was sometimes skating on thin ice is an understatement. I knew if I made one wrong move on my way to recovery, I was going to go under, and there wouldn't be any way back.

One day I was driving to one of my appointments. As I pulled toward the intersection, I swear I saw a fire underneath the car a few yards in front of me. Something inside my mind seemed to whisper, "Slow down." Immediately that silent voice within also warned me that, if I didn't stop pushing myself, I was going to be in for trouble. Of course I knew there wasn't a fire under the car, so that wasn't a problem. It was the voice's warning I needed to listen to. I physically slowed my car down and backed away. I also began to back away from the pressure I was putting myself in while trying to recover my past.

Surgery

I'd like to take a surgeon's knife and cut into my soul.
I'd slice away all parts that hurt so I could make me whole.

This poem, written in early 1989 was tough, and it circled my mind for some time before I trapped it on paper. I tried to finish, but the direction it seemed to want to take was morose. I decided to set it aside until I felt stronger. This enabled me to back away from it the way you would if you found a sleeping lion. "No supper for you tonight, Mr. Lion," I whispered as I slowly and quietly backed away.

This is partially the way I was able to teach myself to change. I sliced my personal self apart in thin layers and held them to the light of the truth—to the light of reality—and examined any little infraction.

Originally I was so focused on slicing into myself I knew if I didn't stop there would be nothing left because everything hurt. Later I came to realize, if a surgeon cuts away diseased tissue, there is room for healthy tissue to grow in its place. In 2010, I came across something that compared a writing pen (or in my case a computer) to a surgeon's knife. As I wrote about all the things that had happened and all I was doing in order to find my way into a better way to live, I was slowly becoming whole.

February of 1988 is where I need to begin the next part of my story. By then, deep inside, I was beginning to feel a caustic burning boiling into every thought and behavior in my life. To tell you I felt tormented is an understatement. I didn't have any idea what might be causing this torture. It was hard to remain focused because of an insane amount of noise cluttering my mind. The level of noise made it almost impossible for me to stay focused. Even though I didn't know where I was going or what I was looking for, I pushed myself into the fray and began hoping I'd find answers. Without going into myself and understanding what was creating this clamoring racket, I never would have been able to go fully into my life to find the cause of my problems.

Noise Alert

In the early months of 1988, I became acutely aware of the noise in my mind. By now it seemed so loud I felt if anyone stood close enough they could hear it. My confusion was growing stronger, and I felt a sense of panic that wouldn't subside. It felt like an impending doom coming from somewhere inside that would no longer be still. Anyone who has experienced this knows exactly what I'm talking about.

Later I found the noise was something classified as hyperacousis. That sounded better than schizophrenia, so I went with it. I researched schizophrenia and found some of my behavior fit, but it wasn't a true diagnosis for me. Instead my husband made the statement that he felt my mother had been schizophrenogenic. Her behavior was all over the place, and when I was a child she hadn't been able to give me any clear messages about life.

Finally, after reading an absolutely phenomenal book, I began to understand where the noise might be coming from and what I might be able to do about it. The noise was coming from what is known as a turned-on mind. In one book I read, the author went into detail to describe two types of minds when it comes to noise. The first is normal and has to do with times when we say we are always thinking about something. The second is about always thinking.

All I can say is, if your mind is always thinking about something, you can go to the park, sit down, relax, and be aware of the birds singing, the trees swaying, and the smell of the grass. When you are always thinking, you are hardly aware of the birds, trees, or the grass.

In my case, my mind was always racing around to check surroundings so I could remain safe. I picked up on every conversation and enlarged it (hyperacusis) so I wouldn't be caught off guard or miss anything. I spent every moment listening for and watching for signs of danger. I wouldn't focus on just one thing at a time like the birds, trees, or grass; instead I would try to focus on everything at once. Trust me—if I went to the park, it wasn't fun or relaxing but exhausting.

Because I was hyper aware of sounds around me as a child, this is how I processed noises in a classroom. Can you imagine trying to learn something new as your mind trips over every sound and every movement? For example, if you are in a history class this is what happens: Columbus discovered America in—what was that? It's over there. Columbus discovered America in 14— wait, wait, there it is again. What's that? As you search for the sound, Columbus sails out the window along with the date 1492. This condition made learning next to impossible. Later I'll describe learning or, worse yet, not learning in another way.

After reading the book and checking with my physician, I was given permission to take the medication mentioned in the book, and it did make a difference in how I felt.

Before I can tell you the difference, I need to explain a few other practices I brought into my life at about the same time. It was a combination of these that helped me align my thoughts in a totally different way than I had done before.

Positive Affirmations

What does it mean to affirm something? It is to state something with conviction, or assert a positive statement. Because of these changes my life began to open like the flowers in spring.

I had a hard time with this at first because, to affirm something, I was supposed to say positive things so I could get positive results. I tried to avoid focusing on negative things, but Mother's words had made deep wounds, so without realizing it, I had always felt negative when it came to me. I never said anything positive to the girl in the mirror. I knew we were the same person, but when it came to breaking her with unkindness, I made sure I could see it in her eyes before I left the room. When I saw "her" brokenness, I knew I had succeeded. It is hard to explain how, when I turned to leave, "she" stayed imprisoned in the mirror as I walked away. I truly hated her. Her sadness went to her core, not mine. Throwing negative affirmations in her face gave me a sense of accomplishment I could never explain. I should have wanted good things to happen to her, but it almost seemed impossible to say even one kind word to her (myself).

In some ways I should consider her as another inner child, but I see her when I look in the mirror. Even now I avoid looking myself in the eyes when fixing my hair or putting on makeup. The others are in my mind's eye—but not her. I always see the question "Why?" after I see her crumble. The problem is that I never could answer her question. I *had* to do it—I just *had* to!

I've read in a multitude of books about consciousness and how it is actually easier to think negative things than it is to say positive things. You'd think it would be the other way around. It almost makes one think that the mind's way of thinking is defective.

When you affirm something, make sure to be specific with the words you use. There can be times when something seems negative when it arrives, but it may be a positive thing in disguise. Learn the lesson the way it has been presented. Sometimes this type of issue can be the most important lesson of all.

When I was a child, I depended on Mother for everything, even my sense of self. Since she was telling me I was hated, should be dead, and should never have been born, I guess I incorporated that belief into my core thinking. After all, Mother had power, and I was powerless to even take care of myself as a baby. In many ways, she was my god because she provided for me in ways I couldn't yet provide for myself. I really had to fight to change what my mind had been trained to think with regard to myself. The message given had been done in a trickle-down fashion, so as I grew up, I continued her chatter, thinking it was my own. I tried with every inch of my being to believe her, but at the same time I had my own internal spirit, which was trying to tell me something different. It was extremely difficult to override the messages she had given me. The same is true for other authority figures such as parents, ministers, teachers, friends, enemies. By the time I began learning about affirmations and realized what fantastic changes they might create, I was ready to try anything. I had nothing to lose and everything to gain by beginning to replace my negative thinking from childhood into the positive ones I needed as an adult.

I carefully culled through a book written by Louise Hay titled *You Can Save Your Life* to find statements I felt applied to my particular needs. Before long, I had a script of affirmations I felt I might be able to use to override my negative thoughts. I went one step further by making my own tapes using a method known as subliminal messaging. In the professionally made tapes, all you hear is the music. The message is layered beneath in such a way that you can't hear what is being said, but your subconscious absorbs it nonetheless. I had purchased several professionally made tapes of the type of music the brain finds most useful in promoting the messages I wanted. Fortunately I had the same piece of music, so I set up two tape recorders. One played the music, and I spoke my chosen messages into the other. After I was finished, when I played my tape, I could hear the music in the background and was also able to hear the messages. The premise of this has to do with part of the brain listening to the music while another listens to the spoken message. Using my own voice raised my level of acceptance because it was an audible form of mind chatter. What I was attempting to do was override the earlier programs set into my psyche from childhood.

There isn't any way to tell you how often or how long I listened to my homemade tapes. All I can say is I took them everywhere. If you saw me during this period of time, you'd see me with a small earbuds in at least one ear so I could barrage my mind with new messages. By listening with only one ear, if I was driving, I could still pay attention to the sounds of the traffic. When I was alone, I'd put both the earbuds in and close my eyes as I absorbed each and every message.

At first, every time the tape made a confident positive statement, I could hear my mind disagree. On one hand, I was telling myself I was smart, kind, loving, and beautiful. On the other hand, my mind immediately tried to remind me that I was stupid, hateful, selfish, and ugly.

Around and around my thoughts went hour after hour, day after day, and week after week. It was like the swirling of a toilet that wouldn't flush because it was plugged with crap. It didn't matter how many times my mind disagreed; I continued playing that tape until I had it memorized.

Finally it happened. I could almost hear and feel the flush of the old, outdated, useless, harmful messages being drained out of me. Every time a negative message tried to sneak into my mind, my new concepts drove it out as quickly as it arrived.

I enjoyed my newfound freedom from negative thinking two months before I hit a wall. One day I woke up and realized something was wrong. My heart sank. The medication had lifted the fog, and the self-help tapes were changing my internal scripts, so all should have been well. Now what?

Hopelessness swept over me like a tsunami threatening to take all my newly acquired skills out to sea, leaving me in its path of destruction. I felt disappointed because I had felt so close to resolution, and now it seemed out of reach. I was sure I could find a way to understand why my mind was slipping back into a negative state, but I wasn't sure how I was going to do it.

I got out of bed and got dressed. I grabbed a book, my recorder and recordings, and set out for the back of our property. Once there, I immediately took out my player, put my earbuds in, and pushed the button. Instead of hearing how smart, kind, loving, and beautiful I was, I heard, "I ammm smmmarrt, kiiinnd, loooviingg, aaannd beeeaautifuul." Slower and slower it went until it stopped.

When I reached inside my backpack to retrieve freshly charged batteries, I realized I hadn't put them in my bag. That was always the first thing I did every day before I went anywhere or did anything, so my heart sank. But I had a backup plan. I put my recorder away and pulled out my book. Reaching deep inside my backpack, I searched for my glasses. I had not only forgotten to bring recharged batteries; I had also forgotten my glasses. After putting my book away, I sat slumped on the log I was using as a chair and stared at the ground. That was when the miracle happened. I heard a bird singing!

Now that might not sound like much, but believe me, it was really significant. At that moment I realized I'd never heard anything like what I was hearing. My mind was focusing on one single sound. I was hearing one sound, and it was a bird singing.

In that instant, I realized how much extraneous noise was missing. Before there had been a constant barrage of it in my head keeping me distracted so I couldn't focus on what was going on around me. Later, as I recounted the experience to others, I compared the earlier noise to sitting in the center of a circle of tables, each containing a radio. Each radio was on a different station, so instead of hearing solitary sounds, I heard noise that was nothing but a jumble of sounds and static.

My mind had been filled with that noise for as long as I could remember, and now I heard one single sound. That was what had been different when I woke up. I was so accustomed to multiple sounds that when all but one disappeared, I'd felt a sense of panic. I knew something was wrong or different, but I never would have imagined it had been such a simple thing. The sound of that bird singing changed my life.

The funny part of that story happened as I walked home—listening to single sounds—and a question entered my head that made me laugh. What do people do with all this quiet? I've never really had all that level of noise return. Can you imagine how wonderful it was for me to be able for the first time in my life to manage my thoughts in an orderly fashion? It was, and still is, absolutely spectacular.

Mostly what I'm saying is that it is almost impossible to imagine how many layers of things had come to me in this trickle-down method just so I could successfully make it through each day.

Visualization

About the same I also started taking part in other modalities that are often classified as alternative medicine. At that time, even affirmations fell under this heading. In 1988 most people were not into what was being called Eastern medicine, but today many of these methods are not only medically recognized but are successfully being used for a broad range of illnesses.

In 1988 I was on the rim of changing my religious beliefs. Because of the way I felt when it came to the mind, I was skeptical. After all, the church was constantly warning people to beware of allowing the mind to be open to any type of mild control, even if you were doing it to yourself. This included such things as affirmations, visualization, and hypnosis. They made a point of saying any of these could open the door for the devil to come in to trick you into taking a path into hell.

The first time I thought about or read about visualization, it was being used for things like cancer, heart issues, blood pressure, and a multitude of other things. The books I read were some of the first written by medical doctors who were using it in outpatient and in-hospital situations. I was fascinated at the level of success they were having.

People teaching visualization said to imagine something familiar you could use to change your circumstance. In my first visualization I used the image of a large map of the United States like the one I'd had as a child, but bigger. As an adult I began to envision this small puzzle blown up in a huge, oversized way. I tried to picture it as if it had missing pieces, just like my life. That was exactly how I felt—as if there were gigantic gaps where various pieces of my life were missing.

In my mind I made the pieces so large I had to wrap my arms around them to move them from place to place. The trick was to see not only the map but also the gaps where the puzzle needed filling. Since I had no idea what fit where, I saw myself walking on top of the puzzle carrying each piece looking for a place it might fit. No matter where I took each piece and no matter how hard I tried, I couldn't get even one piece to fit into my life's gaps.

Now I needed to find a method that might enable me to adjust the pieces to fit so my map would look as if it was complete. As I told you earlier, I accidently dropped an axe on my leg before my father was killed, so in many ways an axe had meaning. You'd think I would have found a less-violent method of trimming the overlapping pieces, but I remembered my father handing me the axe. Whacking my leg and leaving a scar didn't mean anything, but seeing my father's hand reaching toward me did.

I took the gigantic piece of puzzle, placed it in a spot that looked as if it might fit, stepped back and—*chop*—I envisioned the axe cutting the excess bits off the ill-fitting puzzle. If I needed to do it more than once, that's what I did. Before long, in my mind, I could see my readjusted piece drop into the empty spot. The fit might not have been perfect, but now I no longer had to carry the ill-fitting pieces. This gave me a sense of freedom I hadn't had before. I did this again and again until I was relieved of every issue (puzzle piece) I couldn't remember. This may sound bizarre, but somehow it worked and I started to feel more relaxed.

Several days after this I was on my way to the store, and something happened. We live in the country, so to go to the store I had to drive. When I started the car, the radio came on. I don't listen to the radio because it keeps me from being on full alert. Before I had a chance to turn it off, however, someone on the radio said something funny, and I laughed. This may not sound significant, but it caught me off guard and it frightened me.

Our house is three miles from town. Halfway between the highway and town there's a bridge, so what I am about to tell you happened only a few minutes from home.

My first thought had to do with how pretty my laughter sounded. My second was—oh no—if I laughed I must be happy, and if I'm happy I want to live, and I can't live. I *need* to die. Notice the word *need*? Mother's words bounced back into my mind in that moment, and I was in conflict: she hated me, wished I was dead, and thought I never should have been born. That is part of the trickle down I want you to heed. Something deep inside didn't feel I had a right to feel happy because I needed to die. I was an adult with no conscious memory of anything other than "I hate you" being said by mother when I was fourteen. Something at that age had been triggered, and suddenly I began using her entire message. My aunt hadn't yet told me what she used to hear Mother say, but the message had come alive and transferred itself from my subconscious mind to my conscious mind. I was fourteen when I started my mirror messages. Now Mother's words became bombs I threw at myself for the next thirty-three years.

Within a little over one mile, I had a conversation within myself that I had a hard time believing. That was when I knew I had to find a way out of the state of mind that confirmed that I felt I had to die. That trickle down flooded over me like a flash flood threatening to pull me off my feet and into the water under the bridge I was crossing at the time.

Why? Because I had opened a door that had been sealed. Visualizing the act of putting those pieces back, even in a haphazard way, had opened the door to every secret I had been keeping from my conscious mind. The only memory escaping were Mother's words to me as a child. In that moment, I felt I reminded myself I didn't deserve to be happy or alive. Suddenly I recognized what a powerful tool I had found. This gave me more hope than I had been able to muster in my entire life.

Before I explain, I want to talk about our family drama. Suddenly I realized because of a book written by Jacquelyn Small titled Transformers I might be able to change the negative dramas in my life. I realized everyone has had difficulties in life. I don't see mine as being more challenging than anyone else's. We all have varying degrees of problems, but I knew since I was still alive I might be able to change my own. I wanted a peaceful way to resolve family drama, but I wasn't quite sure how I could change other people's behaviors. At the time, I thought it required their cooperation. I didn't yet know that, if I changed, they automatically had to change because a change in me would change the balance within the unit. Each person involved then has to find a new way to fit within the new paradigm. I've seen this happen again and again within my own life.

Finally I came to realize that I didn't need to repeat negative family issues. For the first time I knew I no longer needed to unknowingly pass family dramas on to our children. If I could stop my part in negative drama, I could end the trickle down in a significant way so we no longer needed to repeat the same story year after year and generation after generation.

I knew that not repeating drama wasn't going to mean the issues would be gone; it just meant I was removing myself from the part I was playing. In other words, I would walk off the stage. In that way I could find a personal, peaceful solution and watch from the sidelines instead of being overly involved as others in the family continued to tear each other apart.

I've heard it mentioned that there is a gooey, sticky substance called plasmic streamers. I'd read how this substance could be thrown from one person to another. This is the short version of what happens: The plasmic streamer can create a bond between the two parties so an unhealthy drama ensues. Alternately, the streamer can be cut, in which case the drama must stop. At that point I in a book by Barbara Brennon titled Transformers I had to find a way to stop any unhealthy drama that was being lobbed between me and other people.

Once again I pulled out my axe and saw myself chopping away at whatever drama-loaded plasmic streamer bomb was lobbed at me. Scissors also had meaning, so sometimes I would visualize myself just cutting the drama bomb away.

I began using other visualizations to change the dynamics of my life. I would picture the other party as a charging bull and myself as a bullfighter waving a red cape. If I felt I was about to encounter a plasmic drama bomb, I would see myself stepping back, moving my cape to the side, and allowing the bull to pass. *Ole!*

In another visualization I pictured myself as a screen door. If anyone began to speak ill or move toward me in a negative way, I'd see the problem as simply breezing through the screen without touching me. As the plasmic drama bomb passed, I'd take a big breath and blow it out of my mind and life.

Sometimes I wish I could have do-overs in which everyone and everything behaved in an ideal way. That isn't going to happen. I was coming back into my life, transformed by a new way of thinking, speaking, and behaving. Now I knew it was my responsibility to use my new skills to do what I could to change my place within our family dramas. I knew not everyone was going to quickly accept or believe how different I had become, and at times some fought me tooth and nail to "put me back into place" so they could go on with the drama we'd been sharing. This happened more than once. I had to stick to my new plan even if they weren't willing or able to adjust to our new relationship. Since some were close family members, I didn't want them completely out of my life, so I set boundaries. I just no longer bought what they were selling. It was hard to do this because I wanted everyone to play nicely, but if the family drama addiction had been working, I knew that others might not really want it to end.

If you are interested in any of these methods, it's easy to find books to guide you through various types of visualization. I felt a little odd doing it the first time, but once I was able to see how easily it worked, I found a multitude of ways to use this skill.

Neurolinguistics

I can just hear readers now—neuro *what?* Don't ask me how in the world I got into this type of program. All I know about it is that what we say and what our brain hears being said are two different things. I'm sure most everyone has heard psychologists and marriage counselors talk about mixed messages. There is a way to decipher messages so what I say is heard by everyone the way I want it to be. Changing a message is called reframing.

I am not an expert, so all I can tell you will be how I applied what I learned about my own communication and what I did to change my messages. What I'm explaining has worked for me in almost every case. I don't understand how it works, but that doesn't matter. I don't know how my TV works, but that doesn't stop me from watching it. My only goal was to find better ways to live my present-day life.

The fact is that everything I experience in life leaves an imprint. When I hear something or do something, it is automatically filtered through my own personal experiences, and what I say and what I hear is then colored by them. I don't think the brain plays fair. This is part of the reason that everything said, especially around children, should be said in a clear, loving way.

Even though I might feel as if I'm saying one thing in a very plain, understandable way, I realized my message may not come out the way I intended. The hard part was that I wasn't even aware anything happened, so changing it never entered my mind. Without becoming consciously aware of how what I was saying to others might be twisted, I felt confused when they misunderstood.

I didn't want to be one of those people unwilling to work my way through a problem. If that were true, I would be part of the problem of continuing a form of drama that would never end. I had always felt it was better to talk until I was able to find a collective satisfactory solution. I always encouraged our sons to do that—talk it through—even if it takes more than one conversation.

I've found that something left unfinished can quite easily twist itself into something that grows into a form of resentment, even when the original source is no longer clear. In olden days, this was called a feud and broke families apart, sometimes forever.

I always encouraged our sons to make sure their relationships stayed clean of any form of gooey unresolved issues. The reason this was important to me is how my father left and never returned and how my brother never made it home. No one knows how much time we have left, so I feel it's important to keep my relationships in check. The last thing I remember about my brother is how I had done something kind. It was his job to dust mop the floors, and I offered to do it for him so he could be on his way. I remember this interaction in a good way. I've always been happy that I didn't try to blame myself for doing this since it would have been easy to see how he wouldn't have been on that part of the highway when the accident occurred. Thankfully as a child it never occurred to me to have taken any blame for his death.

My husband and I were experiencing this during twenty years of our marriage. He was seeing what I was doing through the filter of his experience, and I was seeing it through mine. He was bound and determined I wasn't going to control him the way his mother had, and all I was trying to do was behave in the way I felt a good, loving Christian wife should behave. I wasn't trying to be controlling; nonetheless, that's how he was seeing and hearing me. Everything I said was a challenge under the guise of his mother's voice—not mine. In other words, he was trying to finish unfinished business with his mother by putting me into her place. To say I felt confused is an understatement. I could not understand what I was doing or saying that seemed to instantly stir his anger.

As I became acquainted with neurolinguistics, I was able to see how the way I was presenting my words seemed to be part of the problem. Not only that, but I began to recognize how determined he had been when it came to protecting his integrity. Some people aren't nearly as interested in integrity as they are about being right. Something in him wouldn't allow himself to view himself as part of the problem. I guess he felt if something was wrong—it must have been my fault. We were fighting a battle when there wasn't a battle except in our minds.

I can't tell you how many books I've read on the subject of communications so I could learn how to say what I meant without it being taken out of context. Neurolinguists, marriage counselors, psychologists, and psychiatrists try to make it a point to have couples repeat what they "think" they heard the other person say. It is like the game in which one person is told a secret and then is asked to relay it to the next person. That person is asked to relay it to the next, and so on. At the end, the final person is asked to repeat the secret. Many times what is said at the end doesn't have anything to do with the original message. This is an oddity within the brain because it filters everything through our experiences. With each new player, the secret changes and is twisted into a form each individual relates to.

From there I went one step further by considering not only what I should and should not be saying, but how I was saying it. Everything counts. How I held my body during conversations, the tone of my voice, and the look on my face—it all mattered, as well as any type of tell someone might see that even I didn't recognize I was showing. If I didn't do this, what should be a pleasant conversation could easily turn into a full-blown argument over nothing more than a look, a tone of voice, or some other miscommunication or misperception.

I think schools should be teaching communications to students. There are a lot of subjects being taught that aren't nearly as important as neurolinguistics. Correct, effective communication is a life skill, just like learning how to handle a checkbook so I don't spend more money than I have or verbally convey a hidden message I might not have intended to send. It would also be nice if we knew how to do neuro-listening. That might avoid a lot of trouble before it even begins, wouldn't you agree?

There are things I taught myself to do when it comes to what I say. I try to find soft words rather than hard or harsh-sounding ones. Have you heard the saying "Make your words like marshmallows, soft and sweet, because you never know when you'll have to eat them"?

As I began teaching myself to monitor what I was trying to say, I did so in a way that wasn't exactly the same as was being taught by neurolinguists. I didn't want to learn how to assemble a car; all I wanted to do was to drive it to the store so I could buy marshmallows.

Another lesson I taught myself had to do with an addictive, problematic behavior society seems to share, and that is the way we take things personally. Think about this—if I begin a sentence using the word *you*, the other person automatically takes a defensive stance. The rest of what I say after the word *you* may not be heard because the mind is already trying to find a way to avoid being blamed for whatever I might say next. A conversation can become blocked because what might be said next has become contaminated by the listener's past.

One of the other things communication experts pointed out is that, when I am having a conversation and it goes sideways, I needed to stop and gracefully find a way to change the subject or back off. Why? Because when a conversation becomes overheated or confused for no apparent reason, the person I am talking to may have dropped back in time to an unresolved issue. This also applied to me. If I started to feel upset, I was able to realize I was dropping back in time to my unresolved past issues. Minds desire resolutions. It doesn't matter if it is a past issue or a present one. If something is said that seems familiar, all of a sudden the brain makes a jump into the past. At that point there's a ghost not only in the brain but in the relationship. What began as a personal conversation, discussion, or argument can easily spin out of control. At that point the subconscious mind and the conscious mind begin to have their own conversation, and this becomes a no-win situation. When I saw this happening, I found ways to talk about something else or remember something I need to do so I could excuse myself.

I taught our sons to tell the other person they're sorry when they find themselves in an argument or a detrimental situation with someone and the temperature seems to escalate. They should do this if for no other reason than they are sorry the other person is feeling so upset. I told them to allow the other person to interpret the words *I'm sorry* in whatever way they choose so things can cool down. That was always one of the tactics that enabled my husband and me to stay together. We went through some difficult problems, but being right or holding the other person accountable wasn't something I chose to pursue. I don't think there has ever been a time when, after I backed off, he didn't come within the next couple of days and apologize for what happened or for what had been said. Being right isn't nearly as important to me as being happy. As far as I'm concerned, happiness means peace.

There were things I taught myself to say, and words to avoid, after I learned how neurolinguistics works. One example is to avoid attaching feelings. If someone says "you make me mad" or "you piss me off," I've been able to come to terms with the idea I can't make anyone mad or pissed. What I say or do might piss someone off or create a sense of anger, but to be mad or pissed off is a choice the other person makes for himself or herself.

If someone chooses to behave in a detrimental way, I pull out one of my visualizations and allow his or her feelings of anger to pass through me like a screen or whiz by as I move my bullfighting cape. This way I can let go without being sucked in by words. I try to avoid allowing myself to think that someone else has the ability to create a sense of anger in me. I know I need to own my feelings and behavior and not try to make it someone else's fault. I've been known to point out to others that I am more than willing to take responsibility for my own feelings, but when it comes to their personal feelings or thoughts, it's up to them as to how they handle it. The neurolinguistic way to deal with this is to say, "I feel angry when you say this or do that." We have a right to our feelings. By using the word *feel* instead of *make*, the issue dissipates because the negative energy has been pulled out. It's like a firework that fizzles instead of exploding.

Other words to avoid are *always* and *never*. These words can suggest that something happens all the time instead of once in a while. Instead, try using the words *sometimes*, *occasionally* or some other word that avoids a final, unmovable piece of information that cements something into place permanently.

When it comes to the word wrong, I prefer to use the word *mistaken*. I like how one word feels as opposed to the other.

The words *need*, *know*, *want*, *should* or *have to* might be replaced by *prefer*, *feel*, or *think*. After using neurolinguistics for a while, a sense of soft or hard words begins to develop, so before anything is said it is possible to get a sense of whether the sound is going to have a sense of conflict hidden within. At that point I may be in the middle of a sentence, but I stop and rethink or reframe how I might say something. The nice thing about doing this is that it slows down the conversation so there's a better chance of avoiding a conflict or misunderstanding.

Quite some time ago I read something I try to consider every time I talk to someone. Ask these three questions: 1) Is it fair? 2) Is it truthful? 3) Is it necessary? Some of my statements or thoughts might pass the fair and truthful question, but many times they can's pass the third question—is it necessary? I try to question my motive behind what I am thinking about saying. I can't tell you how many times I've asked myself these questions and wasn't able to make it past question two.

Another word I've tried to remove from my vocabulary is *control*. Instead of trying to control a situation or a person, I've taught myself to use the word *manage*. Control is a hard, harsh, in-your-face word that many times isn't received well—not only by others, but by our own minds. I've often told people that I treat my mind like a child, and I'm attempting to teach that child how to behave so she can live a better life.

Many times when we make stern demands on children they seem to have a tendency to want to rebel. Our minds seem to work the same way. Your mind might start an internal conversation that says, "You want to bet? I'll show you!" If instead of demanding or trying to force my mind to cooperate, I find gentler ways to ask for what I would like to have from myself.

As I am working to change my thoughts and behaviors, I've taught myself to first thank my internal self for doing what needed to be done at the time in order to preserve both my sanity and my life. After that I remind my internal self that what I set into place as a child worked great for me at the time, but now, because I'm an adult, those thoughts and behaviors are no longer working in a productive healthy way. It's almost like standing in front of my internal self and agreeing to let go of past unhealthy behaviors because I've now been able to find a better way to handle, or manage, my life. I never fail to smile at the children I used to be as they happily hand the reins over to me, the adult, so we can change our old, outdated method of protection into one that is faster, newer, and better. My inner self almost rejoices after being relieved of the need to control everything so they can go back to just being a past part of my experience without the burden of having to be in charge.

Now I'm going to introduce you to one of the most nonsensical tricks our brains sometimes play on us. From what I've read, I've learned that, when we use the word *not* or *no*, it doesn't come out the way we think it should. If we are affirming or saying "I am not fat" or "I am not stupid," the brain drops the word *not* so the messages which come out says "I am fat" or "I am stupid." Why? The brain abhors a vacuum, so the mind sucks the negative word *not* out of what is being said, and it becomes invisible. I think that's a really mean trick. Life is difficult enough without what should be your greatest asset (your brain) becoming your adversary. Instead of using the word *no* I use the word *stop*. If you say these two words out loud and compare how they feel and sound, you might be surprised.

I've found it is difficult to avoid the word *not* when talking. I'd love to sit down with a neurolinguist and ask if this applies to conjunctions. Just to be safe, I try to find ways around *don't, doesn't, won't,* and the rest of the words that have an altered version of the word *not* hidden within. Trying to avoid using the word *not* is unsettling. What I noticed was how many nots I have in my daily language. Even as I'm writing this book, I've allowed a few to sneak in to what I'm trying to say. When this happens, forgive me. *Not* seems to be a convenient, short cut word. When I began to monitor the way I talked, I began to notice how much longer it took to say things without using the word *not* so my brain was aware of the change.

Neurolinguistic boo-boos fit into the trickle-down process since we speak almost in the same manner of generations past. Our families have sayings that seem to be particular to them according to what part of the country they grew up in. A few years ago, I had to laugh when I heard my words coming out our sons' mouths. The words Mother spoke to me as a child fit in this category. This is the reason understanding even the smallest part about neurolinguistics was important. I wanted to make sure generations to follow understood how important words are.

In my mind's eye, in 1988, the year in which I began my renovation, I felt like a horrible person. I was certain something must have been wrong with me. I was trying hard to be the best possible person I could be, yet our marriage was faltering. I couldn't understand what I was doing that was wrong, or what I could do to salvage what we had shared for twenty-six years. Finding neurolinguistics helped me alter things enough so we began understanding how that trickle down almost put an end to something we wanted to keep.

One of the trickle-down issues that happened when Mother came to live with us was that, if she scolded her dog, I cringed. Something in me recognized how she had spoken to me when I was a child. When that happened, part of my brain went back into my childhood and tried to take the harsh words she was speaking to her dog as if she was saying them to me. I wanted to cower or run away and hide—just like her dog.

As I said earlier, I don't need to know every detail about communicating neurolinguistically, but learning a bit about it definitely was a game changer in my life. I thank the day I happened across this information, and I am grateful for the determination and grit I was able to apply to make sure that what I said was coming across in the right way. I worked hard to change what I had the ability to change. If I ran into an obstacle, I tried to acknowledge that the only person I had a right to change was me. The interesting thing about change is that, even if the only person you can change is yourself, that change still ends up changing everyone around you since that's how it works.

Taking Things Personally

As a child you live in a state of confusion when you are being given mixed messages such as the ones I received.

Now we are supposed to be giving our children a new message, but some didn't get the memo that says that who we are and what we do are two different things. We can change what we do (our behaviors, thoughts, and speech), but that doesn't change our original selves (who we are).

I've mentioned this idea a few times, but this needs its own space. I can hardly begin to tell you how this changed everything in me. This is probably one of the most important things I learned. I wish I could explain how important it is that we avoid taking things personally at all costs. As strange as it sounds, it can also be an addiction.

Finding the information about taking things personally is something that still astounds me. I happened across this seed information in a book I had avoided because its value was questionable as far as I was concerned. Once I began to understand this concept, however, the seed grew into a garden of very healthy, digestible, understandable changes for me. As I began to see the connection between taking things personally and addictions, it became clear to see how trickle down from my childhood of wanting desperately for others to love me had become an addiction. I think in today's psychological language this might also be classified as codependency.

Until that time, I believed internally that, if I behaved in a favorable way, others would see me as being good and would reciprocate by giving me positive feedback. It never occurred to me it took out the idea of free will of how others chose to view my behavior.

Because being liked was important to me, my energy level would sometimes go over the top due to my excitement and anxiety. Instead of being seen as a positive thing, my excited behavior probably came across as controlling. This idea never crossed my mind; neither was it my intention. The more upset others became, the harder I tried to show them how good I was and why they should love me. In other words, I became addicted to the behavior of others. The need I had for satisfying the addiction grew harder and harder to meet as I struggled with the amount of disappointment I felt. As an addicted person does with alcohol or drugs, I would double down my efforts, even going so far as to try to find a way to talk to the other person in order to explain myself. By that time, my frustrated behavior was leaning toward unresolved confusion tinged with anger. Why? I had drifted back into my childhood where I wasn't openly loved as much as I was tolerated.

Eventually, as the issues continued, I went back to my old childhood standby of *avoidance* and just went on with my life as if the other person never existed. The problem with avoidance is that it isn't resolution. If someone came along I wanted in my life, I did my best to try to fit into his or her life, but if it didn't work out, I'd just drop out of the relationship. Finally I began to remind myself that "no resolution is a resolution," but in truth that's nothing more than more avoidance. If I avoid it, then I don't have to confront it, and if I teach myself to avoid confronting it, then I can make it disappear, just the same as I did with my childhood issues of abuse.

In childhood I depended on others to love me so they would keep me alive. In 1990 I realized that, as an adult, I hadn't outgrown that need. I was still doing and saying nice things so I could be seen as good so others might be happy to be around me. The problem was that, if they still wouldn't accept me after I did good things, then in my mind there had to be something wrong with me personally. That may sound irrational, but we aren't taught to think rationally when we are children. Since I was still in the learning phase of my life, it should have been up to the adults to help me see the difference and to see to it that I made the distinction. Now, with this trickle-down behavior, what happened was that, since Mother wasn't taught the difference between what someone does and who someone is, she wasn't able to teach me. She and my grandmother had an extremely tight codependent relationship, and I was an outsider. They had each other, and that was all either of them needed. As a child, for me it was difficult not to be part of what should have been a female bond. As long as they had each other, they didn't need me.

This behavior can become intertwined with our egos. I've heard it said that a wounded ego can be dangerous. At this point, just as it is for a wounded animal, it is easy to strike out because we have mistakenly taken the base part of who we are and twisted it until it becomes indistinguishable from what we do—which is our behavior.

I know children crave attention, but the way they respond can be confusing. If I was told

I was good, I'd go out of my way to prove them right. When I was told I was bad, instead of doing more things to prove them right, I'd just disappear.

It seems easy for the mind to do this since it was easier for me to believe or search my mind for something negative rather than something positive. Suddenly the child would come to the forefront of my mind and began listening with the limited amount of experience I had available at the time the original statement was made. Frantically my mind began to sort through messages given by parents, ministers, teachers, or anyone else who had authority over me to find unresolved issues and resolve them. My adult mind was forced to take second place so the mind of the child I had been could obey past directives given by others in a trickle-down way.

Thinking about past directives given to me by adult family members, siblings, classmates, ministers, teachers, or even a bully from my past was shocking to recognize. I didn't know what I had been told, so it was hard to work to override what I felt or believed was true about myself.

Changing how I might look to others was a horse of a different color. Yes, we can have plastic surgery to change the size of our nose or breasts, and even to a certain extent we can change the color of our skin, but those are superficial changes. The hard part is changing internal messages about how others said you looked to them—too fat or too skinny, ugly, four-eyes, freckle face, and so on. Some of these personal attacks can be worked on and changed, but what doesn't readily change are the feelings still attached to that big nose—which is now adorable—or to thick glasses that have been replaced with contacts. Inside, the child you used to be still sees that old nose and the thick glasses. Even looking in the mirror doesn't give the relief we seek because we tend to see the image of what used to be. Past messages can still be firmly entrenched within the mind, so instead of seeing the perfect body you have attained through surgery, diet, and exercise, you see the body from your childhood. Changing the mind's eye view is difficult. The only way this can possibly be accomplished is by changing our thoughts.

What comes in to us through our ears from someone else's mouth has a tremendous power over how we view not only ourselves but everyone from our past and present. A bully from your past tells you you're fat. Then your present-day sweetheart jokingly remarks about how much you seem to like cake. Suddenly the sweetheart becomes the bully from your past telling you that you are fat. Who do you believe—the smiling sweetheart as we eat a piece of cake, or the bully? The answer leans toward what the bully told you long ago rather than how your sweetheart smiles when you eat cake. Our internal dialogue needs to be defused, but that's hard to do without work on the thoughts and behaviors to which we have become addicted.

Now, let me explain how important this is when we deal with others, especially a child. When we tell children they are good or bad, we need remember we are talking about two different things. Who we are and what we do are not the same and shouldn't be glued together in any way. Classifying a child as a "good girl" or "good boy" or a "bad girl" or "bad boy" when he or she does something suggests that the recognized behavior has to do with the person he or she is. In other words, if the child does something good, that makes that child a good person. And, if the child does something bad, that makes the child a bad person. The fact is that there is a tremendous difference between who the child is as a person and what the child does as that person.

Here is an example: Let's say I go to the store and buy a brand new set of glassware. I take the glasses home and fill one with tea. When I pick up the glass, bring it to my mouth, and drink, I leave fingerprints, lip prints, and smudges on the outside of the glass. After it is empty there's the residue left inside. Looking at the glass, I might say, "The glass is dirty." Is it really?

The gist of this story is that the glass itself is always clean—it merely has some smudges and traces of the tea that was inside marking its surface, inside and out. Now I take the glass to the sink and wash it, dry it, and put it on the shelf. So here is the question: was it the glass itself or the actions I took when I used it that made it appear to be dirty or clean? It was the behaviors applied to the glass that changed its appearance. The glass itself never changed.

At the time children are told they are bad or good when they do something, they may not have learned that who they are and what they do are two separate things. It seems to them it is the act they have done that has created the dialogue. What a child does and who he or she is should be seen as two different things. The child is therefore always good even though sometimes he or she might do something we disagree with or see as bad. That's part of the reason today people are encouraged to tell a child "good job" instead of "good girl" or "good boy."

Another example to think about has to do with when a child dirties a diaper. I can't begin to tell you how many times I've overheard someone tell a baby or a child not yet toilet trained, "Ewe—you stink"! They might even say it with a smile. Just think of all the dialogue you have with children which is similar to this. "*You're* a mess," "What is that smell? Is it *you*?" When one of my younger grandchildren needed a diaper change, I'd tell them, "Whew! That sure is a smelly *diaper*." With that said, I changed the diaper.

Words can seem to the child to represent who he or she is. That's why when my mother was in her eighties and I was in my sixties and she would scold her dog, something inside me shrank down to the size of the child I had been when being raised by her. After all is said and done, we may end up going around trying to get approval for who we are instead of what we may be doing. We can never change who we are, but we can definitely change what we do.

Please think about this and try to absorb this message. Apply this knowledge each time you begin to speak to a child. Changing the neurolinguistic style of your language may sound difficult, but it is like any other habit you want to develop—practice makes perfect. Or at least it can make it better.

Another thing I want to mention is that, when we deal with babies or children, we don't often take into consideration the fact that they will not always be small. These are our future teachers, firemen, lawyers, doctors, and so forth. Be careful not to destroy their future lives before they even have the opportunity to live them.

Rolfing, Structural Integration, Core

Before starting therapy, I never knew this type of body therapy existed, and you might not either.

I had been in therapy several months when I found a book about how the body keeps every physical memory over our entire lifetime. Learning this led me to believe that I might be able to use the author's techniques to retrieve memories.

One of the most surprising things I encountered while going through the process was how one part of the body seemed to talk to other parts of the body. My bodyworker could be working on my arm, and all of a sudden I would feel something in my leg. Since my attention was at such a high level, I found it fascinating. Usually he would tell me the way it worked and explain the connection. He was not only a fantastic bodyworker, but a friend. They day I walked into his office became one of the best days of my life.

Even though my husband hadn't come to terms with all my methods of trying to retrieve memory, he told me to go for it.

Although I live in a farm community, I was only thirty miles from the third-largest city in our state. I looked in the yellow pages and there it was—Rolfing. I didn't realize at the time that there weren't that many practicing Rolfers, especially in our area. The word *Rolfing* doesn't often appear in the phone book, so if you want to find someone in your area, check the Internet. The person I found has now been in practice for over twenty-five years. When I met him, he had just recently started practicing again after being in a small aircraft accident that left him temporarily unable to work.

At times I've heard this referred to as massage therapy. One thing it is not is a massage the way one might think of it. This type of work is known as "deep intramuscular massage or manipulation." By that I mean they work on what is known as *fascia*.

Using the word *massage* when describing Rolfing can be deceiving because any time you are working within a deep layer of muscles, it can be painful. There are lighter versions of this modality, but I never was one to go for anything easy. What I hoped for was some type of memory retrieval, but that never happened.

As I said, I had already started therapy, so when I came across the information about

Rolfing, I thought it might help since I was having a difficult time relaxing during hypnosis. I hoped to relax my body enough to retrieve at least a sliver of memory.

I made my appointment for two hours before my visit with the therapist. It wasn't clear from the book what the Rolfer was going to do, but I had high hopes it would make a difference.

As I said earlier, the man doing the bodywork had been in a small aircraft accident and had been away from his practice while he recuperated. Since he had taken time off, he had subleased his office to someone and had taken a smaller space in the same building in a basement office.

Because sexual and physical abuse is so personal, I always had issues with being touched. Not only that, but our family never were into "touchy feelie," so for me to allow someone to touch my body was in some ways terrifying. My need for resolution about my past was more important to me than having someone touch me, however, so I was prepared to handle whatever he dished out.

Now here I was in a small, cramped office located in the basement. A hanging sheet separated the dressing/treatment area from the rest of his office. I had been into therapy for only a few months, so nothing had been addressed yet as to how I felt about my body.

Here's the difference. There was something about this bodyworker that put me completely at ease. He felt safe. That seemed astounding to me. I had never allowed anyone to touch me without full awareness. The instant I was touched in any way, it was as if everything inside me was on high alert to get away mentally or physically. With this practitioner, however, somewhere deep inside, I felt a level of comfort that comes only when you have known someone quite a while and trust him implicitly.

His first session was called "cracking the shell." The idea is to begin with a light form of the Rolfing technique over the entire body. It is as if you are introducing your body to what is going to be happening. I had no problem allowing him to touch my arms, stomach, legs, hands, neck, and so forth as his hands traveled over my body. That was a surprise because, by all counts, I should have become frozen in fear. To tell you I was impressed in an understatement.

After that session I went directly to see my therapist. By the time I arrived at his office, my entire body itched as if I had hives. When I got to the therapist's office, he asked how my bodywork session had worked out, and I mentioned how prickly my body felt. He said it sounded uncomfortable. I told him it felt wonderful—as if blood was freely flowing into all parts of my body, where before blood flow had been sluggish. My body felt awake and alive. It was my hope that my mind would pick up a cue from what was happening and let me spill my guts all over the floor as I suddenly began to remember traumatic events. I think my mind missed the memo, because it was still tightly guarded and ready to flee at the least hint of danger or stress.

One of the issues I encountered when the therapist tried hypnotism was an absolutely desperate need to touch a wall. This behavior wasn't unfamiliar to me. From the time I was little and into adulthood, I recall this as being one of the things I did when I felt stressed. I'm not completely sure why I wanted to press myself against a wall or, of all things, a refrigerator, but I have a good idea. I wanted the entire front part of my body, especially my face (cheek) to feel the object I had chosen. My opinion was that I was seeking protection, strength, and steadfastness from such a structure. The refrigerator provided one other aspect I wanted, and that was its temperature. It was not only strong, but also cold. When I touched the wall or the refrigerator, it temporarily became my protector. It was my almost-perfect, non-threatening stand-in parent. Everyone in my life felt cold to me, so the temperature of the refrigerator felt emotionally familiar. Another aspect of the wall has to do with going "into" objects. I've found I've always been doing this if I felt stressed or was being abused. By doing this, I didn't have to experience what was happening to my body or my mind. I have a story I'll recount to you later that has to do with cities of children living inside the walls where they placed their minds.

In therapy, not only was the therapist dealing with my need to protect my body; he was also dealing with my need to protect my mind. Both would be at risk if I exposed our long-kept secret. I wasn't aware at the time that I should tell him about my "family." They wanted nothing to do with him. At one point during our first session, I told him there was a part of me that was telling him to stay away. Now I realize this was the part of me that wasn't going to be tricked into spilling "their" guts when he used hypnosis. (By the way, all hypnosis is self-hypnosis, so if any part of a person disagrees with what is trying to be accomplished, it may not work). Even though consciously I wanted to allow myself to go into a hypnotic state, my subconscious mind—by way of my internal family—was overriding that directive. Later I began to recognize that, instead of allowing hypnosis to work, I went into a state of dissociation (which was easy for me) so I could use my version of what I was being asked to do.

Now here we are. I've had my first session of Rolfing, my body itched as if I had a rash, and my internal family was not only pissed, but off balance. The first thing they wanted to do when the therapist began his attempt at putting me into a self-induced trance was to head for the wall so they could hide. The only way I can explain the going into the walls technique is that it is as if there's a magnet inside the wall, and I'm being pulled into it by a strong magnetic force. Before, all I could do was to put myself as close to the wall in his office as possible. At least then my mind would attempt to focus on his words rather than the overwhelming need to hug the wall. As I said, the only problem was that, instead of going into a state of relaxation, I was spinning into the Universe in a dissociative manner. After one session of Rolfing, the magnetic yank left! To tell you I was surprised is an understatement because I had been doing this behavior for as many years as I could recall.

Hugging the Wall

The touch of the wall,
So cold and so strong.
If I hugged the wall,
Nothing was wrong.

If you grab me too tight,
I just won't be there.
If you touch my soul,
It's too much to bear.

So I pull away
From consuming touch.
I'll hug you back,
But not very much.

Walls

No more walls,
But peace of mind
So I can live life
So I can find.

That life for me
Won't be too much.
The walls will be down,
And I can feel touch.

Then I'll not be afraid
Of heaven or hell.
A heart filled with love
And a mind that is well.

   When things happen, I've always been able to step back, look at the situation, and say,
"Hmmm." That's my first clue that I'm in the process of learning something new about myself

or my situation. If we put this into the context of an archetype, this might be called "The Observer." This was another thing that fascinated me. It sounds crazy to describe it, but I seem to have archetypes presenting themselves in my mind. I've never read about others experiencing this, but that doesn't mean I'm alone in this behavior.

Because I had such a spectacular reaction after my first session of Rolfing, I decided to continue and see what else would happen.

One of the other issues I had been dealing with was food. Unless something in me was hungry, I wouldn't eat because I'd end up with a stomachache or a bad case of nausea. The only way to handle this was to drink several glasses of water and throw up. That never makes eating food fun or even necessary. I'd dealt with this my entire life. Not only did I dislike eating, but my stomach felt as cold as ice, and I had a knot about the size of a fist that would never go away. I still remember how much I used to rub my stomach, even as a teenager, trying to get the knot to relax. After my first Rolfing session, I realized my stomach was warm, and the knot had disappeared. Food wasn't making my stomach upset! For me, this was astounding. All it had taken was one treatment, and something I had been dealing with my entire life just melted without any effort on my part.

How many treatments have I had since 1989? I couldn't tell you because even now I go for what I call my tune-up so I can dispose of any new body issues. Trust me when I tell you he knows his business!

Let me briefly explain the fascia he addresses. Fascia is described as being an ensheathing band of connective tissue. When I tell anyone about it, I put it in a more understandable way by comparing it to the thin, white film we see on a piece of meat. This is fascia. If the meat is still on a living animal, it would have fluidity. This tissue is found from your scalp to the bottom of your feet.

If at some point you encountered trauma—either physical, or psychological—this damage is retained by the body. Because of this, the fascia in that part of the body becomes sluggish. As the bodyworker works, he or she is able to find areas where the fascia isn't flowing the way it should. If we were looking at this in a psychological way, we might call it an area in which we have become stuck. It is the practitioner's job at this point to work in that area to readjust the flow so that it can begin working correctly.

It is said that our bodies retain every physical memory. This might mean that, if someone were to slap you and you recoil, the movement backwards from the slap is retained in the muscle memory of your body until it is released. How many detrimental body memories can you count throughout your life? I went so far as to have our grandson worked on twice. He was worked on once when he was a baby for birth trauma and the other after he finished playing football in high school. Even birth can be traumatic. Before my birth, the nurse crossed Mother's legs so I wouldn't be born until the doctor arrived. Contractions pushing me toward the birth canal were met with crossed legs. Now that's not a very good welcome into the world, is it?

Rolfing never gave me even the slightest piece of childhood information, but it relieved body trauma from all my childhood antics. It also would also have taken out the trauma from the whipping I mentioned when I was eleven.

The best thing this did was enable me to feel more comfortable in my body. It lets various parts of my body start a better sort of body conversation as one part speaks to another. It was fun to see how my body was waking to the fact that I was always in a state of disconnection both in my body and my mind. Quite often when I pointed out how working one part of my body had an effect on another, I'd laugh when the practitioner's answer to my questions of "How'd you do that?" was met with a shrug of his shoulders and smile on his face. I believe it was almost as much of a mystery to him as it was to me. It was as if the entire process was connected to something sacred that no one really completely understood.

Another type of bodywork I encountered was done with the lymphatic system. Lymphatic fluid is more accessible than fascia so treatment is done in a much lighter way. Lymph is a colorless, plasma-like fluid that bathes many of our tissues by a system of ducts and channels to the blood circulatory system. The lymph vessels can range in size and can be compared in size to capillaries and veins. They both lubricate and cleanse. That's why this work is addressed in such a delicate way.

I had surgery on a small complex parotid cyst in my neck. A complex tumor contains walled-off areas that make it difficult to determine if each area is addressed individually. Even though three samples were taken, there was no assurance that the tissue was taken from separate areas of the entire cyst. When the cyst was removed, the tissue had to be taken to the pathologist while I was still on the surgical table. Thankfully, the cyst was benign, but the removal of the cyst left an empty place under my skin. Because this would have left a hole or indentation in my neck, the surgeon filled it in with sterile, denatured tissue from a cadaver.

Because the lymph needed to travel through that part of my body, it too became sluggish. Since some of the nerves were traumatized, I was left with an ear that felt like a chunk of wood. I hardly had any feeling in the ear, and it was cold. The Rolfer worked on me first, and then I went to see a woman who did work on lymph. As they worked on that area, they were able to clear the way for the lymph to again begin moving through the damaged area. She then taught me how to carefully drain the lymphatic fluid around the area of my ear and neck to allow better blood flow.

Again, if you want to find out more, the Internet is loaded with information. Fortunately when I addressed the problem, my ear started to stay warm and didn't feel as if it was put there by an inept carpenter.

Study on Depression

Depression was another issue I investigated during the time I was beginning therapy. I noticed an article in the Sunday paper in which someone was asking for volunteers for a study on depression. One of the first things the therapist had mentioned after I took a Minnesota Multiphasic Personality Inventory was that I was in a state of depression. Since I seemed to fit the criteria, I called the next morning and was accepted into the program.

As I heard stories about a childhood I couldn't remember, I felt confused—not depressed. One thing to note is that, just because you aren't able to remember what happened to you as a child doesn't mean the lack of memories has to do with trauma. Maybe your childhood was normal and uneventful so there isn't any reason to recall everything. The mind seems to retain special events or trauma, but other things can be so mundane the mind files them away as not being fun enough or important enough to save. When you are with others and begin to talk about childhood, you may begin to recall more of it as you laugh and compare notes.

I've found that a good way to help children remember their childhood is to begin a family conversation. I used to call this "remember when" with our sons. Today if we play and they bring up things they did that I didn't know about and that I find upsetting for one reason or another, I stop them. They laugh when I tell them, if they survived (and evidently they did), I don't want to hear about the frightening, dangerous, or possibly illegal things they may have done. They had experiences I would have objected to had I known about them. It was my rule to keep an eye on them—at least when they were younger. As they grew in age and were out of sight, that became a whole new ballgame.

I already knew my childhood wasn't normal, uneventful, or mundane. I knew it had been filled with multiple layers of trauma and neglect. There were enough traumatic events that stuck with me that I knew the rest were true as well. Why? Because I had retained snippets of memory as well as thoughts and feelings connected to what had happened. Not only that, but both aunts confirmed each other's stories even though they hadn't seen or talked to each other for over forty years.

What I realize about my type of depression is that it is known as chronic, which means it lasted for an extended period of time. I was depressed from childhood through adulthood. Now that's what I call chronic! I experienced it in varying degrees. It became clear to me that, if the scale for depression went from one to ten—one being the worst scenario and ten being the best—I rarely went beyond level five. If I made it to a six, I was in a total state of elation. My lowest number would at times been about a minus two, but even at that I didn't see myself as being depressed.

I believe that, along with my depression, I experienced levels of unrealized, unrecognized anger. I have never been angry at any of my childhood caretakers, only at what happened to my ability to be a good student, wife, mother, and individual. In other words, I was able to get into a state of not only *depersonalization* and *dissociation*, but also a state in which I *diminished* what happened. I was finding out what had happened, but I saw it happening to someone else, not to me. As I recounted my story, none of it had a personal impact.

This is also what happened when my brother died in 1957. I *diminished* it and *denied* that I even cared he was dead. Why? First, he had been away for five and a half years before he came back. And second, I envied him because I felt he had been lucky when he died. That was one of the reasons I felt upset when I saw the picture of him in his casket without the smile. How could he be considered happy or lucky if he wasn't wearing that smile? I have "head knowledge" that I should feel upset when people die, but I never had the "heart knowledge," and that meant that none of it mattered.

The study was interesting. The problem I had at the time was that my state of confusion had me living in a world in which I was pretending to be living my life without having to participate. I'd dress up and come to the program as if I didn't have a care in the world. Superficially my conscious mind never recognized my depressed state of mind. Making decisions was almost impossible. Every day I woke up in a different world. I never knew if I wanted to dress up and pretend I was a lady or if I wanted to put on a long skirt as if I was living on the frontier. One day I'd dress funky, and the next punky. This also applied to what I was willing to eat. It became so bad that, at one point, I couldn't go out to eat without having my husband order for me because I had no idea what sounded good. It was the same way with my house. I finally stripped it down, boxed things up, and waited until I could decide what to do.

The first study was held in connection with a well-known, highly respected medical intuitive. This person has the ability to know what's wrong with a person physically before that person knows what might be the matter. During this study, the volunteers didn't deal directly with the doctor; rather, they dealt with his staff. After he was given their information, he would talk by phone to the intuitive.

After the first study, a period of time passed, and someone called from the facility to see if I was interested in doing another study. This time both the world renown known doctor and the intuitive would be present and deal with us in person. This felt frightening in some ways because a medical intuitive also has psychic abilities. I still had "churchiness" stuck to me, so I could almost feel something bad lurking in my brain threatening to pounce on me and drag me to hell. Not only that, I was apprehensive she would take one look at me and proclaim me to be a liar.

What if she realized nothing really happened? What if it was only a game with not only my mind but also other people jerking me around with a story that never happened? What if

I hadn't been molested or Mother never said she hated me? Then what? If everything I was coming to believe was true, but wasn't, then that definitely would have led to a feeling of craziness. Besides, I had personal memory of some of the things that happened.

The intuitive made it clear she wasn't going to do any personal readings, so that left me in limbo. Did I want to ask her? Yes! I did some twenty years later meet another person who had the ability to look into my past and tell me if those things happened. What did she say? Not only did she tell me I had found my truth, but she told me other quite surprising things. She knew things I hadn't shared with anyone but my best friend and my husband. I was impressed with her calm demeanor. I never had what might be called a "reading." When I met her, I was more interested in her abilities as a shaman. To top it all off, she was a child psychologist. If I asked questions, she answered to the best of her ability, but she never said anything without following through so I wouldn't close down or become overwhelmed.

Even though all the things I describe may sound like a lot for anyone to handle, I personally don't care. If there had been sexual, verbal, and physical abuse, so what? Snakes in the water or an axe whacking my leg—no big deal. My internal dialogue told me I had survived, so that's all that mattered. Wouldn't that make about anyone depressed—or in my case confused?

Everyone participating in the program was nice. The people in charge were extremely knowledgeable and highly qualified, so I definitely was in good hands.

How did the study go and what did I do? I attended lectures and participated in groups, which I enjoyed. I was given homeopathic medications (vitamins and various herbs) and homework. Because it was hard for me to remain focused at the time, I think when it came to homework I failed.

It was especially difficult for me to sit in front of a flickering candle for a period of time. Doing this when you have a fractured sense of reality begins to do interesting things. I'm not at all sure it didn't have almost the same type of effect a mild dose of illegal substance might have. Gee, maybe I need to rethink doing this and find out what kind of trip I might be able to make.

One of my favorite things was being sent into a tiny darkened room about the size of a closet and shown a flashing light patterned after my brain rhythm. One of the professional medical assistants had recently been to a retreat and shared a chant with us in group that I found interesting. As I sat in the room watching the flashing light, I repeated the chant over and over as a remarkable peace swept over me.

We were also asked to sit in front of a copper wall and concentrate. The idea behind this was to see if radiating energy might make a pattern appear on the copper. Sitting still without doing anything but stare at a wall caused me to be restless. I have a difficult time doing this on any level. I tried, but I doubt my energy projected far. Instead, it almost seemed like an insult to my internal family. Because of this, I had to battle with them as I tried to keep myself quiet, stare at the wall, and think positive things while they were saying, "What the hell?"

The next thing we were asked to do was lie on a narrow prototype of a waterbed with speakers beneath it. As the water absorbed the beat of the music, the beat traveled to various parts of the body. Listening to the type of music being played always sent me into a dissociative state of mind. Images and feelings were alive in me in an interesting way. I think my internal family enjoyed this as the beat of the music projected through my body. I'm sure it had an effect on every organ, muscle, and bone.

Occasionally I was given a brain scan that could be compared with a scan made in the beginning of the program. I'm not sure how this worked or what they expected to find, because they didn't share that with me. It seemed straightforward, but as the scan was being done something interesting kept happening. I could feel my mind go into peaks and valleys. I mentioned this to one of the medical assistants, and she said that what I was experiencing was true. Now it makes me wonder if something else wasn't happening.

One day as I was leaving, I met one of the psychologists involved in the program, and we began to talk about what the intuitive had said about me. The first thing she asked was if I believed in reincarnation. I wasn't sure, and I told her so. Without trying to convince me, she said it didn't matter if I did or not. Evidently the intuitive had noted that I seemed to be moving through lifetimes very quickly. What does that mean? I was transforming myself with every change in thought, behavior, and language into a completely different person.

I found what she told me interesting because I had been telling people the same thing. I felt that, if I could turn around fast enough, I could see my body in a coffin. It was like a movie about pod people in which someone goes to sleep and becomes absorbed into an identical self. No one seemed to know that my original self had been transformed into a duplicate me. Part of me had passed, and yet I had been able to continue from one point of death to the next while still being alive. I could visually see myself in a casket but had no concern about what was happening. I felt happy to be rid of the part that had been weighing me down and holding me back. I especially loved the idea of having the ability to step outside myself and into the position of being an observer.

Reincarnation

I'd hate to think,
In sadness and shame,
I'd have to live

Again and again.

Once through this life
Is enough for me,
Then bid me farewell
And set me free.

I happened to be reading a book written by a well-known physicist. Since I had grown to love bits and pieces of information about physics, I wanted to know what he thought about spiritual things. Little did I know this was a new twist in the tunnel of experiences I would be having. It was surprising to find out he was a shaman. With that in mind, I hit the Internet to find out what that was about. Within no time at all, I found we had two shamans in our area. Imagine that!

I was scared half out of my wits, but I was desperate to find out how I was doing. I called both of them and set up appointments. The first shaman was okay, but I connected more with the second one, Karen. She quite often went to Peru and studied under a widely recognized psychologist/shaman. I made another appointment with her for the next week and bought five books written by her teacher.

The information was both scary and fascinating. Reading one would have been frightening enough, but reading five, one after another in a single week, was mind blowing. He was the shaman who mentioned soul clearing. This exercise sounded like something I might be interested in. From what I gathered, soul clearing had to do with going back into your past experiences and clearing out any "stuck" places. Sounds right up my alley, doesn't it?

When it came time for my appointment, Karen told me that I had already accomplished a great deal of clearing on my own. After the session was over, she told me she saw a girl sitting in a box tipped on its side. The girl kept putting her finger on her cheek as if she was saying "hmmm." Almost everything I encounter gets that treatment. It's like the girl was being very nonjudgmental. I originally wrote a poem in 1989, but I didn't meet the shaman until 2011. The image in the poem is exactly the way she was describing the girl to me. Even now as I write this, I can see her with her questioning looks and her finger at the side of her face. She's really quite familiar, and has been for years.

The Girl, the Box, the Key

There's a girl in a room
In a box out there.

Mary Davenport

I don't know who
And I don't know where.

She keeps my secrets,
She holds the key.
It's hard to remember
That the girl is me.

She's quiet and hides,
But now and again
She screams out loud,
But I'll not know when.

She hates the room
And being alone.
Her mind is calm
But her heart's a stone.

She cries in the night
In a box out there.
I don't know who,
And I don't really care.

Someday I hope
To set her free,
But it's hard to do
When she holds the key.

The key, she says,
I can only find
If I open my heart
And I open my mind.

It's hard, you know,
To find that key,
For I am her

And she is me.

Information about Changing Thoughts and Behaviors

From 1988 until 2010 I thought my coping behaviors were connected only to abuse and neglect. Imagine my surprise when, thirteen years later, I found another condition that may have been contributing to my problems. It is known as temporal lobe epilepsy (TLE) without incidence.

The behaviors that evolve as the result abuse are almost the same as the symptoms of TLE. I can't one hundred percent confirm that I have TLE, because it is extremely difficult to diagnose. For now l will treat the rest of my story as if I do, just to show why I feel this may be part of my problem.

As soon as this information became available, I tried to separate the behaviors of abuse and the symptoms of TLE. Much to my surprise, many were tangled like yarn tossed in a bag and shaken.

All I can attempt to do is list behaviors. I can't tell you how much sleep I've lost trying to decide how to do this. For one thing, I don't have the qualifications to do such a difficult task. I would need a master's degree, not only in neurology but in psychiatry. Since I don't have either, I may not be able to do this the way a professional would. These are my own personal behaviors I'm trying to explain.

I feel the best way to do this is to start at the top of my head and move down my body in order to show not only what I was doing, but how I lessened some of my thoughts and behaviors to a more tolerable level. If I were to underline identical behaviors, most all of it would qualify. TLE does present with a few unique behaviors not presented by abuse, but not many.

My experience has to do with thoughts first and behaviors second. You see, a thought isn't anything other than the movement of energy. They aren't just wispy ethereal things; they actually have a neurochemical element. Even the atom bomb began with a thought. If behavior hadn't followed, it wouldn't have changed history. Thoughts are bombs in the mind just waiting to blow you and your world into oblivion. The only thing that can alter the bomb is transforming the thought so you can modify the behavior, which will inevitably reshape the results. Not only will it revolutionize you, but also it can have a positive effect on everyone with whom you come into contact.

I need to say that changing the behaviors I've used all my life has been difficult. It doesn't take long to recognize when I've started slipping back to my old ways. Thankfully, due to a high level of awareness and determination, I am able to change back very quickly. Part of the problem is that I don't have the memory available that ties me to the reason I implanted the behavior in the first place. This means that the roots to these behaviors are so deep there hasn't been a way for me to cut them away so they will be destroyed.

The point I want to make is this: thoughts and behaviors managed my entire life. They helped to create me and make me the person I have become. These thoughts kept me alive from the very beginning of their creation (by me!). Just like my imaginary internal family, my thoughts and behaviors were my friends simply because they were familiar. Even friends can sometimes turn on you, and this is exactly what my thoughts and behaviors did.

Here is a very important fact I taught myself: when I found out about my past and the effect it had on me, I realized I needed to take time out to grieve over the person I had been and the difficult time I endured just trying to live. Once I found a thought that was no longer working in the way it should—which was to keep me alive during difficult situations—I knew I had to change. I found it extremely important to do this because it was a way to allow myself to begin over. That person—the one I use to be—is forever gone. She has been transformed into a whole new person living a whole new life. The person I am and the person I now choose to become no longer needs to cling to the way I use to be. I must admit that, when it came time for me to grieve for my past self, I have done an excellent job. Since these selves have actual substance in my mind's eye, I could see them as they relinquished control to my new self. There really isn't any way to tell you how I do this.

I first honored the place they had taken in my life to keep me alive. I pictured these behaviors as if they were standing in front of me. I praised them for the job they had done in order for me to survive. At that point, I thanked them for the part they had played, but then I told them their services were no longer needed. I told them that now they were damaging me. I tried to show as much respect and honor for my past behavior as I could. Sometimes I even pictured myself hugging them, and I watched as they walked away into the darkness of my mind where they would be neutralized. At that point, I gave myself permission to replace the thoughts and behaviors with ones that were more appropriate for my physical, emotional, and psychological wellness.

If your changes aren't honored and respected, they can return with a vengeance. By honoring my past thoughts and behaviors, I wasn't showing respect and honor to them; rather, I was showing respect and honor to myself. The last behavior my inner self needed was to hatefully kick them to the curb. They didn't start out in me as bad things; they began as good behaviors with the sole purpose of keeping me alive. I found they may try to come back, but when that happens I simply remind them of our conversation.

Sometimes the mind seems to question our new truth simply because of an ingrained habit. Now the question is, do I trust in my changes or do I want to go back to the way I was before? This is normal simply because habits are hard to change. If you don't believe me, then ask someone who has been a life-long smoker.

My List of Thoughts and Behaviors

Before I begin, I want to tell you this has been excruciating. I'm doing it because I know others might identify with me, and it might possibly give more insight into who I am and what I do and why. With every explanation, I have to dig into myself in a way that is painful because I've put a lot of it behind me. Bringing it back is like digging through vomit to find a ring you swallowed. I'm not proud of any of these behaviors, so this means I feel mildly embarrassed. If my 1977 message is true, I need to do it because it may be part of the dialogue that asked, "How can you tell others if you don't know?" There were tons of things I didn't know about myself until I started my journey in 1988. If I'm able to tell others, maybe that will complete my mission simply because I care how this may help others. Honoring that question has been my quest—so here we go.

Reading

Let's start with the most important behavior I've had since I was thirteen. That was when I first discovered the library. I remembered seeing one before when I was nine, but that one was huge and intimidating. I guess it wasn't time for me to take the first bite of the apple and climb the multitude of steps that led up to that great place of learning. When I remember how far I've come in my process simply by allowing my books to choose me, I am astounded. One of my best assets as far as I am concerned has always been my insatiable sense of curiosity. So many times I've been able to recognize that I didn't need to go to college for a degree. My degree is in what life has taught me through reading. By now I certainly could have had a piece of paper granting me the identification of a college graduate, but I've met some of those graduates, and their knowledge isn't any better than the paper their degree is written on.

I'm not saying continuing your education isn't important. I am saying that there are a lot of us who are smart, but our abusive past hasn't allowed us to pass the test so to speak. Instead, no matter how hard we study, our minds just aren't willing help under pressure. I can't begin to tell you how many well-educated people have remarked that it took a high level of intelligence to do what I've done both as a child and as an adult. They comment about the intricacy of how well ordered my mind was as it layered my behavior in a way I was allowed to survive. What can I say? The Universe was my teacher, and the courses I took were well planned.

Books have played an unbelievable part in my life. It never seemed to matter how difficult life's chosen books were for me, I'd set my plate in front of me, open the book, and begin to slice away. Each piece of information given to me was delicious. As I read, I underlined, highlighted, circled, and commented with a code to remind how I felt about what I read: RR=Reread; TAT=think about this: Initials=people the passage brought to mind. I'd write "cute," "wonderful," "I love this," along with other comments. I'd cover both the front of the book and the back comments and page numbers I might want later. Since I couldn't mark library books, I started building my own library. I have many old friends sitting on the shelves of this room waiting to see if I might want to come and chat. Sometimes we play hide-and-seek when I need one for reference. In the back of my books I've sometimes written full-length poems because my impatient sense of dictation hasn't been able to wait for me to find a notebook.

I've always found I know what the book wants to tell me. I have one book that is over three hundred pages long, and in it I found one word to feast on. That word is *aversion*. My take on the word had a lot to do with what happened to me in my childhood. Inside that word, I saw two words: *a* and *version*. Everyone who experiences something detrimental or even something that might not be detrimental has his or her own version of what happened. My brother and I each had our own versions about what happened in our childhood. In his version of the baby buried in the backyard, it was he who was sent to bury the dead child. I had discovered a completely different version.

Books have a rhythm. When I start reading a book I am unable to understand, I keep reading until I am able to find the heart of the book beating with mine. At that point I begin to understand what is being said. It is my habit to stop reading at that point and go back to the beginning. Once I am able to do that, the book seems to open in a new way. I have purchased books that felt like stones in my hand. I remind myself that I've never purchased a book that wasn't for me. At that point I put it on my shelf and wait until it is needed. Sometimes this takes years. Books draw my hands to them like magnets. They pull me in and note me in their pages. If I had to live one place for the rest of my life, I'd pick the library.

Fat Head

I have a sad dilemma,
It sounds crazy but it's true.
I think of all the books I've read
You'd think I'd find a clue.

What if all the books I read

With all their author's fame
Put weight on my body
And changed my very frame?

I can't seem to stop my reading.
I chew on every sound
Just hoping I can find a way
To turn my world around.

Since I'm sitting as I read my way
Trough ideas that fill my head,
My exercise regime
Puts me in a chair instead.

As my mind becomes obese
My world becomes less thin.
But it's not just all the books I've read
It comes from deep within.

Sometimes when I'm stuck in place
I longed-for release.
That's when I find some food
Then my body becomes obese.

I long to find a way to bring
My body and mind in tune,
To balance my life and make it right,
But it had better happen soon.

As my body becomes rounder
For everyone to see,
I'd like to tell them it's because
I'm looking for the key.

But if my head was fat instead,
They'd smile and all agree

I'm the smartest person in the world
That's how I'd like to be.

The problem I would have to solve,
No answer I could find.
How do I fit a hat atop
This very big fat mind?

Like an octopus I'd drag my head
Over rocks and then I'd ache,
Because my head was so large
This could be a mistake.

So I guess I'll have to settle
For a head that's average size,
Not worry if they don't think I'm smart
Though I think I'm very wise.

You can't call me fat head
For that would not be nice,
But I'll never stop my reading
For that's my best advice.

Books open worlds
With wisdom deep within.
The problem you might ask yourself
Is "Where do I begin?"

Hair

I can't stand to look into the mirror long because of the girl living there. Something in me resists doing this. This makes it difficult to style my hair or put on makeup. From the time I start my shower until I'm fully dressed and out the door, only fifteen minutes elapse. I tried for years to find a hairstyle that works for me. Thankfully I have a hairdresser who understands. He knows to keep my bangs short because, if they are too long, I tip my chin and look out from beneath them. This drops my mind into the imaginary state of the child. He once styled the rest of my hair so short I look like a guy. I've also worn it long, which seems to work best for me. When it was short, my stylist noticed that my hair grows not only fast but in sixteen directions. Also, it is neither curly nor straight, but both. We've chosen to keep my hair long enough for a ponytail, or I can wear it down if I want. A curly spiral perm seems to do the trick. When we first met, I kept cutting my hair—well, not cutting so much as chopping. My bangs were about an inch long and swept to the right so there wasn't any chance the child might show up. Cutting hair was the only way I could control my life. Today I let Kelly manage my hair for me. If an urge hits and the scissors begin to whisper to me, I call him, and he knows to work me in.

Makeup

By the time I've gotten out of the shower, the mirror is steamy, and I'm out of there before it clears. The foggy mirror reminds me of my foggy mind. I put on moisturizer, a slight amount of base, a small amount of rouge, eye shadow, mascara, and lipstick. I use my fingers and put it on like a house on fire. I've been told that, if I did makeup correctly, I would look nice. But at this point, "good enough" will have to do because I might have to look the girl in her eyes, and that's hard to do. Since I am unwilling to look into the mirror for a long time, I do the best I can. When I leave the house, I use my imagination to see my makeup and hair as being perfect. As long as I stay away from mirrors, this works out great!

Vision

Over the years, I've read under all sorts of conditions—good light, bad light, in the car, and everywhere else. I wouldn't just read one book at a time; rather, sometimes I have as many as five books "going" at the same time. That's because they're all located in different areas.

Since money was scarce earlier in my life, I often gave myself home perms. It worked out okay except for the solution that dripped into my eyes.

As my vision changed, I began wearing glasses, usually from the drugstore. This year the ophthalmologist found cataracts, so I had surgery. Instead of implanted lenses, I now have multi-focal lenses so I don't need reading glasses. It takes time for your brain to adjust to this type of lens as you look near and far. I'm doing well, but it seems my vision can begin to blur when I'm under stress. At that point I reassure myself it is my normal and ignore it until the stress is over and my vision becomes clear again. I monitor any type of situation that might be involved such as dry eyes or allergies. I've never regretted the lenses, but I did have to keep reminding myself I no longer need glasses.

One of the things I've always done is squint or furrow my brows when I'm concentrating or trying to decipher a situation. At one point when I was doing this, someone noticed and told me she thought I might want to get my eyes checked. It wasn't my eyes that day, but my need to monitor everything around me in a hypervigilant way.

Looking Around

This is something I use all the time. In the beginning, I told you how I always had a horrible sense of panic most of the time. What I finally learned to do was stop and look around in order to see if there was actually something for me to feel upset about. Generally, if I was able to do that, I could reassure myself that there wasn't any real reason for me to feel upset.

At that point I knew the source was internal, so I'd begin checking off my list of traumas to see if the behaviors attached to any of them might have been triggered or if it might be related to my physical health. I'd ask myself if I had eaten, been drinking enough water, was breathing deeply enough. I'd think about the weather and ask myself if it was similar to the weather in any of my memories such as my father's death in March. Once my checklist was complete, the sense of panic seemed to lessen.

Sleeping

When I was trying to fall asleep, I would quite often ruminate about what I had done and said that day, what I regretted, what I needed to do the next day, and so on.

Hopefully I would interrupt myself so I could remember to allow the next day to take care of itself. If I continued, I'd tell myself to get up and write it down so I wouldn't be concerned I might forget what needed to be done. I'd remind myself it was nighttime and most people were asleep, so I didn't need to feel concerned about phone calls or other things that might be on my list.

Since I hoped one day to be interviewed, I'd begin to rehearse what I would say to a talk show host. Pretty soon I'd look at the clock and see that hours had passed. I knew better, but sometimes I forgot. When I realized what I was doing, I'd back myself out of my imaginary conversation by telling myself that everything I might want to say was written in the book, and I needed sleep more than I needed to play mind games. I first started doing this after getting the phone call from a popular talk show program about amnesia. Each time I had a thought about what I might say to her about my past, I would empty my mind and try to focus on my breathing. The next thing I knew it was morning.

Mouth

Most of my life I bit my lips and sometimes would bite at loose pieces of skin. I also bit the inside my mouth. I finally realized, if I didn't stop, I'd end up with wrinkles around my mouth the way a smoker might. Now, the minute I notice this behavior I ask myself: "What's eating you?" Next I tell myself, "You are!" It has become an inside joke to me, but it helped. I seldom do it now unless I'm under stress and not paying attention to what I'm doing.

Teeth and Jaws

I still sometimes clamp my teeth until my jaws hurt. When I notice I'm doing this, I open my mouth like a lion roaring to relieve the tension. I still do this, but not as often. Mostly when this happens, I'm deep in a thought I'm trying to understand or incorporate into my life.

Another habit was to scrape my bottom teeth on the inside of my top teeth. This darkened my teeth because I wore them so thin that light could pass through. By the time the dentist noticed the problem, my top teeth were extremely sharp and thin. He built them up, and I've stopped doing this as much. The only thing I missed was how sharp my teeth were when I was sewing. They were as sharp as any scissors in my drawer, and I didn't need to look for them when I needed a piece of thread or yarn cut.

It took forever to realize I spell and count by clicking my teeth to phrases or words. This behavior is called automation. I'm sure this can be attributed partly to obsessive compulsive disorder (OCD), but it also fits other headings. I've learned to repeat the word "automation" each time I start and—poof!—I stop. Eventually my mind will get the memo that I no longer need to do this. I've found that, if I can apply an actual name or diagnosis to a behavior, I am somehow able to manage it better. No one seems to notice because the movement is so small. Taking the mystery out of a behavior by knowing its name tends to lessen the behavior.

I still tend to offset my teeth when I'm being scolded or confronted. By doing this, I am able to draw my attention inside to what I'm doing instead of hearing what is being said. I don't do this quite as often as I have in the past, but if anyone begins to scold me, I tend to draw that one out and use it again.

Ears and Neck

When it comes to hearing, I remember how difficult it was to change behaviors in this area. My behavior has lessened. Paying attention to so many sounds is exhausting. Not only that, but it felt crazy. I was concerned it might be attached to schizophrenia, but when my husband told me it wasn't, I was able to breathe a sigh of relief. What I was hearing wasn't individual voices telling me what to do or conversing with me—I just sucked in all the surrounding noise and movement like a vacuum. Things like traffic, music, the conversations of others, and so forth played in my head. I was extremely grateful when I was able to lessen the impact of all my superfluous noise. Being able to have single thoughts still fascinates me. At times I like to not just turn the volume down, but off. The quiet in my mind is churchlike.

I also have a behavior involving my ears and neck that to this day makes me feel crazy. I cannot stand to have anyone breathe on my neck or in my ears. Even thinking about it makes me draw my ear to my shoulder. I'm thinking this has to do with sexual abuse since, to get close, this might happen. I find it extremely difficult to tolerate anyone breathing on me. It is a behavior that seems to be firmly implanted in a very negative way. Until I'm able to have recall about what happened, this behavior is still actively trapped inside. To cut it away from me has been difficult.

Being Hypervigilant

Being hypervigilant is watchfulness, or being on alert in order to guard against harm. This is one of the behaviors of anyone who has post-traumatic stress disorder (PTSD). This was the second diagnosis I was given, and it is an exhausting behavior. Anything that is *hyper* has to do with excess. In the same vein, apply the word *hyper* to behaviors such as sound, smell, touch, and movement can indicate watchfulness for things that should be benign. In order to cancel all of these things, I added hyperactivity to the mix just so I could distract myself from being so hyper.

Hypervigilance when it comes to the body keeps everything in you on high alert. This, in turn, makes it extremely difficult for my body to do what I need in order to remain healthy. The things affected by this have to do with digestion, blood pressure, body temperature, hormonal activity, memory, headaches, hearing, body tension, elimination, and so on down the line until my body remains, even today, a knotted mess.

My startle response also fits into the hyperactivity. When I hear something, it isn't unusual for me to quickly turn my head to see what might be happening. The softer things are, the more I pay attention. For instance, at times I have a hard time falling asleep because I'm listening to every sound. This means I want every extraneous sound turned off—the fan is running, the computer is humming, the heater is running, there are dogs barking. (I quite often count barks and then wait for the next one. I do the same thing if my husband coughs or sneezes.) I have been able to teach myself to turn on the fan and pay attention to the whirr. This is called white noise. The only problem is that I become obsessed with the noise in a negative way. I've tried machines that have choices, but my hypervigilance remains too high for that to be comforting.

Altogether it can be exhausting. If any sound comes from another room, I've taught myself to check it out. I refuse to be intimidated by a noise. I'd rather know what it is than allow my mind to play games. In other words, I want everything around me to be as quiet as possible so I can scan.

Breathing

This is another area of my life that still gives me problems. I tend to hold my breath or breathe in such a way that I'm not filling my lungs the way I should. Since the body needs oxygen, I can at times have a feeling of anxiety simply because I'm not breathing deeply enough. When this happens, I have several methods of relieving the situation. I take a nonaddictive, homeopathic treatment such as B vitamin. If that doesn't work, I might take a mild prescription medication. One thing I believe about taking medication is that there isn't any shame in doing it if you need to. As a matter of fact, there's more shame in not taking it if you need temporary relief.

What I try to do is bring my mind into my breath so I can remain in the present rather than bogged down with some problem I can't remember. I've always been able to recognize why I feel I'm doing this. For one thing, it has to do with past abuse. If I could lessen or hold my breath, I didn't seem to draw as much attention to myself. This may be part of the reason I have a difficult time crying. It is hard to cry without sounds, so both the sound and tears stay inside. When I hold my breath, it gives me a feeling of being invisible or diminished in size, so I can be too small to see. Consciously I realize I no longer need to do this, but subconsciously, when I'm in a familiar situation, it just happens. Even after I've started breathing normally, it never takes long for me to start again. Holding my breath heightens my anxiety. Quite often when I was having bodywork I had to be reminded to breathe.

One of the exercises I've taught myself is to place my hands on my stomach and do what is called belly breathing. The idea is to mindfully breathe so that my hands rise and fall. Shallow breathing is done in the upper chest and doesn't allow a full volume of breath to enter the lungs. I've noticed when I begin to feel nervous or edgy, I check my breath. Deep breathing using awareness releases the tension I'm feeling, and my uncomfortable feelings seem to end. Never underestimate the value of how your breath manages your behavior in silent ways.

Bathroom Habits

Bathroom habits have a lot to do with stress. I'm always in too much of a hurry. This is how I am in every area of my life. This is one area I'd prefer not to talk about, but these habits have a lot to do with how well the body functions.

I try to remember how much water my body contains and how I need to keep myself hydrated. I've heard it said that, by the time you realize you are thirsty, you've waited too long. If you aren't emptying your bladder enough, it is time to begin drinking more water. By not drinking enough, it is easy to contaminate the body with unwanted bacteria growth. Drinking water helps flush out of the system.

When I was little, I don't think I drank enough water. It seems as if I was always constipated. Mother's go-to when I was a child was to use an enema. As an adult, I've come to realize that, if I'm not drinking enough water, I don't have enough fluid in my body to be able to eliminate properly. Stress can play havoc on the bowels. If too much time has passed, I belly breathe in an exaggerated way, especially as I breathe in. If I can extend my belly and hold it long enough, my colon can stretch out so things can move along better. I always know when I'm doing it correctly when I hear sounds that tell me I've been successful. Sitting too long isn't helpful because, not only do I not need to fold myself in the middle, but I need to do a certain amount of activity so things aren't allowed to stagnate in one area too long. Holding my breath is a definite no-no, but this is something I need to be hypervigilant to monitor.

Recently I found an article about the body's flora. This has to do with the balance of bacteria in the gut. The gut is classified as a larger part of our brain's system than the one in our skull. Why? It constantly sends messages about the status of our body. In turn, the brain reads the messages and contacts whatever organ or body part is in need of attention. When I began to see my gut like a major part of my body's brain system, I began treating myself better.

Yeast can also create a problem. Almost every woman has encountered it at some time or another. I read that, if a mother has an overabundance of yeast or bad bacteria, it can be passed on to a baby during the process of birth. If that happens, the newborn doesn't have the ability to fight it off. It is extremely difficult to not only diagnose but to get rid of. An abundance of yeast in the body system of the child can remain for years if it is not caught and treated. It can cause havoc on the body of the child for years to come. Mother talked about how depleted her body was at the time of my birth. Could she have passed yeast on to me as a newborn? Was this part of the reason I was so sickly from the time I was born? At that time, doctors knew most of the things that might cause problems for a baby, but when it came to my prognosis they were baffled. Information about food allergies wasn't prevalent. Could that have been causing my stomach issues? I know that, as an adult, even if I smell of peanuts, coconut, or popcorn I can feel nauseas. If I feel queasy when I smell food, I know I mustn't eat it because it won't digest and I'll be in trouble.

It has also been said that, before a baby is born, it already knows how it fits into the family. It picks up signals given by the mother if she is as highly stressed as mine was. There has been a lot of unbelievable information about stress in pregnancy and how that relates to the infant. Without someone available to tell me about my behavior as a baby, everything at this point is something I would be second guessing. My body's balance is off and always has been. That has been the reason I've tried so many things to regain mental and physical balance. Until I am able to do that, I'll need to try harder to monitor everything to do with my mind and body behavior so I can head off the imbalance or at least slow it down.

Another thing that comes to mind when I think about bathroom habits has to do with the extreme headaches I used to get when we would visit my grandparents. One of the first things Mother did was to give me an enema when I woke up with my lightning-like headache. I'm not sure how much it helped, but everyone was desperate to for answers. One thing I vaguely recall is how everyone would come to the open bathroom door to see if they could help. This also applies to my grandfather. Something in me sees him. I believe he was the reason for the headaches, since I woke everyone in the house with my screaming. By doing this, I thwarted any effort he might have made to abuse me. In some ways, as odd as it may sound, he may have been able to meet his need by watching as I was getting an enema. Anything put into any body orifice can be seen as abuse if it has any regularity to it. From that time on, I assumed if I had a headache it was coming from my gut, so I would also use an enema. Today I've been able to change this for myself, but it takes a lot of awareness as to my body's status. When too much time has passed, I begin looking for natural ways to take care of the problem. I use breathing, drinking more water, and using a drinkable form of fiber. I think about what kinds of foods I'm eating that might be causing trouble, or medication that may have a constipating effect. Since eating isn't my favorite thing, it is easy to not take in enough fiber. By finding another way to get it, I've been able to manage my bowels better.

As silly as this might sound, one other thing I do is to thank my body each time it performs in a healthy way. I talk to my body and tell it I don't need to hang on to something that is no longer useful to me. I remind myself it is now safe to eliminate it from my body and my life. The mind can respond to this message. After going to the bathroom, I thank my body for doing something that is for my better good.

Not long ago, I told my husband I remembered a time before my father was killed when I was in the outhouse wearing, of all things, a diaper. This vision has always bothered me, and I was always wondering why. I wasn't a baby at the time, but a child. I do know Mother bragged about training one of my brothers when he had an accident by putting his dirty underpants on his head. Was this something done to punish me for an accident? That can easily become a reason for a child to begin to have problematic bowel movements. If a child is told she is bad because she messed her pants, it comes across to the child as "I am bad because I went to the bathroom." In turn this can become, "I am bad if I go to the bathroom." That in itself is enough for the child to subconsciously hold on rather than let go. That's why I made sure when I was working with our sons to be careful. I went one step further when it came to grandchildren. I always told everyone, "I'd rather have it out than in." I cringe when I hear people talking to babies or small children in a way that suggests that what they've done is bad and that it has a direct correlation to who they are. It has to do with something they did, and since it is natural, it's a good thing. Yes, I want to train them, but there are better ways than to scream, smack, or shame. I should have been told that going to the bathroom was a good thing, and I wasn't bad simply because I had to go to the toilet. Maybe instead of constipation, I had diarrhea because of a food allergy or sickness. Whatever it was, it shouldn't have been seen as bad enough that I needed to be taught that type of message.

Another thing I've read is that the reason for holding it in can be the same as the reason I used to cut my bangs—it was the only thing I could control, so I didn't feel upset. Subconsciously a child might be thinking, "It's mine, and I'm going to keep it"—even if it makes the parents upset. It's another body/mind message being given and being read incorrectly. How could I know if no one explained that going to the toilet was a safe thing to do?

Smells

Now that's funny—I put smells directly behind toilet behaviors. I didn't do it on purpose, but it is funny, don't you think?

When I was going to therapy, I would sometimes smell pipe tobacco or perfume. My father occasionally smoked a pipe, and I wondered if this had anything to do with him. The perfume wasn't a complicated blend like what we have now, but a sweet, simple one. It had an innocence to it that made me think about times gone by.

Once when I was having a session with my bodyworker, I suddenly smelled something akin to model airplane glue. As far as I was concerned, the entire room reeked of the odor. I wondered how he could work under those conditions. Was someone in the building doing some type of construction? When I mentioned it, he asked what I was talking about. I then asked, "How can you stand that smell? Doesn't it give you a headache?" Again he told me he had no idea what I was talking about because he didn't smell anything. I know my older brother loved to put together model cars. Maybe that was what I smelled. About then something popped into my mind about ether. I had been given ether when my tonsils were removed when I was nine months old, and I had been given it again during the delivery of our second son. Could that be it? I didn't try to button down what it might be, but at the time I didn't know about smells that might be connected to temporal lobe epilepsy. Now the question would be, was it memory or an incidence of TLE?

Sometimes I couldn't identify the smells. When this would happen, I'd try to find something to connect to it. These smells were many times acidic or caustic. Smells like these were so strong I could taste them. One that comes to me quite often smells like burnt wiring. Believe me it's not one you want to smell when you're driving down the highway. I always ask my husband if he smells anything—just in case. If he answers no, then I know it might be connected to TLE.

Smells that I might be able to attribute to childhood have lessened. Even if it happens, I try to think "hmmm" until it fades away.

Faces

To say I make faces is putting it mildly. It never failed to surprise me when my grandchildren asked if I was angry. When they started doing that, awareness about the faces I was making became another thing to monitor. I've talked to each of them when they mention it and satisfied their anxiety by telling them no. "I've always made faces. I promise you I'm not angry. If you do something that upsets me, I'll tell you. Until then don't worry about it. Okay?" Sometimes they may tell me when I make faces, but it no longer bothers them the way it did before our conversation. I never notice I'm making faces unless someone brings it to my attention. I slide in and out of them as things change. I wish I didn't do it, but it's one of those things I make note of and then dismiss as nothing to bother with.

I've found the best way to relieve any tension in my face or mouth area is to exaggerate the muscles so they relax.

Hands, Fingers, and Thumbs

My hands were always shaking as I grew up. I don't think I even noticed unless someone brought it to my attention. When my husband and I were in the deepest part of our marital issues, my hands would shake so much I'd grab something in order to stop. At that point in time, I didn't know about my childhood, so I didn't understand the significance of what was happening.

When it comes to my fingers and thumbs, I have a language that keeps me informed as to where I am. If my fingers are spread as far apart as possible, it feels like a scream. By the time I get to that point, I'm in trouble. I try to notice it and relax my fingers. If I rub my fingers together in a rapid manner, that means I'm beginning to get anxious. If I pay attention to this and stop, I can avoid stretching my fingers into a scream. Another behavior is to fold my fingers over my thumb. To me this means I am trying to become invisible or hide. There are books explaining how various behaviors tie to the mind. It is how our mind tries to grab our attention. Again, as I've said before, the mind first begins in whispers. If I listen, I can avoid trouble. If I don't pay attention, it gets louder until I do. Thankfully, when my body started screaming "Cancer!" I heard the message early enough while it was still treatable.

When I'm startled, my hands fly in the air as if I'm under arrest. This doesn't work well when I'm riding in a car and overreact to someone else's driving. When I notice I'm about to do this, I sit on my hands. I have several things I can do with my hands while I ride in the car. I crochet, read, work crossword puzzles, or close my eyes so I can't see what is happening. I look out the side window a lot. When I catch myself doing this, I tell myself to go ahead and look. If I refrain from looking, my mind conjures up visions of accidents. This may also be attached to the deaths of both my father and brother.

I taught our sons that, if they felt restless, they should look out the window and notice things. Our sons and our grandchildren have all played "I spy with my little eye" when we are in the car. One of the funniest incidents was when our grandson began to describe, of all things, the Statue of Liberty. What were the chances we'd find something like that while driving on back country roads? All of a sudden, there it was—a replica outside a church. We all still crack up when we talk about it. He was familiar with the road, so maybe he was listening to his subconscious mind as it relayed to him what was ahead. Even he was shocked.

When anything happens with my hands, I know I need to take a personal inventory of what may be bothering me and back off. I can generally identify the source of my problem, and once I've taken care of it, my fingers and hands go back into a calm state.

One afternoon in 1974 when my husband and I were having serious trouble, I was working as a teller in a bank. My hands were shaking so badly a customer asked what the matter was. It may have made him nervous to think it might be connected to the money I was counting. I think my hands were shaking on the outside the way my body and mind were trembling on the inside.

Voice

Have you ever been around someone whose voice was so high pitched it felt irritating? Stress can do that. What tends to happen is, as our tension begins to rise, so does our voice. This is simply because our larynx tightens. Usually I cough a few times to break the tense pattern.

I also try to slow down my speech if I begin to notice I'm becoming tense or too tired. When that happens, I tend to jabber or go completely silent. When I first tried telling my story, I coughed uncontrollably. It was almost as if I was choking on my words as I tried to spit them out. I don't do that as much since my story is so familiar. There are times when I'm reading or recounting a psychological story or poem that I still choke just enough so I realize I've stumbled on a secret I still haven't realized.

One of the other things about being traumatized is how I recount my story in a flat or sing-song manner. Even though the story may flow out of my mouth, it is dull and unrecognizable to my conscious mind. It is still difficult to accept this story as mine even though I have enough personal memory to know I'm being truthful. If my voice doesn't have any fluctuation or fluidity, I'm not feeling enough heat or emotion to feel angry or upset. I may feel upset about the story I'm telling, but not at the people who put me in the situations. I am a "Johnny One Note," or in my case a "Mary One Note." I may not like it, but even if I think I'm showing emotion as I speak, I'm not. Can you imagine me in a school play? I needed to have the ability to fluctuate my voice as I expressed the emotions of the character. If I can't do it in real life, it is even more difficult to do in a pretend life.

I believe the pendulum can swing the other way for some. I've often heard spectacular people such as actors, singers, and speakers tell how they use their trapped emotional energy in what they are doing so they can discharge it in a positive way. The problem with that is that, even if they are putting their emotions out for us to see and feel, inside their true personal emotion is trapped nearly to the point of explosion. When that happens, it creates a void that has to be filled with something—drugs, alcohol, or other lesser addictions such as being a workaholic, eating, shopping, and so on. Sometimes the emotions are so confusing and strong they can be ended only by suicide. When that happens, we are all left with questions about how their success could have ever allowed them to feel such internal despair.

Enoughness

This word seems to be built on a foundation of honor and respect and has to do with feeling secure. I'm not talking about honor or respect I have for others; rather, I'm talking about the honor and respect I have for myself. As a child I wasn't able to honor myself and my feelings because I was trying to honor Mother's wishes. Later, I constantly tried to reassure myself I was loved by doing nice things for her, such as spending the money I earned cleaning. I use to do the same thing as an adult. I tried to buy love and respect by showing my respect and honor for others. I'd do things and I'd buy things and go over the top trying to convince others what a nice person I was. Did it help? No! The problem many times was that my desperate need to have others see me as good came across as controlling or forceful. I used to constantly ask my husband if he loved me. I didn't feel loveable and could hardly believe anyone would ever find anything about me that would allow him or her to care. Even through all our marital issues, he never stopped loving me, or he would have left. Even the fact that he stayed wasn't convincing enough to keep me from asking him repeatedly, as if he might have changed his mind.

In 1988 I had a feeling that something was horribly wrong. I had no idea at the time that my childhood issues were beginning to boil inside as they tried to surface. Since I felt so hollow and empty, the first thing that came to mind was that it must have something to do with me as not being enough as a person.

That was why I was constantly asking my husband if he loved me. What I needed to realize was that I hardly loved myself. I felt flawed, and I could hardly believe he couldn't see it. At the time, I didn't really know why I was asking. I just needed him to remind me I was worth loving. After all, hadn't my family instilled in me that I wasn't enough? Having him remind me didn't have anything to do with the sanctity of our marriage—it was personal.

I knew Mother must have loved me. After all, she was my mother. At the same time, she never displayed any true affection for me. When you don't feel the loving attachment to your mother, then why would anyone else love you?

When I asked my husband if he loved me, it was almost as if I was checking to see if he had changed his mind. He always reassured me, but gave me a look that silently asked, "What do I need to do or say so you will quit asking me that?"

Finally, after the light in my brain was switched on, each time the question "Do you love me?" popped into my mind, I'd answer it for myself, remembering that, if he didn't, he would have left a long time ago when we were still having so many problems. All of a sudden, I stopped asking, and before long he was the one needing reassurance, not me.

The lesson: I realized I had to become enough for myself because, in hard times, I was the only one able to be there 24/7 to pick up the pieces. I knew it was okay to ask occasionally if my husband loved me, but if I felt desperate, there was something else going on. I taught our sons to freely say "I love you" simply because too many times in my life people left for a short period of time but never came back. Loving yourself enough enables you to love others even more than you could have ever imagined.

Interrupting

I am aware it's rude to interrupt even as I'm doing it. I've tried to dig into this so I can understand why I continue. It may be the need to change a difficult conversation into one I can handle. In the past, I changed subjects the way someone plays checkers. My mind was so jittery I couldn't stay on one topic long. It isn't that what I have to say is important; I just don't seem to be able to stop. I don't think I'm concerned I might forget what I want to say; it just keeps my mind moving.

This behavior has been difficult to change because the habit is deeply ingrained. Sometimes I get excited when a subject comes up that I'm passionate about. Right now all I can seem to do is stop, apologize, hope for understanding, and ask the person to continue his or her thought.

Dreaming

This is an interesting behavior. Some say they never dream. From what I understand, we all dream; it's just that we don't always try to remember. It was once said that a dream uninterrupted is like a letter unopened.

In the beginning of my process, I did dream a lot. If I kept a notebook by my bed and wrote down a few words, I was generally able to bring back the meat of the dream later by connecting the words into what I felt the dream meant.

My first dreams contained lots of suitcases, boxes, dirty clothes, monkeys, and cars. When I went to see my father's family, I woke to dreams of counting gunshots.

I did purchase a book about understanding my dreams, but only allowed myself to go into my "hmmm" state of mind. I didn't try to make them into anything in particular. Occasionally I found dreams that contained actual memory. We even had an organization nearby that, once a year, you could call and tell them about a dream, and they would interpret them, or try to. The dream I shared with them had to do with a race I was running while wearing red tennis shoes.

I generally don't share dreams with anyone. The only people I do share with are highly trained in a medical way because dreams follow patterns. Sometimes they have to do with what I still need to do, what I've already done, an actual memory, or my present-day cares and responsibilities. I find them curious but don't put too much emphasis on my need to know. If

I do have something I should understand, my subconscious mind seems to find a way to bring it to my attention in the now.

My favorite dreams are ones in which I'm flying. I've taught myself to recognize that I'm dreaming and direct myself to do loops and swoops. This is known as lucid dreaming. Those are the dreams in which, even though you are sleeping, you become aware you are dreaming and you can participate in the dream. I love these because flying is a lot of fun!

No, I generally don't have nightmares. My mind is too plugged into that "hmmm" behavior to let myself be too carried away. I've had difficulty waking up from some dreams, and I've ended up crying out for help. If I do that, my husband reaches over and touches me until I come back into my body. Dreams come from the subconscious mind, and I learned to put up with its antics a long time ago. I just temporarily notice and then drift back to sleep knowing full well it isn't anything for me to feel concerned about.

As a little girl, I had a dream that repeated itself more times than I wanted. It had to do with having a huge boulder in one hand and a feather in the other. I needed to dispose of the feather before I could put down the heavier object. The problem was that I was never able to put down either one. I told the therapist about this dream, and you know what? I never had it again.

Since Mother passed, I've been having more dreams than I've had in years. I know I've been dreaming all the time, but these seem to come back in a variety of different ways. If you believe dreams can contain visitations by others, both living and dead, then you may believe that I've had quite a lot of company. They just keep coming. For the first time ever, I saw my father. I was an adult seeing my father probably the way he looked when he was alive. Part of me wanted to smile and greet him like the adult I had become, but another part wanted to run up to him, put my arms around his waist, and hug him as a child would do. I've seen Mother, both aunts, my uncle, friends, and such, but thankfully, so far, my grandfather hasn't come to visit.

I feel a lot of these dreams have to do with finishing my process. Rewriting this book has helped in so many ways it would be impossible to explain. Versions of the book before this version were jumbled and somewhat confusing. With this new one, I feel a peaceful resolution. It would be impossible to tell you that I am not a bit concerned about getting it edited, published, and out to the reading public. I've always believed in the concept that the right things happen at the right times, and the right people find you when you're ready for them. If this book is meant to be accomplished in an outstanding way, then the Universe will bring it about come hell or high water. I've never stopped believing since 1995 that this will happen, and I'm not about to begin doubting myself or the Universe now—not when I'm so close to watching it manifest.

Just recently I've started turning the tables on what I heard in 1977 with the challenge: "How can you tell others if you don't know?" Lately I've been repeating this question to myself and continue by saying, "Well, I know quite a lot now, and if you want me to tell others, then you'll need to do your part and make it happen." I fully believe without wavering that this book was meant to be, and it will reach others with my message of hope. After all, this is the book I wish I could have found before I started my journey. The saying goes: When the student is ready, the teacher will appear. Well, Teach, I'm ready! Come on, let's go!

Lucid Dreaming

Dream if you dare.
Dare if you can
Wake in your dreams
Upon command.

Walk in your dreams.
Speak if you may.
Your mind will tell you
What to say.

Panic and High Anxiety

Early on in this book, I wrote about my high level of panic and confusion. I have found the word *panic* to be like a shard of glass that is too dangerous for me to handle. Instead I started using the words *high anxiety*. It would be nice if I could just call it a normal level of anxiety, but there's never been anything normal about how I feel. When I see the words *high anxiety* written on the page, it feels softer and more acceptable than *panic*.

It almost reminds me of the difference between art media such as marble and clay. With marble (my sense of panic) it is hard work to even make the slightest change in the stone. With one wrong move the entire thing could crumble leaving nothing but a pile of rubble. With clay (high anxiety) there is a sense of malleability to the medium that makes it easier to manipulate into whatever form I might desire. Changing my wording from *panic* to *high anxiety* has finally started to provide me with the ability to manage some of the harsher feelings I have.

Once I make the shift in words, the rest seems to flow into the spot where I removed the word *panic*, so my life feels better. Over time I've actually been able to lessen even my sense of high anxiety to a level I think is really quite acceptable.

Over Intellectualization—Too Serious

Gee, I'll bet you never considered this about me, did you? My husband didn't have to point this out to me, but he did. I already knew I did this. In some ways, overanalyzing everything is part of what keeps me from being able to feel things. I like facts! That's why I prefer nonfiction. It seems to stand like a wall between me and the processes I should have gone through each time something abusive or traumatic happened in my life.

In my heart of hearts, I don't think I have any other tool available that has worked quite as well for me when it comes to trying to understand. I wanted more than anything to make sense out of my childhood and the issues it contained. When push comes to shove, I now believe it's probably best for me not to remember what happened. If I did, I'd have to feel something, and all I've ever done is to try to keep that from happening, even at the cost of being able to come to terms with what happened to me.

What would I do with it? Accept it? Change it? My intellect tells me to just leave it alone and move on.

Disremembering

Until my husband brought this up, I never heard the word. Before, I was always feeling upset if someone promised to do something with or for me. It felt as if he or she was lying to me from the very beginning. My husband pointed out that, in the moment the person made the promise, he or she probably did mean to follow through, so I really shouldn't see it as a lie. In the moment, the person was telling me he or she was going to do this or that, and it was true. As time passed, if the person wasn't used to following through with what seems to be a promise, he or she forgot the promise. In other words the person simply forgot to remember.

By this time, I fully understood that, in the past, I had issues with being addicted to the way others behaved. Once I was able to put two and two together, I was able to come up with four instead of five, which was what I had done before. I felt a sense of disappointment that the promise had been forgotten, but that was my problem, not the other person's.

Now when someone promises to do something, I just give it my "hmmm" thinking, knowing I might need to eat his or her marshmallow words or make them into s'mores and let it go.

Anger

I've said this before, and I'll say it again. I don't feel any sense of conscious anger about what happened to me or toward the people involved. At the same time, that isn't reasonable. I'm always willing to forgive people; sometimes, however, I think I'm the one I have a hard time forgiving. It may have to do with restricting and deadening my emotions. The problem is, just because I don't see flames or feel the heat of the emotion of anger doesn't mean it isn't there beneath the surface of my mind flashing out at times without my awareness.

I can't begin to tell you the number of times I've been speaking on the phone to straighten out something and, at some point, I'm accused of shouting or screaming. Usually I tell the person I'm not doing either one, but if they want me to, I can show them how I would sound. I think it must have something to do with what I refer to as my bottom-line voice. When I take a firm stand, I think this may be how I sound. It sounds emotionless, and others may be reading it wrong. Then again, maybe it sounds louder than I realize. Both of us need to realize our time is too important to spend seeing who is "king of the mountain." I start out nice, but sometimes the other person is out to be right, and he sees himself as a failure if he doesn't fight tooth and nail to get his point across (of course, this could happen with a woman too!). I try to remember that most of the conversations we have on the phone are recorded now, "for training purposes" and, I think, just to have a record of what was said. If employees don't handle things the way they've been taught, they could lose their jobs. Right fighters shouldn't be customer service people. I can be intense when I point out something and the other person still remains blind to the facts. Convincing me I'm wrong just because he or she says so isn't going to happen. If it gets to the point that I need to back down simply to end the conversation, I'm willing to do that. I pick my battles, but when it's war, I'm not going to lower my weapon and surrender just because I'm the consumer and the other person represents "the boss." I'm more on the side of bipartisan behavior. I give, the other person gives, and we meet in the middle and find common ground.

I suppose I do have anger trapped somewhere inside because that seems reasonable, but it no longer seems reasonable to go on the hunt for it or for the reasons it may exist. I just watch out and stay away from my bottom-line voice.

Once I reasoned that maybe it was just that I had so much anger it frightened me too much to acknowledge, so I avoid it. There was a lot of anger and violence being slung around our house at times when I was a child. Maybe I taught myself I needed to avoid it at all costs and from all sources. I really did try and find anger toward people from my childhood, but that was when I came to realize I wasn't angry at *them*; rather, I was angry at the *acts* they perpetrated against me.

Laughter and Games

One of the things I came to realize early on was how hard it was for me to enjoy life. I started thinking about laughter being the best medicine, so with that in mind I started watching funny shows on TV. Spontaneity definitely was difficult for me. It is hard to be spontaneous when you take life so seriously. That's what happened when I was always on guard for safety. Something had to be sacrificed, and for me it was my ability to enjoy life.

When I started watching funny videos, I started to loosen up, and before long I was hooked. The first time one of our sons saw me he was astounded. I'd looked at him with tears running down my face laughing so hard I could hardly catch my breath. It was almost as if the floodgates of all that contained laughter had broken free from the past. The tension poured out of my body like melted butter.

One of the things I'm enjoying most is a better sense of humor. I'm sure it will add years to my life. You know what they say: laughter is the best medicine.

I'm better about playing games than I used to be, but I'm still not much of a fan. I can sometimes have a strong sense of competition when I play games. Recently I heard it said: you should be able to lose as gracefully as you win, or you shouldn't play.

Sometimes we just don't want to seem foolish if we make a mistake, so instead of giving anyone the opportunity to laugh at us we simply don't play.

Travel and Relaxation

How do you erase stripes off a zebra and replace them with spots? You can't! That's the way relaxation is for me. Why would I want to go on vacation if I couldn't relax? That made things worse. Besides, my inner family didn't like me to take them too far from home.

I think my problem with travel may have to do with people going out and not coming back. My father died without a will, and that had a terrible impact on our family. One of the ways I hope to resolve my unwillingness to leave home is to finish any business that needs to be taken care of. I try to help myself understand that traveling a long distance is probably safer than driving close to home, but I like being close to home. When I go on vacation, I want to do my normal chores like make the bed, pick up the room, and put everything in its place.

As for doing relaxing things, I planned to spend time doing things like yoga, tai chi, and dance therapy. I gathered all the materials I needed, but instead of being able to do it right away, I had to stop and rewrite this book. It's a good tradeoff as far as I'm concerned. All I know is, before I'm finished, I need to be able to claim my body so I can enjoy myself more fully. I'm confident I'll get it done—I always have!

Singing

Pre 1988, I sang a lot. It was comforting to lose myself in the words. Most everything I sang then were songs I learned in church. That doubled down on my sense of comfort and helped fill my religiosity. My singing became different when I felt stressed. Sometimes I couldn't remember the words, so I'd repeat the same line over and over. If I was somewhere I couldn't sing out, I'd do it in my head or hum. Several times I've met other "hummers" and wondered if they do it for the same reason. It didn't matter where I was if I needed to distract myself, what better way than to occupy my mind with trying to remember a tune or the words to a song? Sounds of any type, especially loud, pulsing noises, heightens my heart rate and can increase my level of stress rather than lower it, so I try to choose my songs carefully.

Picking my Songs

When my husband and I were having problems I made myself a play list. In it were the songs I had chosen as fight songs. No, they weren't about fighting with my husband; rather, they were songs that aroused my fighting spirit. Then I had songs that encouraged me to understand that saving our marriage was worth the effort. Several pieces of music I used had to do with bringing out a strong sense of self. Since I had chosen my songs carefully, the effect they had on my mind and spirit was astounding. Without them I'm not sure how well I could have handled everything that kept happening.

If I wanted to work hard, I'd put on loud music with a beat that would rattle my eyeballs and speed my adrenalin. I'd tackle jobs in such a frantic way that I'd be exhausted when I finished. It was almost as if the pulsing of the music would come through my ears and out of my hands in a creative way. By the time I was finished, all the negative energy had been dispersed and transformed. Afterward, I'd feel the quiet sense of contentment after a job well done.

Music and Shows on Television

I began in 1989 to monitor music being played on TV because of the anxiety my body and mind felt. I knew I had enough stress in my life without buying into what the producers of the shows wanted and intended me to feel. Many of the action shows had background music that exhausted me, especially during chase scenes. Because I had hyperacousis (enlarging sounds), I monitored every single note of the music. My heart rate would go up as well as my anxiety, and by the end of the show I would be a hot mess. For me it was not only a distraction, but also the music added nothing to the story. I knew the way the shows were presented wasn't about to change, so I would mute the music, turn it down, change the channel, or turn the TV off if the music began to upset me.

As a matter of fact, I developed an entire list of shows I no longer exposed myself to because of how I felt while I watched or afterward. Even today I refuse to watch programs in which people are fighting, belittling one another, gossiping, or cursing. The only problem is that this leaves out much of what many people see as entertainment.

I no longer watch court TV because I'm not qualified to judge anyone. Besides, in the past, I made a lot of the same mistakes these people are bringing to the judge. It could very well be me bemoaning my poor choices and trying to get justice for a situation I created.

I've found that some reality shows seem over the top in exposing things I don't need to see or hear. If they have something to teach, great. But more often than not, the shows have more to do with deceit and greed than good clean competition. I find it unbelievable that people would be willing to allow everyone in the nation into their lives. Quite frankly I'd be embarrassed if anyone had seen what was happening in my household when I was growing up. Then again, had someone been watching, I might have been rescued. My feeling is, instead of spending time watching others live their lives, I really need to be tending to mine.

Some of the earlier talk shows were helpful because they taught me I wasn't alone. It seemed comforting to know others had not only survived but had been able to regain a new outlook on life. Some, however, had remained trapped in their past, and that was one thing I didn't want happening to me. The experts on these shows were great at explaining situations in a more understandable way. These shows seemed to keep a general rule of decency. Today's programming, however, seems to get worse and worse. This appears to be true especially when it is time for ratings. I now record shows instead of watching them in real time. That way, I can decide if they have anything of interest that might help or if someone is just out for their fifteen minutes of fame. I never hesitate to delete anything mid-program if I find the content is beginning to clash with my internal spirit or sense of fairness or sanity.

I have even gone so far as to stop watching some of the prime news channels. At times I feel over informed. This is especially true when what they are saying begins to instill a sense of fear into my daily life. Most of what they tell in full gory detail is beyond my ability to manage. Terrible things have always happened worldwide, but most of us didn't know or worry about them. I limit news programs to the first few events, check our local weather, turn the channel, or simply turn it off. I do need information, but not so much that it has a negative impact on me. If what I am watching leaves me feeling fearful, angry, or negative, I realize I need to look into my own life to see why I am feeling upset and deal with that.

Since it is hard for me to remain still while I'm watching television, I tend to look at catalogues, check mail, work crosswords, or do handwork like crochet. One nice thing is that we can now pause a program and never miss a thing. If I do miss something, I can rewind and go back to where I lost track. Wouldn't it be nice if we could live our lives that way? If company comes, I push the record button, visit with real people, and then watch programs after they've gone. I also record shows if I want to go somewhere in the real world and do real-world things! Even if I miss out on a program, so what? It isn't as if it is that important. I've met people who can't stand to answer the phone when a favorite program is on. Most programs are prerecorded, so what's the big deal?

A few cooking shows go over the edge when the person in charge begins swearing or diminishing the people. When the food and verbal abuse starts to fly, I switch channels. Besides, I've found that seeing food makes me hungry. I envision myself making what they do, but it's difficult for me to cook now that my family is grown, and there's no one else but my husband and me to eat it. The minute I become stressed, chances are I will begin devouring what I shouldn't be eating. Not making it or having it on hand helps. I've read that watching this type of program adds weight or can put you in a hungry state of mind.

Movies

Going to the movies is supposed to be a pleasant thing. Not for me! Again, I had a big problem with the musical scores. Not only that, if I try to eat popcorn while I'm feeling stressed, it won't digest, so I'm stuck with popcorn in my throat.

My husband likes action movies. It isn't that I don't like them, but until I taught myself differently, all the blood and gore horrified me. When I would be exposed to something like that, I'd tip my chin to my chest and look from beneath my bangs—which, as I've mentioned before, throws me into a different state of mind. The child in me could hardly believe her eyes that I had taken her to something that made her feel so upset.

I knew there wasn't any "her" and that it was me—just in an altered state of mind. I finally started putting my finger beneath my chin and moving my head until my eyes were looking straight ahead. I knew it might feel uncomfortable, but I needed to face my fears head on.

I have a script that I run through my mind when I feel upset about what seems to be happening to the characters in a movie. I remind myself that they are only actors doing their jobs. If they cause me discomfort, that means they are doing a good job. When characters are killed, I picture the actors getting back up after the camera turns away. I picture them going into the bathroom to shower, putting on street clothes, getting into their cars, and going home for supper with their families, or going out for the evening. I remind myself they are getting paid to get me to believe what they were doing was real. I remind myself I paid for the privilege of buying their story so I might as well enjoy it.

Touching or Hugging

As I mentioned earlier, I had a problem with people hugging or touching me. I'm sure part of it is because our family never really did that. Mother never spontaneously hugged me. I was thirty when I realized this. I felt sad when people touched me and inside I just wanted to rip them away so I could run away.

Hugging is an energy exchange. The biggest problem with sexual abuse issues is that negative energy is thrust into you, and it never goes away. That means anyone reaching out to grab you may not be doing it in a loving way, but to molest you.

All people who come into your personal space transmit their energy. That's why sometimes we make quick judgments about people. Something in us is reading energy and questioning if the person can be trusted or if we need to go the other way. That can happen even from a distance. Have you ever walked past someone or been behind a car and something in you somehow doesn't like that person? In some ways it can feel personal without a rational reason.

When I hug people now, I am fully aware of what I am doing. I allow myself to be touched because most people don't want to hurt me; they just want to hug in a benign way.

One of the things I went out of my way to teach our sons was hugging. Still today they never fail to reach out for a hug. I also taught them to spontaneously say "I love you," which is another thing my family never did. I plugged the hole on that trickle down and have always been thankful I've been able to change my behavior so I could influence theirs.

Blending

This is somewhat akin to hugging in a rather strange way. I don't know if other people do this or not. It's one of those things we never consider asking.

During my first session of hypnosis, I felt a sense of desperation about touching the wall. When I was a girl, I pushed my bed against the wall because I wanted to sleep between the bed and the wall.

I hadn't paid much attention to those things until 1989. Just as I was going to sleep one night, my hand went to rest on the nightstand beside me. I had been anxious that day, and suddenly I could almost feel my anxiety physically streaming out of me and into the night stand. It felt really strange because I could hardly believe what had just happened. I lifted my hand, and the anxiety returned. After an emotional day, I still sometimes fall asleep with my hand touching the nightstand or headboard.

Trust

How can you trust others if you can't trust yourself? How could I do that? After all, I was the one forgetting my detrimental childhood. Learning to trust is difficult after you've been brought up with untrustworthy people.

Once I was married, I learned to trust my husband. Then he deceived me, and the trust I had been relying on disappeared. It took years to rebuild my willingness to trust him again, and then one last time he proved he couldn't be trusted. Now where are we? We are trusting each other with the most precious thing we have—each other. Our marriage is solid, and we talk about everything. That doesn't mean we always agree, but with the kind of trust we now have we don't need to.

I'm not one to really trust others when it comes to my body or my safety, but I am somewhat willing to trust what they say or do if I am able to validate their reasoning. I try to be a reasonable person, but when it comes to facts, I'm a fact-based person. Anyone who tells me that black is white or white is black will get my disagreement. I've always felt it was important to research both sides of an argument or idea before making my final decision. I've especially done this in religion. The same was true when it came to some of the therapies I decided to try or people I would be working with during these treatments. I look for pros and cons and then let my inner self make my decision. It's nonsense for people to think I'm going to just take them at their word because of who they are or what they do. Alternate medicine, religious philosophy, medical information, and such have to meet a high approval rate to get my vote. It is insanity for people to think I should blindly obey because they tell me to. Using my mind to find my facts from both sides of the road generally helps me make correct decisions. If I support one stance and then new information comes out showing me I should take a second look, I'm up for that. If a fact isn't solid, it will crumble under the heat of new information if it is researched and brought to our attention. I will change my mind if I am proven to be mistaken. There isn't any reason not to back down. To admit I'm mistaken doesn't show a cowardly stance; rather, it shows strength and willingness.

Lesser and More Benign Addictions

Animals and Pets

This is another thing I'd rather not admit, but it has haunted me for years, and I'm just now finding a way to deal with it thanks to television. As I've learned more about the psychology of animals, I have found it more comfortable and relaxing to be around them. Before I started watching these programs, I think I saw the behavior of animals as similar to our own. I saw them as being angry or happy or using reasoning the way we might do.

For years when an animal would come near and want to be petted, fed, taken outside to go to the bathroom, or taken for a walk, I felt upset. When an animal came close, I'd lift my hand. I always felt a sense of need coming from them that I couldn't meet. Touching them should have brought joy, but instead I felt a high sense of anxiety.

Watching programs about animals taught me that all they want is to please us and be with us. They want to give more than they want to receive. It was their unconditional love that I should have been seeing. I am not quite sure where these negative feelings came from, but over the last few years I've thankfully been able to change much of that behavior. In the past, I found it difficult to take care of pets because I couldn't even take care of myself. Now, because I've seen the humor, grace, and love pets want to give, I'm finally learning to receive.

One of the other things these programs have taught me is about trust. If animals don't trust, they display behaviors that may come across in a variety of ways. They can have issues with aggression, and they can cower in fear. Dogs read our energy to see who will be the leader and who will be the follower. One of the things I tried to impress on our sons is the idea that it is more difficult to be a follower because we need to use good judgment when it comes to picking the one we should follow. A dog will take the lead if the energy is scattered or low and will assume the position of pack leader. In order to change that position, the owner needs to find new ways to become top dog. I love it when I see the changes in a dog. When the right message and behavior is given, the dog can instantly change into the position of being part of the pack instead of its leader. Dogs mirror us so that we can see ourselves through their eyes. The things I've been learning have come to me as a new form of people psychology in which I've been able to see that the dog isn't the one needing therapy—it's me! As a pet owner, I'm now able to stretch out my hand and pet our animals. The need for humanizing their psychological behavior was eye opening. Our emotions and theirs are on completely different plains. As I change myself and my vision of being a pet owner, I am allowing both of us the privilege of one of the greatest gifts ever given, and that is the trust and companionship of animals.

The Behavior of Others

One of my first lessons was learning that I am not responsible for the way other people behave; neither can my behavior cause others to behave in a certain way. Before that my feeling had been, if I was the best, kindest, most loving, generous person in the world, there wouldn't be any reason for others to not see me that way. That isn't true. Others have a right to feel about us how they want to feel, and if they want to see us in a negative way, that's their prerogative. Once I was able to break that false expectation I was more than ready to tackle anything else that might be standing in my way.

There was one person I clashed with in a way that seemed puzzling. It happened in 1986. I wasn't doing anything to deserve the way I was being treated or how I was being spoken to. After I began to understand that the person had a right to her own opinion of me, she called one last time. That was actually the last time I played that game with her. Since we had to be around each other upon occasion, we simply kept our negative opinions and rhetoric to ourselves. Later she called to ask a question because she felt I was one the smartest people she knew. What?

Dolls and Angels

Let me tell you about becoming addicted to buying dolls. I saw a Kewpie in a magazine similar to one I had before my father died. Somehow my baby was left outside and fell apart. I had loved that doll and felt brokenhearted when she was thrown away.

My Kewpie was made of pressed wood, but the one in the magazine was porcelain. She tugged at my heartstrings, and next thing I knew she was in my hands. As a matter of fact, I bought the set. Next I found Shirley Temple dolls. These were also made in a series, and I bought all of them. The next ones had to do with Howdy Doody and Buffalo Bob. I was hoping to find Clarabell the Clown, but he wasn't part of the set. These were characters in a program I watched after we moved in with my grandparents. Next came Charles and Dianna dressed in wedding attire. After that came Raggedy Ann and Raggedy Andy. The final straw was Frank Sinatra dressed in a topcoat and hat like the ones my brothers wore. By then I was thinking, "What am I doing?"

By the time I stopped doing this, I had a lot of money tied up in something meaningless. Next year I hope to donate all but my favorites to a silent auction and let them live somewhere else.

Next came a gathering of angels. I'm not going to attempt to debate or discuss the presence of angels or reality as opposed to nonreality; I'm just talking about them as an idea. The angels I began collecting were touchable and pretty and allowed me to question their possible presence in the world.

I've never really been an angel person since I changed my thinking about religion; nonetheless, last year I started collecting them. A friend asked me why, and I told her I wasn't sure. After I left her office, I laughed because that collection started the same time I put my name on a plaque I'd had for years that said "Angels Gather Here." This year I used a marker to put my name on it so it now says: "Mary's Angels Gather Here." I invited them—what can I say?

Just as I was finalizing my last rewrite, I noticed I had angels absolutely everywhere. It seemed to have something to do with a picture I bought at a yard sale last fall. I wasn't sure if it was an angel, a saint, or a goddess. I brought it home and hung it across from where I sit in the living room so I could contemplate what it might mean. I loved the color, which was the reason I paid the whopping price of five dollars they were asking.

There was a tag on the back, so my granddaughter and I looked it up on the Internet. It was a depiction of the angel Gabriel by an unknown Russian artist.

One day as I sat watching television, a strange thing started to happen. A round orb of light about the size of a baseball came into the room and began to move around. It was hard to believe what I was seeing! I grabbed my phone and started taking pictures. Later that day, I was showing them to my son, and he asked, "Did you see the cross?" "What?" I answered. I looked again, and sure enough, there was a full-sized cross on my wall with the picture of the angel situated perfectly in the crossed section. "There wasn't a cross on the wall when I took the picture," I declared.

The light continued to come into the room day after day for about three months. I never captured another picture of a cross, but there were plenty of other things happening. Toward the end of its coming, it kept making hearts as it traveled from the wall to the ceiling and back again. Did I find where it was coming from? Yes! The sun was coming in from another room and bouncing off a mirrored ornament. As the sun warmed the mirrors, the ornament began to gently move. I also saw rainbow-colored lights coming from the beveled portion of a stained glass cross I had given Mother.

The same thing happened in my office, in our dining room, kitchen, back sun room, and bathroom as well as the front sun porch. Watching the orbs move around the room performing tricks became commonplace. There's no way to explain how mind-blowing the experience was. As for the cross that wasn't there, we never found an explanation. I'm still working on a poem about its antics. I plan to have a friend put my phone pictures together and put it on YouTube for everyone to enjoy. Meanwhile, here's a new poem about all the angels in my office:

Calling All Angels

Calling all angels,
Come sit with me
To define what my life
Needs to be.

Surrounding me here
Around my room,
I need your council
Sooner than soon.

They pray and they smile
And it is quite plain
When I enter in
My mind is peaceful and sane.

One angel stands tall
With wings spread wide.
Next to it a small child
Just trying to hide.

One swings on the stars
Another the moon
While yet another
Hums me a tune.

Many are tall
Others are small.
They seem to be waiting
For me to call.

One wears a crown
Dressed in silver and purple
With two maidens in waiting
Completing the circle.

One shines in silver
Another in gold
With halos atop
And hands in a fold.

One little angel
With outstretched arms
Is missing a hand;
It's one of her charms.

She fell from a shelf
During a storm
And it cleanly broke off.
My heart felt torn.

I found my glue
To put it back on
And readied myself
Then thought, "What's the harm?"

Instead I found
A chain with a locket
And put it inside
Like a coin in a pocket.

I wear the chain
Around my neck.
We all need a hand,
So what the heck.

I have two angels
With hands folded in prayer
Standing over a fairy
Sleeping there.

Another angel,
Her eyes tightly closed,
Watches me work
In her quiet repose.

I have angels here
And angels there.
It seems I have angels
Everywhere.

There are angels in cabinets
And sitting on shelves,
Hanging on walls
Just being themselves.

But the best of all
Right from the start
I've an angel inside
Guarding my heart.

Wearing Apparel and Jewelry:

Fortunately I've never been a shoe person. In fact I have seven pairs of the same black-colored slip-on shoes. They are comfortable to wear, and they fit on my feet like gloves on hands. I don't always wear matching shoes, but since they are all alike, no one knows.

As for clothing—what can I say? I try to stay away from clothing areas in the stores. Soon I plan to sort what I have and make donations. There are some I'm saving for "speaking engagements" after the book is published. Now I'm thinking I should wait until people contact me before I buy anything else.

As for jewelry, I never have been much for adorning myself. I have a few favorite pieces, but then again they aren't very fancy or expensive. If I do happen to wear something, I remove it the minute I get home. I like to wear a locket containing the angel's hand. I also wear my first wedding ring and a larger-sized wedding ring. For several years I'd stopped wearing one, but lately I've started wearing one full time. I think it is because we've resolved our marital issues.

As for the locket, I wear it because it has meaning, and as I put it on I think about having an angel's guidance. Several years ago, I found a bisque angel figurine with her hands out as if she was blessing me. One day we had a storm, a window broke, and she fell from a shelf. When that happened, her hand broke off. At first I was going to glue it back on, but then thought, "I could use a helping hand—especially if it comes from an angel." I found a locket in which the hand fit perfectly. I hung it on a chain and began wearing it. I show it to people sometimes and tell them my story, but mostly no one knows it's there.

Other Stuff

Another addiction I had was buying fabric. Have you ever heard the saying "He who dies with the most fabric wins?" Well, I was definitely in the running. I liked how each piece of fabric felt and looked and could always see myself wearing whatever I might make. The problem with that was that, simply because I could see it in my mind didn't mean I could hang it in my closet or wear it. That would be too much like the story of the emperor's new clothes. I might look nice when I was wearing it in my head, but if I went outside I'd be in trouble.

About that time some of the stores were carrying fabric for a dollar a yard, so instead of buying a yard, I'd buy the bolt. I used a lot of it making curtains and tie-tack blankets. I made lap blankets, nap blankets, baby blankets, bedspreads, and curtains for every room. I guess if I were to put making blankets into a phrase it would be, "I've got you covered." Now my family members roll their eyes when I give them another blanket no matter how pretty or unique it might be. Sometimes I wonder what might be connected to this. I have already donated a lot of fabric to churches and organizations that make blankets for newborns in need or lap blankets for nursing homes.

I had the same problem with sewing patterns. They were also on sale for a dollar. After all, I needed patterns for my fabric. I've donated many of them and try to remind myself not to buy one unless I'm ready to use it. My sewing abilities are passable, but certainly aren't up to the standards of a true seamstress. I've finally stopped buying fabrics or patterns but do sew now and then.

The last items I started collecting are still in my home today. As with everything else, the collection started with one piece and blossomed into an entire garden: art glass. I started putting mirrors of all shapes and sizes everywhere as well as metal art. I've gotten to the point now that I won't allow myself any more unless I downsize. I like swirling designs and the way light comes through glass ornaments and scatters colors across my floor. I like ethereal things like angels and fairies. I dearly love all the colors and shapes they bring into our home. As for the mirrors, they remind me of the reflection of the person I'm becoming—but don't ask me to look at myself!

There are other benign addictions that can create problems such as gambling. I've never been to a casino since 1965, so that hasn't been a problem. The list can go on forever. Some collections come under the guise of being helpful such as taking in stray animals. This can be disastrous not only for the person hoarding them but for the animals as well.

Paranoia

Paranoia can be classified as a mental disorder in which sufferers believe that other people suspect, despise, or are persecuting them. If you are paranoid, you are in a state of distraction.

We all share mild forms of this. We seem to have special, personal reasons that we might find something or someone to be frightening to the point of paranoia.

I remember, as a child, not eating chicken offered to me at a television station because I thought it might be poisoned. Back then people didn't warn children about not taking food from strangers. I'm not sure why I had that thought, but people do make threats about not telling family secrets.

I sometimes feel paranoid about what others might think about what I am writing. I think about people I knew in the past. What would they think? I'm still in contact with people I knew in high school. I ask myself, "Are they going to look at me differently?" These people are adults now and are the nicest people you'd ever want to meet. I only wish I had known how nice they were earlier. Today most of them already know about my past because I have shared it with them. I've been telling them for years that I was publishing a book, but because it has taken so long, I began to wonder if they really believed me. You know what? They all still had absolute faith in my claims.

Some go overboard about their concern about their overall appearance. I love to remind myself that the police aren't monitoring things I so condemn myself for. My hair needs combing, so what? Are the hair police out looking to arrest me for unruly hair? If so, jails would be overflowing. I look dorky? So what? Unless I'm naked, the police don't care what I have on. I talk about what happened and how I feel about it in a book? That comes under the guise of freedom of speech. How can I possibly help others if I'm not willing to stand up and speak out?

Suicide

Like drugs and alcohol, I'm sure you wonder about this. The suicide rate for people who have endured a childhood like mine is high. It is almost expected when a person is diagnosed with post traumatic stress disorder (PTSD).

Fortunately, before I found out about my childhood, my connection to religion was extremely tight. Because of this, I was taught that suicide is a sin. That was why, in 1985, when

I was diagnosed with cancer, I saw it as God's answer for me. The thing is, it wasn't an answer. I was merely being asked to choose between life and death. If I hadn't opted for the surgery and, instead, had allowed the cancer to spread, which it would have done, I would have committed medical suicide by my own decision to do nothing.

Did I have a plan? Yes! I had chosen something that would make it appear as if my death was accidental. Was I serious? Before I was able to discover my childhood issues, every day I felt as if I was more than ready to end my story. Afterwards I could see exactly why I felt such a sense of pain and distress. With that information I knew it was up to me to try in every way possible to disarm my fears. Now I can see that paper-thin the line between life and death. I no longer thought of suicide as a sin, but by that time I was beyond fulfilling that thought.

I find it sad when people feel as if their only way out is to end their lives. More than once I've heard about someone trying to take his or her life and failing. I understand why, but I still find it unnecessary when there are ways to avoid it by seeking help. I once heard someone describe how he tried to commit suicide by jumping off the Golden Gate Bridge. He said the minute he saw his fingers leave the edge, his thoughts were, "Oh, shit!" He was one of the few people to survive such an act, but it wasn't until he actually jumped that he realized he didn't want to die after all.

The side effects of some medications include thoughts of suicide. Pay attention because that's real. By 1989 I was able to realize that thoughts and behaviors were two different things. It was okay to have the thought, but it wasn't okay to follow through.

My advice when it comes to suicide is *don't* do it!

Food and Dieting

Smelling or thinking about food can make me nauseous. Even though *I* might feel hungry consciously, subconsciously my inner family isn't hungry, and this means they aren't going to be bribed, talked into, or shamed into eating.

As I buy food now, I've taught myself a new standard. Not buying from a market or department store helps. This way I'm not wandering through the store searching for things to buy. When it comes to food, I walk past what I shouldn't be eating. My rule of thumb isn't to deprive myself; rather, it is to limit the amount I buy. Instead of a bag of candy, I try to buy only one bar or a small amount. If it's soda, rather than a giant one or a twenty-four pack, I buy a regular-sized one. I've always been what I call a "two-fer" person. I'd buy one to eat now and one "fer" later. If a craving hits, it's my rule to try to not have that food available. That way I have to go to the store to buy it. If I have to make a special trip, I may be able to talk myself out of what I may think I want. Before leaving home or on the way, I try to find a distraction so I have time to hopefully outlive my craving. If that doesn't work, I buy what I want, but wait until I get home before I eat it. If mid bite I decide it isn't meeting my internal needs, I've been known to spit it out or throw it away. I'm not a garbage can, so I no longer try to finish something just because it might seem wasteful not to.

Emotional eating is interesting. Removing excess weight isn't as difficult as removing abuse from the mind. Once the abuse is confronted, sometimes the pounds begin dropping on their own.

Thankfully I've come to terms with weight. I try to keep a reasonable goal in mind at all times, but I refuse to beat myself up if I'm not presently at that goal. Eventually I know I'll be able to get back into a healthy weight once my mind knows it is safe for me to let go of not only my past, but my extra pounds. Even if doesn't happen at the rate I'd like, that's fine. I've seen countless women classified as overweight who are beautiful even if they aren't size zero. A majority of women my age look like I do. They dress to fit their size and age and are setting a new standard most of us wouldn't have a hard time achieving.

In 1988 food was an absolute horror. I had always thrown up even as an infant. As an adult, I watch every bit of food I put into my mouth. This has nothing to do with weight but everything to do with digestion. If I even feel a hint that a particular food isn't going to digest, I won't eat it. I can smell something and know if it is okay for me to eat. So you can tell that food and I have never gotten along well. That was the amazing part about Rolfing. After my first treatment, my food began to digest, and my stomach became soft and warm. My hands and feet were also warm since my body fluids were flowing better. I knew that keeping food down meant I was going to gain weight, but so what! It was healthier than throwing up! One thing I abide by is staying away from artificial substitutes. It is better for me to monitor how much I eat of the real thing than to substitute it with something my body might not recognize.

I once joked about writing a diet book. I would call it *The Dog Food Diet*. No! It isn't about going on a fad diet of dog food. It's an idea that puts food into a different perspective.

Have you ever gone to the store to buy a ten-pound bag of potatoes or a fifty-pound bag of dog food? Think about this. When you go to the store to buy either of these, don't you find it difficult to put it into your basket and then into your car? Would you even consider carrying it around all day as you went about your business? You can't take it to a party or to the pool because people would talk. Well, what's the difference between carrying around a bag of dog food and carrying around added weight? I wouldn't want to carry dog food around, yet I carry that much added weight. It is hard on my legs, feet, and back to carry the extra weight be it dog food or body pounds. I definitely wouldn't want to try to fit a five-pound bag of dog food into my clothing because I just wouldn't look right. Now, do you see where I'm going with this idea?

CHAPTER FIVE

Therapies

In the Beginning

I never intended to look into my childhood so I could spend the next twenty-eight years trying to find balance and wellness. I heard someone say we don't always get what we want, but we do get what we need. I may not have wanted to do this, but I found I needed to do it so I could have a healthier, more balanced life and could show others what I had been able to do and how I had done it.

In 1988 all I wanted out of life was to be the most spectacular grandmother ever, but things weren't working out that way. It didn't help that I was a mother-in-law. Mother-in-law jokes may seem funny to some, but they don't promise high expectations for a good relationship. The thing I wanted was to be part of the most spectacular events happening since the birth of our sons, and that had to do with our first grandchildren. In some ways it started to become a competition. At the time, I wasn't able or willing to battle so I took a back seat. This felt heartbreaking, but as more children came into our family, this issue sorted itself out. Today I have a great relationship with all of them.

My inability to grandparent successfully in the beginning was the catalyst that got me started looking into genealogy. I chose to take my excess energy and look into Mother's Native American heritage. Finding distractions has always been one of the ways I entertained myself, so this was an easy choice.

Genealogy is sneaky because it pulls you in, and it's hard to stop. It was 1987 when I started, and it was a wonderful distraction. My childhood experiences hadn't yet surfaced, but they were circling, ready to pounce at the first opening they were given. All it would take was one wrong misstep on my part, and my experiences promised to take over my life with my past relatives waiting for me to recognize their own tragic stories.

Looking into Native American heritage is difficult. My grandmother, from what I was told, went to visit her grandmother in a teepee. I heard there was also an Indian chief in the mix. In their day, Indian heritage wasn't looked on as a plus. I was able to find one of my grandfather's forefathers in a book in which I learned that my grandfather's grandfather married someone of color. Our family knew this was a person of Indian descendant. With the Internet, tracing family lineage is easier now. When I was doing it, all I had was the public library and the Mormon library nearby. I also was able to check some records by mail. I was surprised at how many courthouses had burned, along with the records they held. I didn't have full names because our personal records had been burned. That had been our only hope to find family names. At that point I began looking beyond Native Americans and started looking into everyone on Mother's side of the family.

Now with so much information on the Internet, I might one day try again to find our Native American heritage, which by the way, I am proud of. The problem with researching genealogy is the amount of time it takes. It can be like a shark in the ocean swimming around looking for shreds of time to eat. One nibble leads to wanting the next and so on until years have passed. I find that knowing my heritage is spectacular, but if it is to be compared to life with my present-day family, it should take second place. I have just enough information now. I may one day return to my search, but I'm not ready yet.

One of the things I did before Mother passed was get her DNA. I joined an organization that helps find your roots by way of DNA. I still remember the day I had to take an empty vile to the care center to have Mother spit in it. She'd spit then look at me and ask, "Now what?" I'd tell her, "Spit again." It took quite a while to get the level of spit they needed in order to run the test. Since this was done so many years ago, I didn't follow through as well as I should. I do plan to contact the agency again and start over. I'm thankful I gathered her DNA before she passed. I understand that tracing Native American roots can be difficult, and determining tribes can be nearly impossible, but we'll see.

One thing led to another until one day I remembered I had two parents. I decided maybe I should check my father's heritage too—not him as a person, but his genealogical history. I knew his family were of German descent and thought it might be easier to trace than Mother's family. Besides, there were more family members still living on his side. This idea sounds easy, doesn't it? Instead I became bogged down in a fight with my mind that I hadn't expected because that was how I began to recognize something had been wrong with my childhood.

Every personal story became horrifying. Keeping all that unrecognized information pushed down and had been exhausting. At times I think about how much energy I put into this part of my life. As my journey to my past came to a crossroad, I did the right thing.

Genealogy at that point took a back seat. Looking into my personal past became my new mission. I wanted—no needed—to know more. Who had I been all those years ago? I couldn't recognize myself as I walked into my past. Whose body and mind suffered through all those things as a child? It surely wasn't mine. I felt I should be able to remember, but I couldn't. Finally, after fifty years, I began to learn even more than my mind could ever hope to comprehend.

I wanted to know who I had been—not in a genealogical way, but in a personal way. We could never have been the same, that girl from my past and me. Where and when had I lost her? Who had been living my life all those years? Was it me or was it a part of me that kept hiding and moving in and around the secret parts of my mind? A mystery began to develop, a secret that had to be solved if I was going to be able to live the rest of my life in peace.

After trying to recall the tiniest piece of personal memory, I gave up. From that point on, I was determined to find a new path. If I couldn't recall what my life had been, or what others had been telling me it had been, maybe I could find out what I had done with my past. How had my brain trained me to forget as if deleting my life as quickly as it had happened?

Following my mind down the path of its deception became the new focus to my story. It was no longer about genealogy or what happened to me, but about what I had done to myself in an effort to stay alive and pretend to be living my life. The mind can be deceptive and destructive, but I wasn't about to let it finish me. I became the commander of my ship and sailed into my soul to find the person I had been. The path to my survival twisted and turned. I took more than one detour as life provided obstacles that I had to conquer. It was strange trying to chase down my mind's antics. At times it threatened to turn on me and not allow me to find a successful end to my story, but I tamed it and corrected its misbehavior. I originally hoped I'd have to do this only once and that would be the end to it. My mind proved to be a worthy opponent. Sneaky little electrical impulse server that it is, my mind proved to me that I'd never be able to retrieve memory or put those forgotten pieces completely out of my life. I correct my thoughts and behaviors on a moment-by-moment basis now. I get tired of fighting with my mind, but the more I succeeded in changing things, the easier it has become.

So this is not only how therapy came to be part of my life; it is how I was able to focus on how I was going to help our sons as well as our grandchildren. This enabled me to recognize our trickle-down issues and hopefully change, redirect, or stop them from going any further.

Getting Ready for Therapy

There were things I took into consideration before I started formal therapy. For one, I needed to understand family connections to learn who may have caused the damage to begin with.

Again I want to point out that I see no need for blame when it comes to my family. I feel my grandfather could have been less of a letch, but he wasn't, so I'm willing to deal with that and move on. He definitely had a big part in how the trickle down went into the lives of his wife, daughters, and grandchildren, and so forth. It is my hope as I speak up and step up that I can be a good example to others.

I wish my stepfather hadn't isolated me from everyone in our family. He was the one who insisted I could no longer see my father's family. Not just that, but he isolated me from her sister (my aunt) and her husband. I believe the worst thing he did was isolate Mother. Once they were married, she stopped being my mother and became his wife. Almost anything and everything having to do with me had to pass by him. She never came to my home to visit unless he was there. When our children were born, he told her they were my children and I was expected to take care of them alone and she wasn't to help. We already had two sons when we moved back near her, which meant I was already an official mother. I didn't need her help raising our sons. I did, however, hope she might be able to enjoy her grandsons. None of our boys remember either of their grandparents fondly. I tried, but there was only so much I could do. She never was around our sons without her husband's eagle eye watching to make sure she wasn't overly helpful or affectionate. Shame on him!

My husband and I are still doing reconnaissance with our sons, but it is happening. We are both determined we will continue helping with past issues caused by the family trickle down. I'm determined the time I've spent changing myself, starting with therapy in 1988, will help us all have a fighting chance of plugging the leak and claiming better mental and physical health and balance for our families.

I went to see my aunt in October 1988 so I could ask questions about my childhood. This was the first time I found I had an assortment of serious problems. This discovery might never have happened had I not started searching my genealogical past. It wasn't until after I talked to her that I made an appointment to see a therapist.

As I waited for my first appointment, I began writing every memory I could bring to mind. I then wrote down the details about what my aunt told me. By the time I was scheduled for my first appointment, I had my homework ready to turn in so the therapist could put the information into his files. He should have known when I stepped into his office and handed him a stack of papers that I might be hard to control.

The most difficult part of therapy in the beginning was that, if I talked to anyone about what I knew, I would start choking and coughing. I was fine unless I tried to talk about my past. Then every word stuck in my throat like a chicken bone. By the time I started formal therapy, I was physically and emotionally exhausted. I could only imagine how I was going to handle talking to a professional about things I couldn't recall or speak about without choking.

Formal Therapy

I made an appointment to begin therapy in January 1989. When I went in to see the psychologist, I briefly told him what I knew about my past and how confused I felt by not being able to remember.

Again, every time I tried to tell my story, I was dealing with symptoms that were almost like pneumonia. Part of this I'm sure was because of the high level of stress I was feeling. I kept trying to remember to slow down, not pressurize my voice, and speak quietly. This choking lasted through several sessions before it finally gave way so I could talk and breathe normally. I was bound and determined I had choked my story back long enough, and I was ready to talk no matter what the price might be.

One of the first questions I asked was how long therapy was going to take. At that point, the therapist said it would take seven to ten years if not the rest of my life. Little did I know this was going to be truer than I imagined. I was still naïve; what can I say? I told him I wasn't about to become a professional patient, and I would be participating in formal therapy for only a year. I knew how others dedicated years to therapy, quite often without resolution, and I swore that wasn't going to be me.

I'm not sure how he felt about my unwillingness to continue beyond a year. I'm guessing most of his patients stayed for as long as it took. I was fortunate in many ways that the therapist I was with allowed me enough leniency to have a say over the direction in which I would proceed. Then again, maybe his idea was to give me just enough rope to hang myself.

One other thing that impeded my progress was my internal family. The therapist knew nothing about this behavior, and I didn't realize I needed to tell him. To me the family was as familiar as daybreak. They didn't pose a problem, so why mention them? When he tried to direct my thinking or use hypnosis, my internal family would immediately take charge and challenge his authority. I could almost feel them as they reacted to his challenge. They weren't about to relinquish control to a newcomer.

What I wanted wasn't the talking part of therapy; rather, I wanted to be hypnotized. I had the wrong idea about hypnosis. The rule is that all hypnosis is self-hypnosis. I had seen programs on television in which someone was hypnotized, and it seemed simple. It was a "wham, bam, thank you, ma'am" procedure. I really thought I'd spill my guts on the spot and the whole story would be lying on the floor between us so we could pick through it and see what actually happened. Did that work? No!

I also suggested he give me "truth serum." In spy movies, it works great, but I received a resounding *no* from him. There would be no truth serum or gut-spilling hypnosis, so that meant we were on our own as we attempted to retrieve my story.

The second diagnosis I was given was post traumatic stress disorder (PTSD). Even though I know the diagnosis fit my situation, it always seemed disrespectful. After all, there were soldiers returning from war who had PTSD. I hadn't served in a wartime situation, or had I? As you have been able to tell from what I've told you so far, I had been in my own personal war. The only problem was that the enemy I'd been fighting was not only my family members, but myself.

Most everyone knows about this disorder. Every year the list of people who are diagnosed with PTSD grows longer. With every soldier returning from active duty, there were terrible stories. Not only that, but presently we can hardly turn on the television without hearing about random shootings and other acts of violence here in America and around the world in areas that should be safe. Natural disasters are also rampant, and they too can leave behind a long list of people suffering from PTSD. Sometimes entire communities can be affected. The difference is that, when a lot of people share the same experience, they support each other in a way that lessens the burden on each person. Sharing the load makes it lighter.

One of the biggest lists, however, is the list of people traumatized by abuse. Again, like war and natural disasters, abuse can cause a list of terrible effects that happen in every walk of life. Since abuse is experienced on a personal level, it cuts into the soul and leaves scars that have a long-term effect both physically and mentally. At times it happens to single individuals, but there are times it involves entire families, as was the case with our family. In our family, even though each of us was at war within the group, no one was experiencing the same thing. Every person had his or her own list of secrets caused by abusers. There wasn't any sharing of burdens, and there were no helping hands because we were all broken. The burden we carried weighed us down. Not only did it have an effect on our lives, it had an effect on the lives of everyone who came into our lives in the future. It is impossible to count the number of people in our society who suffer from undiagnosed PTSD due to this problem. That doesn't even begin to take in the amount of abuse left unreported or forgotten.

What is PTSD? It is a psychological disorder following or resulting from trauma. It may develop after any traumatic experience—an accident, a natural disaster, abuse of any kind. But, as I said, it gained recognition in the United States in the 1970s as a result of the difficulties experienced by Vietnam War.

Symptoms begin with a feeling of numbness as the victim attempts to assimilate the traumatic experience. Some of the behaviors involve hypervigilance, irritability, difficulty in concentrating, exaggerated startle response, depression, a sense of guilt for having survived, and emotional difficulties with relationships. Nightmares, flashbacks to the traumatic experience, over reaction to sudden noises, and outbursts of violence can also occur. I actually have a newspaper article written after early world wars in which the term was used and described.

I definitely shared a lot of symptoms the books listed; they were the side effects of my traumas. I've already told you some of them, and I plan to go into more detail as I go along. The part I dislike more than anything is the inability to relax. It also created havoc for me in school because I taught myself that, if I felt stressed, everything involved had to be forgotten, such as test answers, history dates, and such. I also find it terrible when I have to deal with high levels of hypervigilance. I'm always scanning, always listening, always filtering through everything around me in order to monitor my sense of safety. And I nearly jump out of my skin when startled. The last one I'll mention here has to do with being far too serious. I envy people who seem to be enjoying their lives without having to work so hard.

I originally believed these behaviors were only a result of stress and the behavior I developed and maintained in order to stay alive. In 2010, I found that some of these same behaviors are caused by TLE. I'm of the opinion that both of these things—PTSD and TLE—were filling my life with more trouble than I deserved. It was bad enough to have been traumatized by people who were supposed to have been protecting me, but to be re-traumatized by my own mind seemed savage.

I used the description having to do with war victims to my advantage as I started therapy. There were so many coping techniques I came across that I began to see myself as a soldier on the field of war. Former thoughts and behaviors were foxholes where I could hide until I felt safe to come out.

Fight, flight, and flee or feel are the behaviors we choose from when we encounter a problem. These are basic behaviors used by our ancient ancestors to keep themselves alive. If danger came, they would use their instincts to choose from one of the four reactions that would work most effectively for them. After the danger was past, they could drop the high level of awareness, which in turn would lower their heart rates and lessen the amount of adrenalin needed for dealing with a dangerous situation. They could go back into their normal lives. For those with PTSD, this is impossible.

As a soldier in my own war, every time someone dropped an abuse bomb, I'd run to my coping foxhole and stay until the trauma passed. I began to teach myself to visualize coming out of the foxhole as quickly as I had dropped in. As I looked over the landscape of my personal war zone at all the foxholes where I spent my years hiding, I envisioned myself with a shovel quickly filling in each imaginary foxhole. In that way, I could face my fears instead of dropping into old familiar behaviors. This type of visualization did make a difference. Before long I could recognize my escape areas before I had an opportunity to use them. Doing this was the first thing that enabled me to know I was on the right track.

During all of the time I was in therapy, I was in communication with my mother's sister. Each time a question popped into my mind, I would write her or call her to see if she might help me. With each new discovery, I put the information into my packet of typed information, took it to the therapist, and we'd talk about it. I did the same thing after I began writing to my dad's sister. The information they were both giving seemed on track. As I stated earlier, both women seemed to be giving me the same descriptions about my family's dynamics. I especially liked the way what they said fit into my own feelings.

Once I asked my husband to describe a few of my detrimental coping techniques. I was hoping we could go through them like a grocery list, and I could check them off one at a time and be done with them. That's not how it worked.

Our conversation quickly became sidetracked after he mentioned the first one. What was it? I constantly change the subject. I understood what he was talking about because I don't remember being able to stay on topic for long, especially if the subject matter became too intense to handle.

When I went to see the therapist, I told him about the conversation. At that point he asked me to explain what I thought my husband meant. I was sure I could explain without any trouble. Instead I became embarrassed as I tried desperately to stay on subject. The second I changed subjects, he would stop me and ask how I had gotten to the new subject. I tried to back track so I could show how one subject loosely tied to the next. This became a tedious job; in fact, during the next twenty minutes, I changed the subject seventeen times. During most of it, I was tracing the way I hyper-jumped from subject to subject. When we finished that session, he told me that, even though he had already noticed how many times I changed the subject during our discussions, it hadn't bothered him. He said it always took him a few seconds to recognize that I had moved in a new direction, but he was also able to see my connections so he could keep up. The only problem he had after that was that just as he came to recognize my new information, I changed the subject.

I'm still bad about changing the subject, but as soon as I see myself do it, I try to stop. I go back and finish my last thought before I allow myself to move to the next. Another form of this seems to do with interrupting people. I've found that the minute I begin to get uncomfortable because I've been on one subject too long, I interrupt. Once I've done that, I move our conversation in a different direction.

As we made each new discovery, the therapist would ask how I felt about what I had learned or what I had been telling him. I always said the same thing, "I want to scream." Why? Maybe I just wanted to find a way to discount or override all the new information. If a scream filled my mind, it kept away all the things I should have been feeling. The last time I told him I wanted to scream, he encouraged me. I looked at him as if he was out of his mind. I knew his office wasn't set up for this behavior, and I told him so. Someone would have been in his office with a straight jacket so fast I wouldn't have known what happened.

On the way home, as I thought about what he had said, I decided the truck might be safe enough. So that's what I did. I screamed as loud as I could. The sound that came out of me was far different than the one I had heard in my head. The scream I always heard was that of a little girl. You know the kind—the ones that are so high pitched and shrill they almost make your ears bleed. Here's the thing: I immediately felt better. It was almost as if someone had finally heard those tightly wound screams I had been holding in all those years. After that I never answered his question by telling him that I wanted to scream.

Rage

There's a part of me
Screaming inside.
A rage I guess
That never died.

Catch my heart
And I'll kill your soul
With a part of me
That's never whole.

Screams

I heard this child
Screaming in my mind.
I needed to know
A way to find

How to set her free.

I screamed out loud
With all my might
Hoping to hear
Her screams from the night.

Hoping to set her free.

My disappointment
I could feel.
It wasn't her,
It wasn't real,

My screams to set her free.

A woman's voice
Was what I heard,
Not the child.
I felt perturbed.

I had wanted to set her free.

She was trapped tightly
Within my brain,
And day by day.
Still remains

Me.

Before abuse began to be a subject that was acceptable in open conversation, people were saying "just get over it." The only problem is, I never knew what it was. One famous television psychologist tells everyone, "You have to own it before you can change it." Again, my problem is that I can't own something if I'm not able to remember it. I decided I'd examine everything I was learning about my past in a nonjudgmental way. I would engage in more of my "hmmm" thinking for which I know I don't really have to own anything other than the fact I'm attempting to become whole.

During my process I wrote poems about trying to locate the source of what was creating my pain. As you read, you are going to see how desperately my conscious and subconscious minds were struggling with the issue of letting me have the information I needed in order to move forward.

Mary Davenport

The Edge of the Wall

How close can you come
To the edge of the wall?
How close can you come
Before you fall?

Can your eyes peer down
To the depths of hell?
Can you still remain sane
And make yourself well?

I've asked that question
Again and again.
Is taking your life
An ungodly sin?

Your eyes well with tears.
Your heart fills with pain.
You go to the brink
Again and again.

How many times
Can you walk the edge?
That razor-thin line
And still keep life's pledge?

Life's full of blindness.
We're all blind, you see.
None of us knows,
Not you and not me.

If it weren't for God
I know I'd find
One day I'd awaken
In a new world sublime.

But I have to trust
To an upward sky
Not asking reasons
Not asking why.

I try and I try
Time and again
To keep my faith whole
And try to stay sane.

I just want my life
To feel better today,
To laugh in the sun
To run and to play.

At times life's too heavy
For me to bear.
If it wasn't for God
I don't think I'd care.

His merciful hands
Cover over me
Till someday pain's gone
And I am set free.

Winning

I fell into the darkness.
No way for me to live.
I felt it was unkindness
I had nothing more to give.

I felt less than nothing,
No way for me to tell

Because where life led me
It pushed me into hell.

I decided death was winning.
Why should I struggle so?
Where it had led me as a child
I now was doomed to go.

But a whisper from the darkness
Screamed wildly in my brain.
I shouldn't go so willingly.
What was my life to gain?

I fought the fight so valiantly
To win my way again,
But it's a battle daily won
If I truly am to win!

During this same period of time, even more traumatic things continued to happen. One crept up on me in March of 1989. This was soon to be a turning point in my life.

In 1989 my best friend's mother-in-law died when the car she was driving was hit by a train. The interesting part is that this happened in the same month my father died in 1951 when his truck was demolished by a train. I've always had a problem with that month. I guess because, even though I consciously didn't own the death of my father, my subconscious/conscious minds tended to come together during the month of March and point out something I was never able to acknowledge. Maybe it was the weather, I'm not sure.

Part of me really dreaded going to her funeral for fear of what it might bring up inside me. At the same time, I knew that, if anything was going to wake me inside, this might be the opportunity I needed. I want you to understand that this is not a made-up story like one I'm going to share later. This happened in real time.

The funeral was to be held in a small community church much the same as the one where my father's funeral had been held. It was a gloomy March day. I had been in therapy for not quite three months and had barely begun scratching the surface of my feelings about my father's death.

I walked inside the church, and as my eyes adjusted, I looked to the far right of the front of the church and saw a full-sized train engine. Let me explain before you pass judgment. It almost seemed to me as if it had been waiting for my arrival. I knew it wasn't real, but that didn't make it any less astounding. Physically, all I wanted to do was sleep. Later the therapist he said it might have been a perfect opportunity to do hypnosis because my mind was overwhelmed and wanted to shut down until the train went away.

The train stayed in the church during the entire service. I noticed that the train seemed to have been cleaned for the occasion. What I felt toward or about the train was interesting. I loved it! I wanted to talk to it and to be with it. I feel it is clear to see that I was probably feeling the same way about my father. Since I had never recognized his death, this was my mind's way of wanting to take care of unfinished business.

Evidently I had gone into a dissociative state of mind. This term is used to describe those defense mechanisms through which a person, for specific though usually unconscious reasons, keeps wishes, actions, images, memories, and so forth, outside his or her self-image or ego.

The thing I always found fascinating about my experiences with dissociation is the many ways I seem to be able to stay in both worlds at once. I am fully aware I'm experiencing a state of dissociation, and it doesn't frighten or bother me. I can't imagine explaining how I am able to do this, but it has been a common behavior. In some ways my state of dissociation seems to be a dream, but I'm awake and functioning. I do this without others around me becoming aware of what is happening inside me. To everyone I must appear to be quite normal; but internally—in my mind—part of me has temporarily gone to another place until the coast is clear.

The only thing I dislike about admitting I dissociate is it that it qualifies as a neurotic behavior. As an adult I find that mildly embarrassing, but it helped save the life of the child I was when I was developing this behavior. Not only was I unaware of what I was doing, but I also didn't have any idea it was unusual.

The day after the funeral, I had an appointment with the therapist and told him about seeing the train. I doubt he had many patients telling him such things in such a nonchalant way. I talk about these things as if they are nothing new. As far as my own personality is concerned, it I take it in stride.

At his suggestion, I went home and wrote my very first psychological story. A psychological story is one written by your subconscious mind. No fair thinking. The only thing to do is write what comes. Don't think about the construction of your sentences or spelling, just write. Be as nonjudgmental as possible, and don't stop to read until it's finished. Even after it's finished, I've found it's best to wait a few days before I read it. Not only that, but I like to read aloud just to see how it sounds. Since Mother's death, I've been surprised by the unguarded feelings that seem connected to each of my stories or poems. When I did this first story, I wasn't sure quite what to expect. I had a book on self-hypnosis, so I picked a page and read it. Then I just started typing. I typed three full pages before I finally broke free.

The words started flowing out of me like butter melting on hot corn. I could hardly type fast enough to keep up with the words coming out of my head and into my fingers. I was only mildly aware of what I was typing. In many ways it felt silly, frightening, intriguing, but *fantastic*!

When I come to the part of this book in which I tell about a few of my stories, I'll tell you more about the train story. I won't include any full stories that I wrote in this manner; I will share only bits and pieces. Since this type of writing is psychologically entangled and strange, I feel it is best to leave original stories to highly qualified professionals to decipher. In my words, I generally find a truth that applies. Some seem to have a universal theme.

What I will say is that this story goes in several directions. The first is the train. The train refers to my father as "the man in the red truck." The other participant is the child I used to be. It seems as if the train is trying to prove his point as to why he needed to destroy not only the truck, but the man inside. At first he doesn't see the child and the conversation is only in his mind. Part way through, he suddenly notices the child. Then, even though he feels regret, he is still convinced the man needed to die. The train was in many ways both proud of and boasting about what he achieved—"the child be damned." The story seemed to go on forever without any way to end it. I finally did it by making the train into a small toy and putting it beneath a Christmas tree. I'm not sure how long the dialogue would have lasted if I hadn't purposefully stopped it.

As I said earlier, I went through formal therapy in 1989, but I didn't find out until June 2010 that psychological writing is a behavior that is known as hypergraphia.

Several times during therapy I had serious issues that sometimes threw me into overload. I almost lost it because I was doing so many different things I felt might help—my way, that is. At one point I almost went overboard because of the stress I felt as I searched to find my story and also worked on coping techniques and behaviors. I considered having my social security number tattooed on the side of my foot just in case I lost myself and literally couldn't find my way home. At least with that piece of information, I felt sure that someone would figure out my identity and get me back to the people who would surely by then be claiming I was a missing person.

Everything that happened seemed to be something I could turn into another building block. When I'd lose my footing, I'd step back and begin moving forward in a new direction. It was like watching my world coming into place, but in this instance the world was in my mind. It was like a sculptor had his hands on me, turning me into something and someone new.

During the time I was doing formal therapy, I was also doing body therapy, incest survival therapy, neurolinguistic training, visualization, affirmations, yoga, aromatherapy, the study on depression, and a whole pile of other things including changing my handwriting. I think you can tell I was determined I was going to find a way to either break into my mind or break out of my shell.

One of the other things I was doing at the same time was reading a great many books. I *never* casually read a book. I study each as if there is going to be a test. I dissected and cut apart every word and every thought and chewed it over in my mind until I could spit it out of my mouth in an understandable way. If I found a book to be especially useful, I outlined it, and then I outlined the outline. Then I made a point system out of that outline. There were times I felt that, if I were to be hit on the side of my head, words would fly out in every direction. I was so full of words written by others I was becoming what I jokingly called a "fat head." If reading and learning new things enlarged your head the way food enlarges your body, I would have had a head like an octopus. I had books everywhere. Usually I had four or five going at a time. I had them in my purse, in my car, by our bed, where I sat watching television—everywhere! This is why I said that, if I had put the same effort into getting a degree in psychology, it would have been a piece of cake.

Even while I was doing formal therapy, I was reading voraciously. In 1989 I started reading the newest books on sexual abuse. Somehow they didn't meet my need. Most were written about clients by psychologists, psychiatrists, ministers, or counselors. Those that were written by the person who had been abused were usually more about what happened than what had been done to change the situation. This is what is different about my book. I'm the patient learning and applying techniques and ideas to myself. By doing this, I have first-hand knowledge and don't have to wait to talk to the patient—because it's me! I psychoanalyzed myself, and as far as I'm concerned, I've done an excellent job.

Next I decided one of the things that might help was to study childhood mental development. I knew how old I was when abuse happened, so I wanted to see if I could understand where my mind was developmentally at that time. This helped. I was able to see myself at various ages of development. I even went so far as to find pictures of myself so I could try to imagine what might be in the child's mind. It didn't matter that I was that child because I wasn't able to make the connection. I'd look at the girl's face or into her eyes to see if I could find any trace of myself as that child, but I never did.

As I tried to imagine how "she" felt, I began to think about how I might have been processing through behaviors like love, grief, compassion, generosity, peace, joy, happiness, anger, fear, jealousy, envy, and other emotions. I felt that, if I found an emotion that seemed to hit home, I might find a way to understand so I could either build on it or tear it down. Books were not just parts of my therapy, but my teachers. I can't express how thankful I have been for all the authors who wrote the books I used for my mind's education. I explored ideas, emotions, thoughts, religious beliefs, quantum physics, brain science, and more. Someday it would be my greatest joy if someone were to come to me and tell me how much this book helped.

At one point I had an entire room, ceiling to floor, with shelves for books. The only place in the room not lined with books was the doorway. Finally, I had purchased and read so many I not only ran out of room, but I was no longer able to find favorites. I sorted and packed books until I was exhausted. I made three piles. One was for donation to the local library book sale. The next were ones I wasn't quite ready to part with, and the last were my favorites. These are the ones that still occupying space in my office. To me they're like old friends I like to visit with so we can catch up on old times.

I wish I could share the title of each book so you could read them, but that would take too much time and space. Sometimes the entire book would be meaningful; other times there might be only a paragraph or a word that helped me make changes in the way I spoke, thought, behaved, and felt. It was interesting that, every time I needed an answer, I was drawn to the right book.

I could never begin to tell you how crazy my therapy was because I took over my own process in a very strange way. It was almost as if I had multiple therapists as I read. Each and every author filled me with information and ideas about how I could change my life in a positive way. With each idea or suggestion, my internal spirit weighed in and made my final choice.

Each time I spoke to my flesh-and-blood therapist, we would engage in a ritual. He would ask how I was doing, what I was reading, what new things I had learned, and how I was feeling. By the time we finished with all those topics, there wasn't time left for much else.

I would recount new information I had gained from my aunts and others. He would ask how I felt about what I was learning. Felt about it? That was a joke. I didn't feel anything about anything. All I was doing was telling him pieces of information as if I was giving a class report. My sense of depersonalization was solidly in place. The events I told him about had more to do with "her" than with me.

My appointment schedule was more like in-house therapy. By that I mean the type that has to be done at a facility where you stay for a period of time. In-house (or in a hospital setting), the therapist can fully monitor your progress in case things became too intense. At one point the therapist told me there wasn't an insurance company he knew that wouldn't have been willing to take me for six to nine months at his request. Part of the reason he allowed me to work so hard toward my wellness was that my husband was a physician, and it was agreed that if he saw me flounder, he was to immediately let the psychologist know.

I went twice a week for the first four months. After that I decided, if I was going to be finished with the year I was allowing myself, I needed to begin cutting back. I went from two times a week to once a week for three months. After that I went once every two weeks for two months and then stopped. All together I went for nine months and then ended what could be called the last of formal therapy. Since I had promised myself I would go for a full year I made one last trip in January 1990.

This was how my farewell visit went. The therapist hadn't seen me for several months and was interested in my progress. First he asked how and what I had been doing. Next he asked how I felt physically and mentally. We talked about what was happening in every area of my life. Finally he looked at me and said he could tell by the way I was holding my body, by the sound of my voice, and the look on my face that I was doing great. He continued by telling me he didn't know what I had done, but without a doubt I was better. All he knew was that he hadn't been the one to get me there. Then he told me he guessed that was his problem, not mine. At that point I agreed and left.

I was really grateful for having the opportunity to work with him. Mostly what therapy did was keep me focused. My behavior during therapy really wasn't any different than it was for any other job I took on. I worked really hard to find a way to find out what happened and to find anything I might be able to do to make life work better.

Inner Child Work

I'm sure some readers will have heard about this therapy. It can be an extremely powerful psychological tool, and it is preferable not to do this on your own. In the next section, I will be talking about one experience I had that could have been dangerous if I hadn't experienced it before.

There is a lighter way to do this. One method I tried was to find pictures of myself as a child at various ages. These helped me envision the child I wanted to reach. The first thing I did was honor the child I use to be and thank her for helping me survive what happened. It's like the old adage that tells us we can get more bees with honey than with vinegar. The child in the picture going through the experiences I wanted to change had done her best to keep me both alive and sane. It didn't matter at the time how she did it—doing it was all that mattered. If I survived and was alive, that meant I was still capable of changing thoughts and behaviors about what was resistant to change.

I envisioned myself sitting down to talk with her the same way you might do with your children. After thanking her for keeping me alive, I told her that what she did then was okay, but now, because I had become an adult, it was no longer working. At that point I told her what I wanted to change and how I intended to do it. I was completely aware of what I was doing. I was addressing my own self in the visualized form of how I used to be. It was kind of like me talking to me.

If there was any sense of anger, I knew I had a right to my feelings no matter what they might be. After all, my thoughts and behaviors had a right to be there, and that needed to be both acknowledged and honored. I then reminded myself that the only shame in not changing was not doing it.

Cognitive Therapy and Talk Show Call

I want to explain what was happening both during formal therapy as well as during a crossover therapy known as incest survival therapy. In formal therapy, my therapist was using what is known as cognitive behavioral therapy. At one point, the therapist remarked that he didn't understand how I was able to have good cognitive thinking. His statement both puzzled me and kept me off of the most popular talk show on television in 1989. I had sent a video to the show months earlier and never thought about it again. One afternoon as I was studying what the therapist meant about my good sense of cognition, the phone rang. The man on the other end of the line asked if I still had childhood amnesia. I was very deep in thought as I had been reading an in-depth textbook trying to understand what the therapist meant. Since my mind was being held captive by my reading, my fractured sense of reality was being fully used. Now out of the blue I was suddenly being asked to change my thoughts and have a conversation with someone from this talk show. His question was "if" I still had childhood amnesia.

At the time, I had written that I was only partly aware of my story. Since that time, I had been able to make giant steps into my psyche and into researching my childhood. Shifting gears at the drop of a hat was impossible. I was shocked and excited to receive a call. It was still hard to believe I was talking about myself on the video I sent. It felt as if I was telling them about someone I knew—not me.

I was surprised by the question about childhood amnesia. My big mistake after I answered yes was to pull a trick rabbit out of my hat and change the subject. Instead I told him how the level of stress I experienced messed with my hormones and created a scenario I felt listeners might find interesting.

Let me ask a question. Do you know three words you should never say to a man you don't know? They aren't *I love you*; rather, they are *menstruation, menopause,* and *hysterectomy*. Suddenly he needed to answer another phone, but said he would call back. Did he? No!

Now let me explain why I said those words to him. Remember how I wrote about the continuance of my periods for eight years after going through menopause? It was due to stress I felt throughout my life due to abuse, trauma, and neglect. I never would have known that if I hadn't tested positive for cancer and opted to have a hysterectomy. Personally, I found it

222

mind-blowing and felt that the talk show hostess's audience, since it was mainly female, deserved this information. I wanted to explain something no one else considered at the time as another problem attached to what had happened to me as a child and later as an adult.

The reason I wasn't upset when he didn't call back was that I realized that an interview would take me on a path completely different from the one I was pursuing. I had already adapted my thinking to the idea that everything that was happening was out of my hands. Instead I felt led by something I never understood. If it had been meant for me to be on that show, I know it would have happened. Because it didn't, I knew it wasn't the right time or the right message for me. It would have definitely been the right talk show host because she, too, had been involved in incest as a child and understood the long-lasting effects it had on the body and mind.

That particular talk show is no longer on the air, but I would still like to finish what I wanted to explain since I received a call, and I would someday like to meet Oprah or chat with Dr. Phil.

I learned a long time ago that everything comes in its own time. For one, if I had been on that talk show in 1990, I would have gotten sidetracked from the real message. My focus and attention would have been shifted. The notoriety might have been enough to damage me since I was an entirely different person from the person I am now. I wasn't strong enough mentally or educationally to have taken on critics. Now I am.

On some talk shows, the main interest is drama. Some want an all-out screaming, hair-pulling brawl to show fury is being felt. Not me! I would have sat as cold as ice talking about what happened, telling my stories as if I was describing the weather. Believe it or not, there are probably more people who feel the ice-cold sensation of depersonalization and dissociation than there are people who are filled with fury. We are the ones who didn't tell, or still aren't admitting that anything ever happened even though, in the back of our subconscious minds, we know all too well that it did. I might freeze you with my coldness, but believe me when I tell you, don't chip the ice too fast because beneath there might be a red-hot fury that could spew out at a moment's notice.

On my own, I became my own in-pocket therapist. I was able to do these things for myself. I constantly searched for and identified errors in my rational thinking and irrational thinking so I could make changes I felt I needed to make. In other words, I was gathering information to confirm, refute, or modify my own assumptions in a way that even I didn't understand.

By the time I talked to a therapist, I was doing this on my own so he didn't need to direct me to use what he wanted to do. Instead I took over and sorted through every piece of information before my first visit. This enabled me to bring about my own results. By doing this on my own terms, I felt empowered. As I began to take charge, it seemed easier for my mind to accept. At least that's how it worked for me. I didn't find the need to talk to the therapist about a lot of things because I already had my answers long before he had the questions.

If this work was being done by the therapist, he would have been following a set of guidelines. The therapist was supposed to gradually teach me so when my process was over I could monitor automatic thoughts and find a way to test assumptions so I could remain balanced and stable by myself. The wonderful part was that I had done this before he had a chance to teach me what to do and how to do it. I did this by listening to my internal self and doing what I felt I needed to do, and it worked! It has been twenty-eight years, and what I taught myself held in a way that surprised even me.

Incest Survivors Therapy

One of the first words I want you to see in this type of therapy is the word *survival*. Since my body survived the crisis, I knew there needed to come a time when I should do everything possible to remove its stigma and pain from my mind. It isn't enough just to physically survive this terrible act. As long as you don't deal with it mentally, it will still have a negative effect not only your life but in your mind. Even though I can't recall what happened, my subconscious mind remembers, and it reacts when something seems familiar. Even the slightest idea that anyone might breathe in my ear or on my neck makes me cringe. I want to draw my ear to my shoulder to prevent this from happening.

Acknowledging my childhood trauma was the best thing I ever did. At times, during my journey, I wished I could un-ring that bell, but in an instant afterward, I knew I had done the right thing. My advice is to never let anyone talk you out of taking your journey if you think you are ready. I won't kid you; it was horrific at times. I found out more than I ever imagined about what happened in my home as a child.

I never knew this type of therapy existed until I was watching television one Sunday and saw a program in which the participants were talking about a young girl who had been fondled and molested. She was fourteen. The perpetrator was a neighbor who had picked her up as she was walking home from the store. After she got into his car, he touched her in an uncomfortable, inappropriate way. The girl, for good reason, freaked out, and when she arrived home, she told her mother what had happened, and her mother had the man arrested.

It is hard to explain the impact this story had on me. By this time I had been in formal therapy five months, but felt nothing about what happened to me sexually; neither had it been fully addressed yet in therapy. The story on TV intrigued me. The child was visibly upset by what had happened. It wasn't until then that I questioned why I hadn't been more upset about the incest that happened with both my grandfather and my older brother. I guess the question left behind was, shouldn't I feel upset about what happened to me?

The girl in the TV program had been taken to see counselors at the local rape crisis center. It never entered my mind that I might need to talk to a therapist who dealt specifically with sexual issues. At the time I felt that formal therapy was all that was available to me. I checked the phone book, and sure enough, there was a rape crisis center nearby. Later I found out that the center ran an incest survival therapy program.

Early the next morning, I dialed the number. When the phone was answered, I explained my circumstance. I told the person how evidence pointed to the fact that I had been a victim of incest by at least two people, but I didn't have memory of it. I recounted the story about the man by the river. I mentioned to her that, since I didn't have memories, I was going to see a regressive hypnotist later in the week to find recall. The woman freaked out and asked if I would see her before I did that. She seemed to feel it could be dangerous because I had so many blocked issues. With the deaths and the verbal abuse along with the sexual abuse, she felt I might possibly begin having random, spontaneous flashbacks.

I didn't know I was talking to the director of the crisis center. She asked me to postpone the appointment with the hypnotherapist and talk to her the next day. The urgency in her voice left me feeling as if I may have been overlooking something I needed to check.

I saw her the next day. One of the things she later mentioned was how I was dressed. I wore a full skirt with a blouse. My hair was in a ponytail. She said she felt if she looked at my feet she would have seen bobby socks and saddle shoes. What can I say? I was in that frame of mind at the time, and my inner girl was in charge.

One of the things I noticed as I phased through therapy, as I said before, was that I couldn't seem to land in any time frame. Every idea, feeling, and behavior kept changing. It was as if I was finishing business at various ages and was dressing appropriately for the era I was going through. By the time I had come through the door at the rape crisis center, I was more confused than ever. I felt as if I was in a time warp because everything I was revealing about myself kept my mind in flight, going into and out of various ages and issues.

After I told her what I knew about my past, she again told me she didn't feel it was a good idea to forcibly break into my mind. She said that, because there were so many unaddressed and unresolved traumas stacked one on the other, the entire structure I had built in order to protect myself was in jeopardy. For instance, I could be driving and have a flashback. I'm not sure that was what I wanted to hear, but I guess it was what I needed to hear. I abandoned the idea of forcing my mind to let go of hidden information. I canceled my appointment with the regression therapist and made a personal agreement: if my mind willingly gave me memory I would deal with it. I also decided I was no longer going to attempt to break into my mind in a harsh demanding fashion. On one hand, I felt disappointment, but on the other, I felt a deep sense of relief.

She immediately set me up with a crisis counselor and suggested I begin attending an incest survivors' group. This was an outstanding idea since what I had seen on TV left me wondering how I should be feeling and behaving about being an incest victim. It was my hope that, by attending meetings and seeing how other survivors felt, I might be able to mirror their behavior so I could begin processing my own issues. I hadn't ever felt anything about any of the things I learned had happened. As time went by, the other women in the group envied the idea that I had blocked memories, and I envied the idea that they had theirs. My theory is that you can't deal with something if you don't know what it is. By that I mean that it is difficult to finish something you never started.

The main theme emphasized in this therapy was that we had survived the original act perpetrated on us, and now it was time to work on ways to shake it off so we could view both the act and ourselves differently.

Going to both incest counseling and incest survivors' group was exactly what I needed to do because this part was not being addressed in formal therapy. My therapist was male and probably uncomfortable confronting this issue the way it should have been addressed. At the time, the counselors in the crisis center were women and had special training for this exact problem. Later I found there were also men in the program who counseled to men because women aren't the only ones raped or victimized by incest.

My hat genuinely goes off to anyone who does this kind of work, and to those who seek answers to problems from their childhood. I'm of the opinion it is best for people working with survivors to not have deep unresolved detrimental issues. If they share things in common with people they are working with, it becomes easy to subconsciously begin to identify with them. If the therapist and the survivor begin to share issues, it becomes harder and harder to separate problems. I felt the women working with us were exceptional. I can't even begin to imagine what it would be like to go home at the end of the day without being affected by the things told to them. It takes someone with an extremely strong sense of self to do what they were doing. If you did find a counselor who shared experiences it was because she had been highly trained so she could understand on a sublevel not available to those whose childhoods had been incest free. This was the reason I knew I should never try to become a psychologist. Since I will never be "finished" because of my inability to recall memory, I might do more harm than good. I've talked to some counselors who felt that, since they'd had similar experiences, they could be more understanding. It isn't hard to tell them apart from those who have a healthy sense of balance. Being able to separate yourself from the act perpetrated on you is extremely difficult.

Just recently I decided that I might be able to help people by becoming a cuddle therapist.

These volunteers go to hospitals to hold, rock, and cuddle babies who are lacking the kind of nurturing that should be given to them by their family members. It makes sense to me that, since they are babies and my deepest concern is to help babies avoid some of the negativity I encountered, I would be well suited to do this. Since there isn't any way to counsel or talk to babies about their situation, all I would need to do is lovingly support their tiny little bodies in a way that would add a bit of silent strength they can unknowingly take into their lives. It would be the best of both worlds for both of us. It would feel nice to feel as if I helped this tiny adult-to-be in some small way.

I also found out I can volunteer to sew for babies in need. By making blankets as well as other necessary items, I could give of myself for a cause where the need is great. As I've said, one of my favorite things to do is make blankets. What better way to meet both my needs as well as theirs? As the saying goes, "When the student is ready the teacher will appear." In this case, the teacher would be tiny, and would allow me to give back in a healthy way while not over thinking or becoming overly involved in an unhealthy way.

By the middle of 1989 I was doing both formal and incest survival therapy at the same time. All together I did formal therapy for nine months and incest survival therapy for five months. They overlapped for only a three-month period. It almost seemed as if, between the two, I was able to make more breakthroughs than I could have with only one method of reaching into my mind to find my truth.

I had already started writing psychological stories by the time I began going to the crisis center. The number of stories increased to the point that I'd finish one issue and was immediately challenged with the next. My mind wasn't left with anywhere to run and hide, so the stories were becoming not only more interesting, but extremely painful and intense. Recently I was going through notes and stories I created from late 1989 and early 1990, and I came across some I forgot I had written. I don't know where my mind was when I wrote them, but believe me when I tell you I don't want to go there again. As a matter of fact, the minute I found a story similar to the train story I stopped reading. It was a pretend conversation between the perpetrator and the child. Ick!

At one of the meetings, the counselor in charge allowed me to read one of my stories. I had titled it "The Infant and the Bath." Everyone seemed visibly upset as I began to talk about an infant being abused as she was given a bath. After I read the story aloud, the women in the group talked about the effect my story had on them. One woman surprised me when she said it sounded to her as if the story was being told by the perpetrator rather than the one being traumatized. I feel this has to do with dissociation and depersonalization. I wasn't doing anything other than observing what was happening to the child (me). Had one of my internal family members come forward to make themselves known? I know that, in my reality state of mind, I wouldn't have written the story of the infant and the bath. I had to bring out my "hmmm" state of mind so I wouldn't consider that the story had anything to do with me. I know I had always been very careful with our sons; I remembered the messages I heard repeated in my mind when I bathed our sons—never linger, never avoid. I had always thought that was a peculiar "rule," but after I found out about my childhood, it was plain to see it was my way of avoiding any trickle down into the lives of any of our sons, especially when it came to how they viewed their bodies.

I always find it interesting how our subconscious minds address issues our conscious minds can't touch. It was that way with the stories. Not only did I never know what would present itself on paper, but I was never able to recognize any part of it as being true for me. If I take time to read the stories aloud, I always come across a "tell"—a catch in my voice and a recognition—that makes it plain to see I had written about something my subconscious mind felt I needed to address.

The psychological stories became my uncomely children. Finally, after I had written so many, I decided I needed to stop pressuring myself into prying into my mind in this manner. At that point, I let go of my willingness to just to continue to let the stories go rampant. I felt this was a good decision on my part because writing this way is exhausting and unsettling, and there is no market for selling the stories.

After several months of incest survival therapy, I ended it and told the group good-bye. The help they had given me was perfect. As individuals, the women in the group never bonded in a way that would result in us being forever friends. We just came in, did what we felt we needed to do, and left. I did decide do something for the program by making trauma dolls for the adults and the children's groups. I made two sets of two dolls each. One was as large as an adult, and the other as small as a child. I sewed a piece of plastic on each face in case anyone wanted to insert a picture of an abuser or themselves inside. I dressed the dolls in casual clothing and took them in to the center. I heard later that the children wouldn't go near the larger doll, but they held the smaller one as if they were protecting it.

In order to make these dolls, I had to make my own patterns, cut them out, and sew them and stuff them in a way that would ensure they were pliable. I made a smaller identical sample doll for myself, which I still own. I made one more with rip-off parts. It contained both male and female parts that could be put on the body then ripped off if someone wanted to act out feelings about his or her perpetrator. I gave this to the director of the program after she opened her own practice. It turned out to be too powerful to use in a program outside of a hospital. I wanted to give back in the only way I knew how, and I felt good about doing that for them. I also donated books I had used during my search. They now reside in a library at the center to be used by the staff as well as those needing the services.

My First Encounter with New Thoughts

I feel it is only fair before I move into the next few sections to tell how I found two books that made me look at my life in an entirely different way. Barnes and Noble are to blame! They sent me a coupon, and it was burning a hole in my hand. My intent was to buy a crochet book for a common crochet pattern for a blanket for my first great-grandson. Even though the pattern was one I had made before, it had escaped my collection. Believe it or not, I couldn't find it at the bookstore either. With my coupon taunting me, I moved from the craft area to books on science. Bad mistake—or was it? My mind was screaming, telling me to run. Get out of there! Your life is in danger! That didn't deter me. Once I was in that area, I was in quicksand, and there wasn't any way for me to escape! From what I've heard, my chances of finding the next few pieces of information were quite small. If the first book title hadn't captured my eye, I doubt I would have read it, let alone bought it; after all, it was a whopping 694 pages long.

I want to share two books that gave me new pieces of information I never considered before. The first book was written by David E. Comings, M.D. and was titled: *Did Man Create God?* In his book he addressed the question about who created God. I was curious to see what the answer to the question was because I had already answered it for myself years earlier. Six hundred and ninety four pages or not, I was hooked by that time, and I was ready to be reeled in! Believe me, I was one happy fish.

One of the first things I looked at after being caught by the title were the author's qualifications. He is a physician, neuroscientist, and a behavioral and molecular geneticist. Winner!

The book was written for those who are spiritual but would like answers to some of their doubts and questions. It proposed that spirituality is genetically hardwired into a specific part of the brain, is pleasurable, is critical to the evolution and survival of man, and will never go away. That was all I needed to hear—that along with the fact he has written over 450 scientific articles and three books, plus he is the past editor of a well-known magazine on genetics.

If this book had been written by a psychiatrist, psychologist, counselor, or minister, I never would have picked it up. I read it with as much gusto as a hungry man at an all-you-can eat buffet created by the most highly qualified chef available. Yum! It was delicious, and I devoured it from cover to cover. Don't let me fool you into believing I understood all of what he wrote, because some of his subjects included: evolution, intelligent answers to intelligent design, cosmology, the neurology of reason, and spiritually. The material covered was definitely above my C-average high school abilities. Time and time again I caught myself smiling as I encountered pieces of information that I had been exposed to in my earlier reading. That alone encouraged me to continue finding out what he had to say about spirituality.

My interest began to peak in chapter twenty-five when he began writing about "Consciousness, the Spirit, and the Soul." My mind went over the moon when I reached chapter thirty when he began to write about "The Spiritual Brain." I'm sure my neurotransmitters were excited because I began to experience almost a firework-like explosion in my mind.

The author explained that, when the temporal lobe is electrically stimulated, the following effects may happen: a feeling of being detached from emotions (depersonalization); feelings that everything is unfamiliar, strange, and not real (derealization); a sense of timelessness and spacelessness; hallucinations; ecstasy; dreamy states; joy; and other experiences that foster a religious interpretation. He states there is something uniquely spiritual about seizure activity that emanated from the temporal lobes.

In 1983 an experiment was carried out in which magnets were placed over the temporal lobes of normal individuals. It was reported that 80 percent had a mystical experience in which they sensed the presence of a sentient or emoting being, often interpreted as God. This magnetic equipment was referred to as the God Machine. We wore a low-quality magnets on our heads when I was involved in the study on depression.

Stresses likely to produce God experiences include death of the spouse or child or parent, marriage, divorce, loss of a job or starting a new job or new responsibilities, being involved in a serious accident, leaving home for college, or midlife crisis. Stress is likely to release pituitary hormones such as cortisol, vasopressin, or oxytocin, or neurotransmitters such as dopamine, serotonin, epinephrine, or endorphins. It was found that it is common to experience the presence of the deceased person, smiling and stating, "Don't worry. I am in heaven with God."

Later he began to talk about LSD, the temporal lobes, and spiritually. Remember when I mentioned that my therapist said it was a good thing I hadn't tried LSD? When I asked why I was told I was able to do naturally what others took drugs to accomplish. I asked what might have happened if I had taken LSD. He said I probably wouldn't have been able to come back out of the drug-induced state of mind. I laughed because I could see myself as a hippie doing a peace sign and talking like a hippie and still driving my wonderful old VW van, not in the seventies but in 2017.

This is where it starts to become more difficult. There are two types of temporal lobe epilepsy. One is a complex partial seizure in which there might be such things as freezing of motion, posturing of one arm, staring, lip smacking, chewing, and other automations, and impaired consciousness or memory loss. If a person had a seizure while crossing the street, he or she might freeze in place. The same could be true if he or she was driving a car. People can do things during a seizure and not remember what they've done. Afterwards there's lethargy and confusion that can last up to fifteen minutes. During this time there can be fatigue, memory impairment, depression, confusion, or headaches. My husband had a patient with this condition, and it took eight tests before he was diagnosed. He had TLE with complex partial seizures.

The other kind (the one I may have) is known as TLE without incidence. For someone with this condition, seizures last from a few seconds to a few minutes, and the condition is difficult to diagnose because a patient must have the seizure at the exact time he or she is being tested.

Did I have the test done? Yes! Did they find anything? No! I did it because I didn't feel I had the right to mention this information without attempting to see if temporal lobe epilepsy without incidence might need to be considered part of my condition. I personally paid for the test out of my own pocket even though I knew the chances of achieving a positive test result were low. Do I still feel there is a possibility this may have been part of why my childhood had been so difficult? Yes! I think the stress of my childhood influenced by TLE might easily have been part of my fractured sense of reality.

Since I'm one to use more than one book to prove information to me I found one other book that honed in on hypergraphia. This book was written by Alice W. Flaherty, M.D. and was titled *The Midnight Disease.*

This information enabled me to hone in when I feel I may be at risk for having an incident. That's why when later I write about going back in time, I was aware I was in a state of dissociation and took the stance of the observer. Watching it was astounding, but explaining it in a reasonable, intelligent way was difficult. My husband called my trip back in time a cosmic correction, or as I like to see it, a slide down a rabbit hole. Being able to do this is something I find astounding and fascinating. It enabled me to feel and see my situation on many levels. This behavior has been familiar to me, possibly, from a very early age.

From here I will explain an overview of epilepsy. Then I'll explain how TLE may have been a resonating factor. I must tell you this idea is only a supposition on my part. My test was done locally with a machine that had a minimal chance of having a positive result. If a machine was used that actually showed the activity of my brain in real time, the chances would be much higher that my rabbit might have been caught and put into a stew.

A General Overview of Epilepsy

I'm not an expert, but I feel it is important to look at epilepsy and what the medical community has to say about it. Epilepsy was originally referred to as "the sacred disease." Depression and mood disorders are common among people with epilepsy. Misinformation about epilepsy in eras gone by had to do with the idea that seizures were contagious. This issue was among the most-often used to identify witches during the time when witch hunting was happening in Europe and the United States. Also, if someone showed signs of the disorder, he or she might be forbidden to marry or have children; in some instances people were sterilized.

I'm not going to take you too far into this diagnosis because I don't want to get off track. More information can be found on the Internet or in a bookstore. Epilepsy can be genetic. It can also begin from brain injuries, head trauma, infection, abnormal brain architecture, birth trauma. It can be accompanied by occasional jerks, which made me think of a family member with this problem her entire life. An official seizure is noted in a book written by Orrin Devinsky, M.D. titled Epilepsy to be: "A brief, excessive discharge of brain electrical activity that changes how a person feels, senses, thinks or behaves." He writes most people with epilepsy have normal intelligence, behavior, and enjoy seizure freedom with medication without side effects. Evidently it can be compatible with a normal, happy, and full life. Mostly he says the reaction of other people to the disorder can be the most difficult part of living with epilepsy.

Learning New Words

Fugue

I experienced a fugue event in March 1989 when I saw a train inside church. I knew as I sat there staring at it that it was a figment of my imagination. After I got home after attending the funeral of a woman who had been killed when her car was hit by a train, I was desperate to put a name to my experience. That was the first time I heard of the word *fugue*. The vision seemed so real.

When I write about my trip back in time, I talk about a dissociative state of mind in which I became the observer and was able to come back and tell my story. I found this to be amazing. Who knew I could do this type of thing? Not me, that's for sure.

Qualia

The next word was *qualia*. It has to do with how consciousness connects to a physical entity—such as the brain—then connects it to a personal individual experience. I knew we all had our own way of looking at our experiences as opposed to the experiences of others, but I didn't realize it had a name.

Qualia are private, subjective experiences of sensations and perceptions. Describing them isn't the same as experiencing them. William James states that consciousness is a process, one that is private, selective, and continuous yet continually changing. Our experiences may seem similar, but they are never exactly the same because they're individually private.

The reason this word stood out is that it is difficult to explain my issues. This has been especially true when I talk about my absence of memory. It is impossible to make comparisons. My lack of memory is more than likely due to multiple types of abuses. When others tell me they have a deficit of memory, our conversations become almost a "my dog's bigger than your dog" challenge. The question then becomes, since I don't have memory, is it because something bad happened to me? Sometimes we lack memory because things are mundane and not necessarily worth remembering. When families get together and talk about the past, it is surprising how suddenly memories resurface during the conversation. The memories are there; they just hadn't been important enough to take up space unless they are cajoled out during a time when everyone is sharing in a non-challenging, fun way.

Trust me, if I could share my own memories with you, I would lay my cards on the table. The problem is, I have only enough memory to point out that something was really wrong in my childhood. These memories are hanging in midair like a spider dangling from a tree. I can't tell you how many times I've run into my own dangling spiders during my journey.

Comparing personal experiences is like comparing apples and oranges. I also take into account the fact that there are those whose issues are much larger, more like watermelons. Sometimes others share their stories with me because I've touched something that seems familiar. It is always good to find fellow travelers willing to share your burdens by sharing theirs. It takes courage and determination from both people to do this. This is the reason I chose not to become a psychologist—too many times the stories of others run head first into mine, and both of us begin to suffer.

I'm not sure it's a good idea to compare war stories. Maybe it's because my lack of memory makes it difficult for me to know where their story ends and mine begins. This over identification sometimes makes me feel as if I need to defend not only my story, but myself. It might be too easy for me to begin to take things personally. I'm trying to allow myself to understand that it only means we have traveled down a similar path. I am trying to sympathize with the other person's plight, but as I've said before, sympathy isn't something I'm capable of doing well. I know I still need to work on this so I can learn how to not only share with others, but also to allow them to share with me without either of us being damaged.

Infavore

In my favorite book, the author explained that one of the most pleasurable things humans do is acquire new information, new knowledge, or insight into the unknown. It is gratifying and brings us pleasure. This enjoyment is connected to an innate hunger, or craving, for information. It has been suggested that human beings are designed to be *infavores*—seekers and devourers of new information and knowledge. It was also suggested this craving for and acquiring of new information has adaptive value in evolution.

As I read this, I could see a dinosaur stomping around looking for something to eat, be it flesh, vegetation, or words. I felt like a dinosaur that had been on a fast and needed to find something—anything—to devour in order to remain alive, so words were, to me, absolutely delicious. I understand that acquiring knowledge plugs directly into our pathways and works much the same as an opioid drug. It contributes to a general improvement in mind. See! I told you I felt better.

Geschwind Syndrome

This was introduced to me in a way that was fascinating. According to Dr. Coming's book it can sometimes also be referred to as 4H syndrome. This is a distinct but fairly rare syndrome associated with TLE involving behavior changes associated with TLE. These behaviors include religiosity (Hyperreligiosity), alterations in sexual behavior (Hypo or Hyper sexuality), loss of a sense of humor (Humorlessness), and a tendency toward extensive, and in some cases compulsive, writing and drawing (Hypergraphia). It was first described by Wasman and Geschwind. Other features might include aggression, pedantic speech, a "sticky" or compulsive personality, and psychosis. The personality structure includes increased concern with philosophical, moral, and religious issues, and extensive writings on religious themes, lengthy letters, diaries, and poetry. Endocrine studies showing a decreased responsiveness to luteinizing hormone-releasing hormone may explain the hyposexuality. Luteinizing hormone, which is produced by the pituitary gland, regulates the menstrual cycle and stimulates ovulation.

I plan to take these one by one and describe how they may have worked in my own life. I have never been diagnosed with Geschwind Syndrome, but when the four H aspects of this condition are seen separately, I think you will find I fit quite well.

Hyperreligiosity: I went to not only one church, but three. I couldn't get enough of the feeling I had when I was in my Father's house. I talked to my Father constantly about everything. I really don't think what I was doing could be called prayer; it was like an internal, running conversation a child has with a parent. I loved talking to my Father. I not only talked, but listened intently for answers. I remember several times I was trying to talk about things that were bothering me, and I became upset because, before I could finish, I was given the answer. That was how intense the relationship was between my Father and me (or, put in another way, my conscious self and my intuitive, spiritual self). I never had to wait to discuss problems with anyone else because my Father was always with me. I trusted that internal voice more than I trusted anyone with a solid form.

Hyperphilosophical writings are also included in this area. Philosophy is the love of or pursuit of wisdom or knowledge, whether religious or philosophical. In some instances, it may include both.

As far as hyperreligiosity is concerned, I think I've shown on multiple occasions how involved I was in religion at a very early age. I sometimes have written things of hyperreligious content, but I don't allow myself to do it often. Generally when this happens, my writing starts out looking normal, and as I write, the words become bigger and bigger as I delve fully into whatever thought has caught me in its grip. I definitely must be in a dissociative state of mind when I'm doing this.

When it comes to hyperphilosophical writing, I'll let you judge for yourself. I definitely have been on a path of seeking wisdom and knowledge where I need it when it comes to finding and keeping my life in a state of peace.

Hyposexual/ Hypersexual: Out of the two of these I would more than likely fit into the hyposexual category. Hyposexuality has to do with an aversion to a person's ability to experience sex in a pleasurable way, and I can tell you first hand that it doesn't do much for a marriage. After I found out about the incest, I began to attribute my inability to really enjoy sex as an after-effect of the incest I had experienced as a child.

I did believe that everything having to do with my sexuality, or lack of it, had to do with incest. This may have also been part of the experience I had with menstruation and menopause. This has to do with luteinizing hormones regulating menstrual cycle and stimulation of ovulation. In 1985 when I had cancer, after the dilation and curettage, the doctor told me I wasn't anywhere near going through menopause because I had such high levels of estrogen and progesterone. After the hysterectomy, the surgeon seemed puzzled when he had to tell me I had finished menopause years earlier. I had a seemingly regular period for seven to eight years after menopause. After the surgery, I went on with my life as if nothing happened. That was what I wanted to point out to Oprah. I felt my childhood issues were the possible cause because of the high level of stress it created. I never thought about taking TLE into consideration.

As for hypersexuality, yes I had a brief encounter with this behavior about the same time I was going through menopause. It may have been because estragon and progesterone levels started to spike, and my body's chemistry was off. I was also at an age where I was processing my way through a midlife crisis. Our marriage was absolutely insane at the time, which I doubt was helpful. I was, however, able to work my way past this behavior, but only when my childhood issues began to present themselves in a detrimental way. It seems that both my body and mind were screaming that I needed to take care of something I had been ignoring before. Why would I have done anything about it? I didn't know I had a problem.

Humorlessness: You tell me! My behavior was more impish when it came to being funny. I never really would let my guard down enough to find anything in life to be very funny, because it wasn't.

Hypergraphia: This was the word that jumped out in the monster of a book. What is it? It is extensive writing about a lot of different subject matters. Generally it has to do with religious or philosophical issues, but also includes lengthy letters, diaries, and poetry.

The minute I found the word I ask my husband if he knew about hypergraphia. He told me he was familiar with it, but they studied it for only ten minutes in medical school because it was irrelevant to most of the patients they might encounter. Unless they wanted to go into psychiatry, it wasn't necessary to go into it any deeper. I still wondered why people I worked with hadn't picked up on this since I was writing constantly. He didn't have an answer for me, so I went back into the other room and started reading.

Within only a few minutes, I was back asking about temporal lobe epilepsy. That was when he told me how obscure this piece of material was. He also was unsure about how it might fit into my own life. What wasn't to see? The book was describing every behavior I believed was only due to my high levels of stress due to abuse. I still find it hard to believe someone hadn't picked up on this. My writings from 1989 through 2010 should have proven there was something more to be seen than just my prolific amount of writing.

As I said, I did go into that behavior in 1957 after the death of my brother, but I didn't follow through because I didn't know what to do with what I wrote. Instead, I began to dissociate even more and physically work in a frantic way. I started to write again in 1989 after seeing the train in the church. After that, I began writing about dreams. I also wrote psychological stories and notes to take to the therapist. It wasn't until 1995 that I began writing books. It was never my intention to do this anymore than it had been my intention to investigate my childhood.

Before reading how hypergraphia works in the mind, I struggled to tell people where my stories were coming from. After all, they came out of me so quickly, and I felt both sickened and shocked by this. I compared it to taking dictation or to watching and hearing a movie and just writing down what the characters were saying and doing. It felt otherworldly and kind of creepy. The feelings the stories and poems brought up helped because they lessened something negative in me, so I felt more peaceful.

I found that the various themes of this type of writing usually are highly meaningful for the author. They are often philosophical, autobiographical, or religious. This, for me, was a check, check, check situation. I don't think it takes a brain scientist to see this fits me to a T. I never knew my writing had a name and diagnosis.

I think the funniest thing I read about was how TLE or hypergraphia was diagnosed in 1970. The doctors mailed a short letter to patients with epilepsy asking them to describe their state of health. The patients who did not have hypergraphia replied using an average of seventy-eight words. Patients the doctors felt could be classified as having TLE or hypergraphia sent replies that were, on average, five thousand words. I'm positive there wouldn't have been any doubt in their minds if I had taken the test. In the past it wasn't unusual for me to write a ten-to twenty-five-page letter to members of my family.

One of the things that should be pointed out is that this excess doesn't always have to do with writing; it also includes music and art.

Scientists, psychiatrists, behaviorists, molecular geneticists, and other professionals put together a list of people who had passed who had probably had hypergraphia. The list was astounding. Since there was no way to test people who had died, the criteria used for diagnoses consisted of descriptions of the candidates given by either the person or by those around them. Some who might have been diagnosed with hypergraphia are Ezekiel, Paul, Joan of Arc, Teresa of Jesus, Joseph Smith, Ellen White, Moses, Dostoevsky, Vincent van Gogh, Henry James, Robert Schumann, Black Elk, Flaubert, Tennyson, Lear, Byron, de Maupcissent, Moliere, Pascal, Petrarch, and Dante—to name a few.

It appears that anyone in any creative field who produced an unbelievable amount of creative product might very well have had hypergraphia. I can think of quite a few of today's authors, musicians, and artists that I feel may have it too. All I can say is, if I have hypergraphia I'm in good company.

With the word *hypergraphia* under my belt, I began to find an entirely new world open up to me. Quite often I would be in awe of something I had written, almost as if it hadn't been written by me. With each new book I'd write, I never felt a sense of panic. One day I'd be looking at blank pages, and in no time I'd be finished.

The book I wrote before the one I'm writing now wasn't the one I felt I was being called to write, so I took a pair of scissors and cut the book apart. If you don't think that can feel intimidating, try it. Part of me was frightened by what I had done, and at the same time I experienced a spectacular amount of peace. Each piece seemed to show me where it wanted to live.

One caution I was given is to never edit my own material. This reminded me of an attempt I made to write a book coauthored with the director of the crisis center. I was going to present psychological stories, and she was going to explain what she felt each one meant and how it connected to the issues of other survivors. Even though she hadn't been my personal therapist, she sat in on the incest survivors' meetings, which disqualified her from writing with me until one year after I finished the program. One of her complaints had been my tendency to rewrite rather than to edit. Every time I tried to work on my part, it came out totally different. This was exactly what others had warned against. What happened to our project? She died of a rare blood issue before we were able to get fully into our project.

One of the problems I had with the book before this one was that I had to do two things in order not to rewrite my story. First, I had to not read any other new information. Second, I had to stop writing.

In order to do this, I had to start physically trying to distract myself from learning the newest information being published. Since I have subscriptions to a multitude of scientific and psychologically centered magazines, it was pure torture to read while resisting the urge to share my new information.

Editing seemed to take forever, and about the time I thought I was close to publication, I was being asked to go back and start over. I had just had eye surgery, and Mother's health issues were taking a turn for the worse. At that point, I was ready to take the book outside and burn it.

Not long after that, I was told by my former editor that she felt I hadn't reached any level of wellness, but was still quite unbalanced. It took time to recognize that my reactions about going back to chapter one had nothing to do with being unbalanced; rather, it was that I wasn't being allowed to tell my story. One thing people should realize about myself and other victims is that we should never be challenged in this way. I needed to be fully believed and fully supported. Recognizing that I wasn't attempting to throw anyone under the bus had to do with telling my truth the way I felt it should be told. It had nothing to do with Mother or any other people involved in the trickle down into my present day life in a detrimental way. That was a "whew" moment for me. The last thing I wanted was someone who didn't personally know me to believe that, after twenty-eight years, I was still angry or unbalanced.

At that point, I legally canceled our contract, cut the book into chunks, and rewrote it into what I'm sharing now. A lot had changed as I waited for publication, so it felt wonderful to update my text with new information and progress. As I breathed in my new book, I rejoiced at how far I had come. I also recognized that I needed a time out so I could finish the last of my issues. Shortly after that, Mother died, and I was free to write this in the respectful, honorable way I wanted from the very beginning.

Poems and Psychological Stories: an Overview

I'm putting poetry here because I don't want to ask the poems where they want to live in the book. It isn't because they wouldn't show me, because they would. It's because I've already invested a lot of brainpower doing this earlier, and I'm tired. Here they are—enjoy.

First, let me try to explain. I'm sure as you've read earlier poems, you've probably noticed that I don't always follow rules. I believe this has to do with hypergraphia. From what I understand, this is the reason someone with hypergraphia shouldn't edit themselves. It is a messy behavior when it comes to length, grammar, and sentence structure. I learned early on not to interfere with the process and take dictation without judging what I'm writing.

In the beginning, I used to call that part of me that writes "My Rude Children." That is the description I gave them in 1989 when, at any moment—day or night—my inner children would run into my mind and bully me into writing what "they" had to say. It sounded crazy, so I tried to not talk about the process. When I use the word *they*, I'm talking about what felt like six children. They remind me of what I use to do to Mother when I wanted to be heard. I'd peck, peck, peck on her arm trying to get her attention. Well, they were peck, peck, pecking my mind in an irritating fashion. There have been times when I've tried to ignore them, especially when it came time for me to write a psychological poem or story. The story "They Never Call me Mary" was one of those I tried to put off. When it came to writing "The Coat of Many Emotions," I felt as if they were gutting me. I was sick during the writing of that story. As for the book I've not yet published titled *Slow Train Coming*, I felt angry when consciously I was ready to write but they weren't ready to give it up. All I wanted to do was get the title out of my head. Instead they taunted me with the vision of what was to come. I tried to write it on my own, but they weren't pleased and wouldn't allow me to tell them what to do. Instead, they dangled a science fiction book in a taunting way so I would become distracted and let them play—and play they did. It started as a short story, but before long it grew into a full-sized book. All of the characters in the science fiction book are still hanging around waiting for me to write the third book. The funniest part of my explanation about the rude children is how I am able to hear their feet pad toward me for our odd conversation. After they finish, I hear them pad away. I know this sounds bizarre, but what can I say? Excuse my children when they don't abide by the rules; after all, they haven't gone to school and are uncontrollable and insistent when it comes to what they want. In other words, they are mind brats! I've found it best to just do what they want and be done with it.

I refuse to allow anyone to judge my process, because it's just that—a process. I know there are explanations for what I'm doing, but it is what it is, and I'm just going to go "hmmm," tip my hat out of respect for the process, and move on. You must admit it's interesting.

239

Alabaster White

Alabaster White
Was the color of her skin.
Alabaster White,
But she was dark within.

Inside her mind
Was as black as night,
But outside her skin was
Alabaster White.

To me the words *alabaster white* represented my innocence and unknowing. Outside, everything appeared to be okay. But more than anything, I wanted to find something to help me out of the black place in my mind where I existed. It seemed that no matter how hard I tried, I failed. I needed people to understand. I didn't mean to bring my sadness along when I was around them. I hid myself and my past in the darkness so no one could touch me. The problem was that I wasn't able to touch them either. In other words, the life I was living was a sham. I gave only the appearance that I was innocent and unknowing, but that wasn't really true because, deep inside, my mind knew everything and was just keeping it from me.

Fringe:

I have sadness fringed with joy.
The core of it I do employ.

I need a path in me to find
A way for me to use my mind

To open up my very core
And empty all that keeps the score.

I want no measurement in time
To keep me from that which is mine.

The infant smile of which I dreamed
And threatened in a way which seemed

To keep me distanced from my past
To separate us until at last.

I saw her only yesterday.
This time she asked if I would stay

To help her from her fear and shame
And promised we were both the same

Because of past warnings I couldn't trust,
But again she promised I really must.

I know her well, this tiny seed.
I've seen her signs in my growing needs.

She is the child who dwells inside.
My love for her has never died.

She calls but I refuse to hear
When she tries to empty all her fears.

"I won't destroy," I hear her cry,
"It will be like singing a lullaby.

I'm not afraid and so you must
Find the need in me to trust

The way is clear. You will be free.
All you need do is listen to me.

I am your core, your fear and shame.
If you keep me dark, I'll keep you in pain."

"What is my choice?" I ask again.
"Set her free? Or keep her within?"

There is still this joy with a fringe of pain.
I need them both if I wish to remain.

This separation lets me see
This division can lead to harmony.

It's part of life; there is no fear.
I'll keep this baby close and near.

Her pain was frozen in my mind,
But now it's time to let her find

Our joy has burst forth, and outshines all else.
With her peace inside, we are now—Myself

When so many negative things happened to me as a child, I became adept at learning how to deal with everyone and everything, just to go on living. The problem arose when my body kept growing and living, but my mind became damaged. My mind was harmed, but since there wasn't any blood to show the horror of it, my injuries became internalized. All those around me went about their daily business and, to them, I appeared to be hunky-dory. My life definitely wasn't hunky, and it certainly wasn't dory. It was scary and filled with confusion, uncertainty, and agony. Not only did pain dwell constantly in my mind; there was a lingering sense of panic I never seemed able to defuse.

Stories

The stories be upon the page
Because I have become enraged

That present life should have the gall
To treat me so, to take it all.

My heart, my pain, my memory.
There's more to life. There has to be,

And so I search the written page
To find out why I was enraged.

I take them out and play my game,
The things I hear within my brain.

Each one of us creates our own.
We sharpen selves to finest hone.

The shining blade will cut us through
With words unheard our lives undo.

In praise I lift my voice above,
Not out of shame, but out of love.

Cut off the fat from written page
And leave behind that hidden rage.

It runs its course, it does display
Itself throughout each living day.

And then at last I will find
Rest in body and peace in mind.

The Coat of Many Emotions

I have a coat I wish to share
With all of you if you would dare.

Its strands are strong, its colors dark.
It freezes your soul and it freezes your heart.

The terror that lies within its weave
Is one I'm choosing now to leave.

This emotional coat is heavy and hangs
Until you find you feel deaths pangs.

You'll soon want to be set free;
At least I find it's that way for me.

The coat is old; its threads are strong,
But it kept me alive even though it was wrong.

I've hated this coat. It was too much to bear,
But one final time, for I'd like to share

So I can feel joy, instead of pain
In this coat I can't remain.

So I'll slip away and let it be
Another way—from the coat set free

Poetry

It's pain that writes for all to see;
My pain comes out through poetry.

Don't Touch Me

I'm a touch-me-not—a fairy wing
In a magic shell—just a thing.

Now I Lay Me

Now I lay me down to die
Not time enough to say good-bye.

I pray the Lord my soul to keep
And no one o're me to weep.

But if I live before I die,
'Twill be God's own sweet lullaby.

Without a Me

I thought of what all life would be
Without a me.

I thought of all my friends and family
Without a me.

I felt though the world a better place—I did agree
Without a me.

But then I found the secret key
I made me *we*!

Wait

Wait—don't turn the page or close the door.
I've never been here quite before.

It all seems strange and very new
That life has finally given clues.

"A clue to what?" I asked my friend
"Is my journey at an end?

Is this the answer? Have I found the key?
Am I now the person I was meant to be?"

The answer chimed within my soul.
At last I was able to see my goal.

It isn't what I thought would come
But when all was said I knew I was done.

Not with living, but at an end.
Now life has become my friend.

I'll lead the way and show you at last—
You can find a way to live beyond your past.

Evermore

I'm watching it all
Evermore
Vigilant to see
That it happens no more.

One thing I have always loved about my stories, poems, and advice is that I am always ending in a way that is filled not only with success, but with peace of mind. It starts in one place, cycles down, then ends on a higher note than existed in the beginning. I call this my "at least" way of thinking. Nothing is ever as bad as it seems because "at least" it isn't as bad as it could be.

Psychological Stories

Now when it comes to the psychological stories, I am not overly comfortable sharing them For one thing, if anyone wanted to understand them, the stories would need to be read exactly the way they were written without editing. The mind seems to have its own language when it comes to this. As I said, I am willing to share a synopses of some of the stories I was writing in 1989 and 1990, but not the full stories. When you write something like this, there are multiple layers of meaning that can be interpreted only by a highly qualified mental health professional.

Some parts of the stories are written in a generalized way, meaning they can have personal meanings for a lot of people without the necessity of being specific. I have always been able to fully understand what it means to me. These stories are life lessons.

It would be foolish for me to vaguely pretend that I fully understand the meaning of any of these stories. Some are about a specific issue I was dealing with at the time, and by writing the story I was able to recognize what happened. Because I could do this in even the slightest way, I was able to step beyond what happened as a child and freeze it on paper so I could view it in a way that enabled me to deal with things in a more harmless way.

When you team up psychological stories with hypergraphia, the result can be entertaining, albeit a bit frightening as well. Letting your mind free to write whatever comes forward can tell you a lot about things you aren't consciously aware of.

The Train

I had just agreed to let go of typing hypnotic dialogue, and this story became alive and took over my paper. My fingers were hardly able to put the words down fast enough. The story started slowly and then began to pick up speed. Suddenly, instead of the story being told from my point of view, it changed so that the train began to tell my story. I wasn't sure what was happening, but it was fascinating, so I got out of the way and let it happen. When the train took over my mind, it told me that it was flying down the track toward a far-away destination. Not only was I writing the story, but pictures came into my mind, almost as if I was watching a movie.

The train began to describe seeing my father's red truck in the distance. To the train, the man in the truck was known as the train racer. One thing the train hated more than anything else was to be challenged to a race. He decided this time that the man in the truck wasn't going to win. As the train went faster and the truck came nearer to crossing the tracks, the train's excitement grew. For the first time ever, the train decided this race was his to win, and he began to move even faster.

I described the sounds of metal hitting metal as pieces went flying. The train's excitement grew even more as he pushed what was left of the truck down the tracks in front of him. All of a sudden, the engineer pulled the brakes, and the metal wheels of the train began to screech loudly as he was forced to slow down. Stopping was the last thing the train wanted to do. Instead, he wanted to blow its whistle in celebration and acknowledge he had won.

As the train slowed to a stop, people raced to see what had happened. It was then that the train saw the man in the truck clearly for the first time. Blood was everywhere. He could hear the radio in the truck playing a tune. "Toot-toot-tootsie good-bye—toot-toot-tootsie don't cry."

By now people were gathering near to see the carnage. Suddenly he saw me watching and asked who I was and why I seemed so sad. I told him it was my father in the truck. For just a few seconds, he seemed to feel sorry, but then he remembered how many times the truck had played the game and whizzed past in front of him. He felt upset when "she" told him it had been her father in the truck. As the train and the little girl talked, my mind was reeling. I had a headache, much like the one I have now as I'm typing this. Finally I knew I'd had enough and didn't want to remain trapped in a story that just didn't seem to be slowing down. It was then I remembered what the therapist had said about the toy train under the Christmas tree. Almost as quickly as the story started, the now-small train began to circle under the tree and toot its horn as it circled not only the tracks, but also my mind.

The Blue Swimming Suit

My next favorite story was titled "The Blue Swimming Suit." I envisioned myself at the pool when I was eight wearing a hand-me-down-woolen suit once owned by my aunt. The problem was that moths had nibbled away until there was a small hole the size of a quarter on the left side so my butt could be seen. Even at eight, I was embarrassed. The story ended as I said: "The sky was blue, the water was blue, my suit was blue, and so was I.

Metamorphosis

Another story I love is titled "Metamorphosis." It started when I began seeing myself as a worm, talking about myself as being a bad person and saying no one wanted to have anything to do with me. At that point I went away, wrapped myself in a self-made cocoon, and went to sleep. During the time I was sleeping, I began to dream about being a completely different person. Finally I woke up and broke free of my cocoon and stretched my wings. At this point in the story, I think I temporarily returned into myself and when I realized I had wings. I said, "Wings? I have wings?" I immediately dropped back into my story and began writing about how others were no longer able to recognize me for the "worm" I had been before. As a butterfly, I circled above those I had outgrown, and I cried. My tears fell on those below, and all they did was look up to see if it was raining.

The Sleeping Giant

"The Sleeping Giant" is another story I loved simply because of the pictures I was seeing in my mind. This story reminded me somewhat of the giant that washed up on the shores of the island of Lilliput in Swift's *Gulliver's Travels*.

In my story, my mind was the giant, and I was one of the little people trying to communicate with him. My giant was sound asleep when I found him. I tried to wake him, but nothing seemed to faze him. Finally I ran inside his ear and began screaming for him to wake up. Suddenly, while I was still inside his head, I felt movement and knew I needed to get out of there quickly because he was finally awake. After escaping back out through his ear, I stood back and watched as he rubbed his eyes and then looked at me. This is my favorite part: when he saw me looking at him, he threw his head back and laughed with glee. Even now I can still hear his roaring laughter and see his smiling face as he looks my way. To me, all it meant was that I was trying to wake myself out of a sleep I had gone into years ago. Once I was finally able to do it, even in the slightest way, I felt a tremendous sense of joy.

The Shop of Many Abuses

This story starts early on a foggy, dreary day. There was one individual rushing down the wet street toward a destination he was eager to find. When he came to the Shop of Abuses, he stepped inside. He was surprised to find a line already formed. Everyone was quietly waiting his or her turn. Suddenly a door opened in a darkened corner of the room, and someone stepped out with a satisfied look on his face. Before the door closed, all the others stretched their necks to see if they could find her—the one they had come to see. They could see only a glimpse, but she seemed upset as she sat on a straight-backed chair with her hands folded. As soon as the man stepped out, another moved toward the child in the room and closed the door. All the people shuffled their feet as they moved one step forward. After the sound of the last man's steps stopped, the people in the line began to murmur. Finally one asked another, "What are you going to do when your turn comes?" Without hesitation he said, "I'm going to beat her up. I'll hit her until she begs me to stop." One by one, they began to share what act they were going to perform when it came their turn to go into the room to confront the child. The list was sickening: "I'm going to sexually abuse her," said another. "Well, I'm going to tell her how much I hate her and how stupid and ugly she is," said yet another. One by one, they shared what they were going to do until they came to the newest member of the group. Without hesitation, he told everyone what he was going to do, and one by one, the people in the line lowered their heads or shrugged their shoulders. One by one, they picked up their things, buttoned their coats, opened the door, and left until the only person left was the last one to enter the store. Do you want to know what he said he was going to do? "Nothing. I'm not going to do anything."

Can you see the implications in the story? One of the worst things you could do to me when

I was a child was be nice. Something in my mind always felt suspicious and uneasy while I just waited for the other shoe to drop.

Children of the Walls

I've already told you a how much I loved walls and refrigerators. My favorite place to sleep was in the crack between the wall and the bed. I don't know how comfortable I was, but at least it met a need in me that enabled me to finally fall asleep.

In this story, I was talking about a child being abused, and as her abuser continued, the mind of the child went away and found itself going into the wall where it could remain safe while the damage was being done. She was surprised when she found she wasn't the only one living in the wall. There was a city inside the wall—a city filled mostly with children who had also gone into that place of safety. The story tells how they came to be inside the walls and how long they planned to stay. The uncomfortable thing about this story was that I could see them in my mind—these hollow children—just looking for a safe place to be. I wrote about how terrible it was that they ever needed to be forced into that place. Once inside, they stayed. Sometimes they shared their stories, but mostly they remained uncomfortably quiet.

They Never Called me Mary

I told you most of this story earlier. The problem was that it wasn't a story, but a memory. I remember how terrible I felt waiting for my turn to open a gift. I don't remember being embarrassed, but I'm sure I must have been. It wasn't until I began incest survival therapy that I came to realize that what was done to me at the Christmas party was abusive. My grandmother's name was the same as mine, or maybe I should say mine was the same as hers. Who could have been this mean? My grandfather!

The Infant and the Bath

I hate to think this story might be true. The day I wrote it, I worked on a series of three stories. I didn't mean to write this one; it just happened. It wasn't until I told my aunt about this strange story that she recounted how unwilling I was to sit in the bathtub. Mother was in the hospital at the time after she lost (?) her baby. I was about eighteen months old. Mother kept a small wooden child's chair in the bathroom. I don't know if it was my aunt's idea or if I told her. To get me to bathe, she put the chair into the tub and let me sit on it. She soaped me as well as she possibly could and then poured water over me to rinse away the soap.

My other aunt told me something similar. I was eleven, and mother was newly married. I was spending the weekend with my aunt when she received a call about Mother being in an accident. While I was at their house, I refused to bathe. Finally my aunt gave me a washcloth and a bar of soap and convinced me to stand in the tub and wash and rinse myself while I was still standing. I was adamant that I was not going to sit in the tub. Why?

I never have been able to understand why I wouldn't sit in the tub on either occasion. It felt strange that both of my aunts told similar stories about me. The stories I was told along with the messages I heard in my mind when I bathed our sons makes me feel suspicious that something about the story might be true.

Since my internal family members seem to be of the same age as traumatic memories, it even makes me more intrigued because the youngest member of my internal family is about eighteen months old. If they are personality splits of some kind, then the age of the child would be important.

In the story someone comes to help the mother. While the mother is making supper, the person volunteers to bathe the baby. Both the baby and the mother are thrilled. The baby gladly lets the visitor place her in the tub along with her favorite toys and begins to play. Suddenly the person begins touching the baby in an uncomfortable way as he envisions not a baby, but a woman. The baby's behavior at that point turns from happy to fearful. I wrote about droplets of blood in the water and how, after the bath, the baby might seem clean, but a new kind of filth has come into her life—one she would not be able to understand as she grew into a woman.

The Man by the River

This was the first in the series of three, and I wrote it because I have partial memory of this happening to me. I don't recall details of any sexual abuse, but, definitely, the allegations of sexual abuse are quiet high.

I wrote this story after I heard a man remark that, when women are raped, it is because they are asking for it. The question in my mind was how could I, at eight years old, have asked someone to do something to me I neither wanted nor understood. I was hoping, as I wrote this story, that a more in-depth memory would reveal itself to me. That didn't happen. All I was trying to do was prove to the man we knew that, in my case, I had nothing to do with what happened.

In the story, I recount my memory: "I was standing in a cove on the shore of the Mississippi

River looking at the water. A man came up from behind on my left hand side, turned me around, took my hand and put it on the front of his pants and said: 'I'll bet you've never felt anything as hard as this before.'"

In the story, I fill in what I thought may have happened, but mostly what I wrote about was where the girl put her mind. She was looking at the leaves, a squirrel, and the birds.

Trading Places

This was the last story in the group of three. In it there was a stairway leading upward to a door. One extremely tired woman trudged up the steps, and when she reached the top, the door opened and an identical woman stepped out. They looked at each other, and the woman who had come through the door began to descend the steps while the first woman went through the door and closed it. Since both women looked the same, the premise was that they traded places.

Before writing these stories I had been asleep, and I woke up thinking about how I could show the man that women weren't "asking for it." After all, I hadn't asked for it. Once the three stories were finished, I folded the pages, put them in my drawer, and went back to sleep. It seems oddly suspicious that I was in a dissociative state when I wrote them, and wasn't fully awake at any time as I was doing this.

The Coat of Many Emotions

I became physically sick when I wrote this story. The title and the idea had been circling in my brain for quite some time. Finally one evening I woke up, went into the kitchen, and started writing. We had overnight guests, so I lay on the kitchen floor as I wrote it because I felt so sick. My head was throbbing, and I did go into the bathroom several times to throw up. I drank hot tea in an attempt to try to stop from feeling so terrible, but nothing helped. It took several hours to write this because I had to go into the bathroom repeatedly to vomit. Instead, I finally vomited the story onto my pages, folded them up, put them in my dresser, and went back to bed.

The idea of this story centered on the coat of many colors in the Bible, but instead of each color representing a piece of cloth that made up the coat, each color represented a different kind of abuse sewed together to make me into a garment I couldn't free myself from. At the end of the story, I was able to quietly sneak away from the coat. Even after I trap my stories on paper, *they* never leave me. It is almost as if they become part of the fabric of who I am.

The Chair Girl

This story is based on the inner child work I did when I was watching a program on television. It would be hard to describe this to anyone, because it is extremely troubling to even recall. All I can say is that I found another part of me that had mentally buried itself in an open grave. The gist of the story still makes me cringe. I'll never forget how, when I put my hand on the doorknob, the house became alive. I also can't forget how badly I wanted to throw my inner self against the wall and run for my life away from the house where the baby lived. The feeling this story left behind was terrible. I left it for the therapist to take care of, but he didn't seem to know what to do with the residual effect the story had on me after I wrote it. The visualization I did with the inner child was mind-blowing. I was finally able to dispose of the way I felt by doing a visualization in which I pictured the child breathing life into me rather than trying to suck the life out of me.

Hypergraphic Books

Yes, I've written several books, and even paid to have some of the work edited, but about the time the editors were finished, my story changed. Part of this problem is that everything I write is connected to hypergraphia and, as I mentioned, if you are hypergraphic, it is best you don't try to edit yourself because it is next to impossible. In the beginning, I promised I wouldn't self-publish because I wanted what I wrote to be able to walk into the world accompanied by an agreement with an official contract. It wasn't the contract the Universe wanted; rather, there seemed to be concern over the contortions I kept doing inside after I completed a book. I kept reading and rewriting, which meant I was going to continue twisting and morphing as I made internal changes in myself and grew into someone new.

I'll do this for the rest of my life, and I accept that about myself. The process that took nearly four years was difficult because I knew I needed to remain the same for the period of time it was going to take to move the book into a completed form. Now that I've abandoned the book that was under contract, it became obsolete. Just like Mother's death, this needed to be honored for what it was and laid to rest. I changed Mother's form from an actual body into ashes in order to accomplish the goal of laying her to rest. The book I had written also changed form as I took scissors, cut it apart, and began a new project, reformulating what I had done. A surprising thing happened—hardly any parts of the earlier book made it verbatim into this book. The only true things left were the poems, and I've even struggled with them because I would like to have shifted personal pronouns.

Once I decided not to spend more time writing psychological stories, I thought I'd begin writing a self-help book. Who was I helping then? Myself! I had been given the title, but the book still had square wheels and wouldn't go anywhere. What did I do? I wrote a short story that turned on me and soon became, of all things, a science fiction book. It was fascinating. I'm not a science fiction fan because I like fact-based books. Writing it, however, became a hoot. It kept performing every line with all its antics like a movie in my mind. Sometimes I'd be in the middle of writing something, and then suddenly my characters would do or say something that surprised me. I loved being lost in that world with all these sad, miserable people just trying to make sense of their lives. The worst part was when I added aliens from another planet. Just as the book was nearing an end, I told my husband and best friend I was going to do away with my psychotic killer, and they went nuts. "You can't kill him!" they both proclaimed. "I like him," said my friend. "It's not his fault he's a killer." My husband said, "Besides, he's been so nice to Sally." It seems they not only liked him, but identified with him. "What?" I asked them. "How can you tell me you identify with him? He's a killer!" "I don't care," they both told me. "Just don't kill him." I kind of liked him too, which bothered me, so instead of killing him, I had him captured by an evil general and taken to an island where he met, of all things, a witch doctor. Oh dear, did I just say that? The second story was as wild as the first and called for a third. I wrote the first few pages and set it aside until later. Even now that story wants to be written.

The worst part about the first book was that, as I reread it, I found it to be a science fiction account of my life. Every character contained pieces of me, and I'm not at all sure the main character wasn't also part of my psyche as well.

The book I wanted to write still wouldn't come so I wrote a "between" book about my grandchildren. Since our oldest grandson was a dinosaur nut, that was the direction I took. After that I wrote three or four books for small children. Most of them contained dinosaurs too.

Finally the book I originally wanted to write came to the surface of my mind, and I began writing. Its title was to be *Slow Train Coming*. The premise had to do with all the detrimental things that happened to me over the years and were still on track to kill me the way the train killed my father. The book ended up being quite different from what I had believed it would be. I was shocked. Nonetheless, it poured out of me and onto my pages like a prewritten script. I'm positive a psychiatrist would love to get his or her hands on that one. I was so sure I could make that one fly I had it edited. By the time the editing was finished, I had moved on to another book, and another, and another. The book you are reading now is actually the sixth writing of the same information. One is a fictional account of my story so I didn't have to own up to all the things that happened. Each book became a stepping-stone out of the hole I'd dug for myself. Each step led me into a place where I was able to find solid ground to build on.

CHAPTER SIX

Falling Back Through Time and Beyond

In May 2015 I was trying to fully come back into my life. There were two things I needed to complete. I needed to go back to the areas where both of my aunts were buried. I wanted to pay my respects and lay flowers on their graves. I also wanted to honor how much help they had given me as I reclaimed my past. It had been fourteen years since I was there, and my return was long past due.

The first aunt I wanted to honor was my mother's sister. My aunt's husband remarried, and he and his new wife had been to visit us numerous times, and I thought it was only fair to go to see him. I wanted to give him one last thank you for how supportive he had been. I hoped the next year my husband and I could go together, since he and my uncle enjoyed each other's company.

I made my first trip with a friend who runs an antique store in our town. She's always up for a trip. When I asked her, she was happy to accompany me. Mother was still in the care center and doing fine. Since I was only going to be gone a short period of time, I felt at ease going on my trip back in time.

Trip One: May 2015

When Monday came, we were on our way. My friend had mapped our journey through out-of-the-way, off-the-beaten-path towns where the antique stores hadn't been picked over by professionals. The traffic was light, and the weather reasonable. It rained once, but it didn't last. The trip turned out to be quite enjoyable. I felt that this trip was meant to be.

Suddenly, four hours into our journey, I saw a sign that indicated we were close to the town where my brother was killed when I was fourteen. This was the only area I hadn't visited during my process. It was on my list, but I didn't think it was connected to my wellness.

The next sign provided not only the name of the town, but how close we were—seventeen miles from my past. In my mind I could see the town as it had looked years ago. I had been sixteen when we moved, and I remembered it as being small, clean, and well ordered. This was how I expected to find it fifty-seven years later. Silly me!

I asked my friend if we could go into the town since we weren't in a time crunch. Besides, maybe there would be some antique shops. She said yes. At that point, I ignored our original turn-off, and we were on our way. Before long, I was driving down the same highway my brother was traveling the day he died. It felt strange. Traffic seemed to move aside like the parting of the Red Sea as we began inching toward this river town. It felt as if a large magnet was pulling us toward our destination. That's when it all started to change.

Suddenly I began to recognize that I was beginning to dissociate and go into a conscious but dreamy state of mind. Now I felt as if I was driving through a time warp into my past. The truck began to shape shift. Its size grew until I felt it was more the height of a semi than a passenger truck. At the same time, I felt myself shrink to the size of the child I had been at fourteen. Things began to come alive in my mind, and I felt as if things around me were breathing. I could feel myself begin to withdraw further into my mind to find a safe place where I could watch what was happening from a distance.

This is a description of behaviors I had experienced before. When I first found out about my childhood, I hadn't been able to recognize how often I had withdrawn from my body so I could stay in my mind. By now I had taught myself to recognize what I was doing and how to stay in both places at once. In the past, going into dissociation had been normal so I could get away from something or someone fearful. Now that I was an adult, nothing in me was afraid of what was happening. It felt odd as my state of mind began to slide down the rabbit hole into another world. She (the child I used to be) wasn't alone now—I was there—and believe me I wasn't about to let anything happen to us.

In my mind, I could see my brother's Future Farmers of America jacket hanging in my closet at home. Suddenly the image of the bucket of blood sitting at the bottom of the stairs came to me. I could only imagine the fear he felt as he lost control of the car. I wished I could have recognized the spot where the accident happened, but what had been open road back then was now filled with houses and businesses, separated by only a few open pieces of farmland.

I knew that, over the years, the town would have changed, but I wasn't prepared for how different it would be. It was situated with the Mississippi River on one side, and it was closed in on two sides by hills with no place to build as it grew. The only way that could happen was if they doubled up the houses and businesses on lots already occupied. Now, instead of being orderly and clean, everything was jammed together like sardines in a can.

The truck kept its oversized form in my mind as we entered into town. To me, it barely seemed to fit through the narrow streets. I was aware I was going in and out of a dissociative state, but I maintained my balance. At that point, I relaxed and waited to see what would happen.

Eventually we found ourselves driving on Main Street. By now most of the businesses were closed and had been changed into other things. Most everyone living there was in some way or other connected to the orchard or one large factory.

All the landmarks I remembered were gone, and I wasn't sure I would be able to find the house where I had lived since things were so different. Before long, we passed the post office, and I recognized where I was. The building looked the same except for new handicap ramps. I could almost see myself as a girl walking past the post office as I made my way to the library or to the local movie house. I now knew how to find where we had lived. I had to drive around the block, but then, sure enough, things began to come into focus. First we passed the Christian church where I attended teen group on Sunday afternoons. A block from there was the Baptist church I attended every time I had the chance. Across from that was the Methodist church, and directly next to it was the yard where the Methodist minister was standing as my stepfather chased me out of the house while swinging his belt. A ghost of my past memory returned, and I could see my stepfather chasing me as the minister watched in horror. Immediately upon seeing him, my stepfather lowered his belt and returned to the house and disappeared. I envisioned the girl as she safely escaped and ran farther down the street and evaporated into thin air.

I looked directly across the yard from the minister's house, but the duplex where we lived had been demolished. It may have been gone, but my feelings about it were still tightly churning both in my body and mind. A shudder traveled through me.

I continued pointing out other places I remembered. Some were gone, but those left were jammed next to newer buildings. I found the grocery store on the corner where Mother worked. The windows were black; the building was now used for storage. The flying Mobile horse twirling in the air next to the corner gas station may have disappeared, but I could see it in my mind. A block away from where I lived was the firehouse/community/government building where one of my friends used to live. Her father had been the custodian. Across from that was the house where another friend lived. With so much crammed into what had once been open space, the area looked small and cramped.

I began remembering the names of friends I'd known and places I'd been when I was sixteen. In most of the towns where I lived I didn't make friends since we never stayed. It felt different to be remembering some of my past. Blurred and blunted pieces of memory began to fill my mind.

Finally we drove down the main street to see if we could locate an antique store. Sure enough, we found one. I parked the truck and, for the first time in fifty-seven years, put my foot on familiar ground. As we opened the door to the shop, we were welcomed like long-lost friends. I began looking around, and then I asked the woman behind the counter if she had a phone book. I opened it and gasped as I saw the names of the couple who had lived in the other half of the duplex that no longer existed. I adored these people.

I mentioned them to my friend, and the woman behind the counter said they were still around. It may sound terrible, but I was surprised. Within a few minutes, I began to dial their number. When the answering machine came on, I started to leave a message mentioning my maiden name and how I once had lived next door to them. All of a sudden there was a voice telling me how excited she was to hear from me. We talked, and then she invited us to her home.

I had been in her house when I was sixteen, but now I was seventy-three. I found her decorating style was just as eclectic as mine. The years melted away as we visited. She looked the same, except older, but then again so did I. She and her husband had played an important part in my life when I lived there, and my memories of them were comforting. One of the odd things was that she didn't know anything about my brother's death even though, when they moved in, it had been only a year since his accident. By then his death had become a moot point, so I never talked about it.

My friend and I started off on our journey again, and I finally began to come back into my body. When we arrived in the area where my uncle lived, I called him, and we headed in his direction.

My uncle always lived on the farm, so when I pulled up to the address he had given me, I was shocked to see he lived in town. The only farm-like thing was an antique tractor sitting out front like a yard ornament. Suddenly my slide down the rabbit hole started again, and I began to dissociate again. It was wonderful to see him. We visited and then went out to eat. After that he took us past the farm where he used to live and showed us the changes in the area. We drove past the cemetery, but since I was off balance, I felt that stopping there needed to be done another time. I spent the night with my uncle and discussed my childhood. He added a more pieces that clarified things even more, which helped a lot.

After we were back on the road, we found more out-of-the way places and laughed as we passed a barn in the middle of farm country and saw three camels in a corral. What were the chances we'd come across something like that? We found as many antique stores as we could, and then found a rather large one near the town I lived in when I was sixteen. Everything in the area kept throwing me back into my past.

Finally, even though it was past closing time, the antique store was still open. We poked around for an hour and then decided to find someplace to stay for the evening, hoping we could return the next day. Nothing decent was available, so we talked it over and decided to head home.

Once we got close to home, we called our husbands. My friend's husband met her at her shop, and we unloaded her findings. Even though we had been gone for only a few days, it seemed more like a week.

When I stepped inside my house, my state of mind was still in a state of dissociation. As I began to tell my husband about my side trip back in time, he laughed and called it a cosmic correction. I knew what he was talking about because that was exactly how I felt. It was plain to see this had been something I needed to do. Without visiting those places, I knew those untouched memories would have stayed frozen in time in an unrealistic, unnecessary way.

Trip Two: August 2016

I didn't take my second trip the way my husband and I planned. Instead, the purpose of this trip was to take Mother's ashes and lay her to rest. Since Mother's ashes would be interred in the graveyard with the rest of our family, I knew it was the perfect time to finish that part of my past.

I made my trip into town and purchased flowers for my mother's, aunt's, and brother's graves. Instead of buying premade bouquets, I wanted to do the arranging myself. I was pleased with how they turned out.

When it came time, as I put the flowers and the newly decorated box containing Mother's ashes into the car, I began to feel a sense of relief that her pain was over.

My husband chose the route this time, and believe it or not, we were soon seeing the same signs I had seen while traveling with my friend. I asked if we could go into the town since it wasn't out of our way. This way he could see the famous orchard he had ordered trees from. This time I wasn't the one driving, so my mind seemed to stay in place, and I didn't go into a dissociative state. I still wanted to come back later to walk the town and visit my friend and her husband. I didn't dissociate when I pointed out where the duplex had been.

Within a short period of time, we were back on our way to where my uncle and his wife lived. As we pulled up in front of their house, I had to laugh because now there were two antique tractors along with a few farm implements.

Once we were inside, the visiting started. It was wonderful to hear how much my uncle and my husband jumped headlong into discussions as if they had seen each other only the day before. We talked about Mother's passing and what the plans were for burying her ashes.

The next day we were up early and headed out for a tour of all the new things my uncle wanted to show my husband. After a tour of the farms, we decided to eat.

There was a local restaurant a few blocks from where they lived. Since a deck overlooked the Mississippi River, we sat outside and watched the river traffic. It was a very relaxing day.

From there we went back to their house and sat outside watching the road traffic. My uncle was thrilled to show my husband his yard ornaments. It wasn't long afterwards that my cousin and his wife came to visit. It was a nice evening.

The next day we were to bury Mother's ashes. The box for her ashes was dark brown faux leather. On top I had placed a small white wooden plaque with the dates of her birth and death. I had also put the names that were to be put on her headstone along with the words "Little Songbird." On the lower half of the box I had put a cross.

As we arrived at the cemetery, I could see the small opening where the box would be placed. It was a perfect fit. My husband put the box into the ground, and we stopped for a few minutes to remember her. After that, we tossed in a handful of rich, dark soil. Next we placed the flower arrangements by each headstone. My uncle took one and placed it between my brother's stone and my cousin's. My brother had always been more of a son than a nephew to him, so it seemed appropriate.

Gathered nearby were the rest of the family members' stones. I was more than happy to see the dog hadn't done his duty on my grandfather's grave. As I walked around the cemetery, I saw one stone with a small cement bird on top. I thought it was a perfect match for the one etched on mother's stone. I decided that, upon my return, I would place a similar one on mother's headstone.

After that we went to eat. Even though there wasn't a family dinner waiting, we did the next best thing. After all, our family could now fit comfortably in the car with room to spare. We had a nice meal then drove to see more places from my childhood. The mission to take care of Mother's ashes had been completed, and now I knew I could rest easy knowing she was where she had longed to be, in the cemetery with the rest of our family. The next morning we talked again before we packed up our car and headed home.

My Trips Yet to Come

My last trip—or perhaps there will be more than one—has to do with what I want to be done with my ashes when I pass. I know it may sound like a strange idea, but what else is new when it comes to my way of thinking? I plan to deposit part of the money I receive from the sale of my book to be held in trust until I have passed. The purpose of this fund will be to portion my ashes into separate packages, each of which will then be given to someone of my choosing.

I want these people to take part of the money to take my ashes to a place of their choosing. It will be according to how well the book sells as to where they take them. If the book doesn't do well, I may not go far, but if the book sells well, I might be spread all over the world. Now how much fun would that be?

If someone would prefer to distribute my ashes locally and use his or her portion of the money to purchase something tangible, that's fine with me. All he or she needs to do is put me somewhere near where the purchase is made.

The idea behind this is to enable those distributing my ashes to remember me in a wonderful long-lasting way. It would be nice if, later, the group could meet and discusses where they had taken my ashes and why. It might even be a nice memorial in book form. I've told them to go the mountains, the ocean, or to a volcano. Put me somewhere that will always live in their memory, and then share those memories in joy and laughter. Wouldn't that be a spectacular way to finish my journey?

CHAPTER SEVEN

Questions I Ask Myself Today

Who Am I Now?

Yes, everyone changes all the time. As years pass, we learn new things and adapt to our new lives. Since 1988 I have made monumental strides toward being a happier and better person.

In 1988 I was churchy. In 2017, you would never see me that way. I feel the presence of a higher power and feel he/she/it/whatever will always be there. I'm more satisfied with that than I would be if I stayed under the umbrella of "organized religion."

I am still learning information in a way that seems to be coming from inside as well as outside myself. Without hesitation I could easily attribute this to the higher power and like doing so. I make choices on a daily basis and do so in a reasonable, honorable, respectful way.

At times my journey was more fun than a barrel of monkeys. I tried things other people would frown on, and sometimes I wanted to do the same but went ahead. Now I no longer let others or even my old self direct my behavior.

What Are My Regrets?

There aren't enough words to express the relief I feel. I have a peace of mind that, to this day, still astounds me. I find it hard to believe I have the ability to manage my reality better simply because I'm aware of it. I never had any idea that my 1988 reality could change so much.

I've finally come to terms with things that will never be available to me, such as spontaneity. It's hard to let myself go when I have so many ingrained habits still warning me of impending danger. I'm better, but I do wish I could be more spur-of-the moment. Hopefully someday I'll spontaneously surprise myself. It would be great not to work so hard to get by emotionally and mentally. I think this will happen as I begin to feel more comfortable with my newfound sense of peace.

I would like to have gone to college so I might have helped with family expenses. We survived, and because I'm writing this book, I still have an opportunity to continue helping our family and those I care about live better lives.

Having a perfect TV family would have been nice, but the truth is they don't exist. I tried to make my family like the prim ones on television, but I don't wear heels or pearls. We have regrouped as a family, and a lot of things are better because of how I changed my own life.

I'm no longer living in a fight, flight, or freeze state of mind, but I haven't quite made it to the feeling part. Even if I begin to move toward any of those behaviors, I'm able to quickly regroup, stop, and shift my behavior into something more comfortable and workable.

I'm sure many other people have similar regrets, no matter what their background is. It would be nice to have an undo command like we have in computer software. I would have worn mine out. I'm not going to bemoan my life. What I do want to tell you is that, by using awareness, I've found a way to pull myself out of the state of mind and behavior that I found myself in before 1988.

Each year had its ups and downs, which is true in all our lives. The thing is, over the years I've been able to make more strides forward than backward. Sometimes these steps were slow and painful; other times I felt as if I was on a rocket ride. With each lesson I found reasons not to remain the person I had grown up to be. It's nice to share my lessons with others and show what can be done.

I've pointed out how I honed my awareness skills and listened to my inner spirit and how I was able to manage my life in a way that helped me be happier. Earlier I had condemned myself to living a life in which I felt miserable. Now it no longer makes any sense to continue doing that. Yes, it was hard to make these transformations, but not as hard as it would have been to remain the same.

I don't want to imagine how my life would have been if I hadn't changed. For one thing, I don't believe I would be alive today. The stress in my mind and body was disabling, and stress kills. I never needed to consider suicide because my mind was doing it for me.

With all the new information I have today, I can still make changes in not only my life but in the lives of those around me. I don't need to nag or be preachy; all I need is to drop a few words here and there. I can set an example for others so they can see what can be done.

I still look forward to learning new things and applying them to my life. Having the ability to know which changes lead me forward is important. I ask myself, "Why am I doing this? Who am I doing this for?" Before, I wasn't doing things *for* myself but *to* myself.

What Haven't I Been Able to Change?

I have armed myself with the information about what happened and why. Even though I now have a more complete picture, I have been unsuccessful in permanently changing my childhood coping skills.

Why haven't I been able to do this? In 1989 my therapist told me about "the things I didn't know that I knew." I researched it until I discovered that this is tacit knowledge. Something tacit exists without actually being stated in words. It is silent. In my case this was a silent killer. My tacit memory, which I had created to save me, had become deadly. I no longer needed protection from others, but now I needed it from myself. Tacit memory held information that kept me locked inside my own prison because it saw me as much of an enemy as those who abused and neglected me.

The information I sought was no longer accessible. Yes, hypnotism might have broken into that part of my memory, but what I retrieved would not have been true memory. I did get part of my memories in dreams or when I wrote in a dissociative way. The dreams were jumbled chunks of truth combined with thoughts and memories my brain wasn't about to share because of the harm they might inflict. These experiences remained concealed from my conscious mind but were producing measurable negative effects. There are gaps between knowledge and what the brain keeps quiet. The silence in my mind seemed deafening. I wanted to be able to remember one actual memory, but that hasn't been possible. At times I hated myself for not being able to retrieve information so I could heal my mind and soul. In the end, I made peace with that part of me knowing it was for my better good. I convinced myself it was okay that I wasn't able to remember because it meant I was still protecting myself from my abusers and from myself. If even one piece of information was freed, it might have caused other memories to surface. The last thing I needed was a domino effect. If one memory opened, it might have broken through to the next until everything came apart. Can you imagine what might have happened if I had remembered the horror of one of the things I've told you? It seemed that, with each question I asked, another abuse was exposed. It was my own personal Pandora's box. The psychosis it might have put me into is beyond comprehension. I made a pact with my mind knowing that, if ever my mind wanted to reveal anything, I needed to be prepared to deal with it. If nothing was given, it meant my subconscious mind knew best, and was still protecting me from my past.

What Did I Learn From This?

From what I understand, tacit memory directly influenced everything in my world. It governed my behaviors in a way that I've never been able to understand. I let it protect me from what I never needed to know. I've taught myself to recognize when that part has taken charge. When this happens, I know how to stop whatever behavior has automatically come into place. It's a constant vigil, and I doubt it will ever be any other way. I've been able to lessen the effects of what tacit memory holds and acts on without my awareness. I find this to be a victory. Maybe it wasn't what I originally felt I could accomplish, but it's close enough to keep my world steady. It's harder to knock me off my axis now. I might temporally tilt, but I have reprogrammed myself to regain my balance quickly.

Now What?

Writing my story using the sense of reality my friend and my husband wanted me to use has been difficult. Why? Because my reality seemed normal, and I wasn't sure what they wanted me to do. Even they weren't able to give me the slightest idea of how I was going to accomplish this. I finally reached out to that unknown quality within and followed that.

As I've written this, and especially as I've waited for it to be read, I've tasted more of both realities than I wanted. I've found them to be both bitter and unrelenting. Why don't others who live in a dissociated reality like mine give up? I think it's because this is the only world we know, and there's nothing to compare it to. When I visited the real world for an extended period of time, I was surprised how trite and flat it felt. In that world I could see my story, but it came with an overwhelming sense of sadness. There definitely are two different types of reality. I live in both of them. One is dull, and the other shines like a rainbow across the sky. Which one would you choose?

I've never lived in the real world full time. For me to visit long enough to get a sense of how it feels has been horrible. I'm still thankful I have two realities, so when things get rough, I can escape. I see why people might feel it necessary to find an addictive substance of some sort to take of the edge of their reality. It numbs them and takes away the cutting limits so they don't bleed to death.

How Have I Done This?

In the beginning, I used a teaspoon to dig myself out of my past life. Later I exchanged it for a shovel so I could dig faster. Once I no longer felt the shovel was working, I brought in an earthmover. The thing is, I knew that, even if some of the earth were to slide back into the hole, I was never going to stop digging. Using these tools didn't wear them out; it made them sharper.

In some ways, I'm sorry I've had to force myself to use both worlds equally. Before I found out about TLE, I could see what I was doing as mysterious and mystical. It was fun, but at the same time, it wasn't stable. I was determined to understand both realities so I could choose which I wanted to live in rather than let my mind choose for me.

Both worlds—the realistic one and the dissociative one—can be excruciatingly painful and confusing if you don't know what you're doing. Before I changed, I had a sense of "oh my God, oh my God" constantly running through my mind. I felt like a trapped animal looking for a way out of a cage. I was willing at a moment's notice to gnaw away any part of myself just so I could be free.

Who Can Profit From My Journey?

I ask myself that question now on a deeper level than I have ever asked before. "Who do I think I am to be sharing my story with others? What have I learned over the past years that I feel anyone should be interested in? Why am I doing this?"

At first I felt that, when I told you my story, it might appear to be contrived, trite, and insignificant. I'm sure I'll hear the phrase "Just get over it" from some people. I wish I could. It isn't that I can't get over it; it's deeper than that. Today it came to me. As much as I hate to admit it, my mind is still sometimes in a fog. At times I feel confused and befuddled. Sometimes this fog of confusion and self-doubt seems supreme. Suddenly a flash of understanding comes out of nowhere. The flash contains what I need to know or do next, and I have perfect clarity. How can this be explained unless this was predestined and meant to be? I allow myself to accept this explanation because it connects with both my worlds and makes them into one perfect orb. It is a beacon of light. If I can change my past into one that no longer haunts me and instead brings more to the table, then I'm thankful for that. You're not alone! That's all I can say.

The funniest thing happened this year. I bought a picture at a yard sale and put it on my wall. I wasn't sure if it was a saint, an angel, or goddess. Later I found it was a copy of a Russian depiction of the angel Gabriel, who was known as the messenger.

I wanted to contemplate the picture, so I put it on the wall across from where I watch TV. One day as I was watching the news, a light began to bounce across my ceiling, floor, and walls. Eventually it did the oddest thing—it landed over the picture of the angel as if making a halo. It took me a while to figure out where the light was coming from. Once I did, I found it to be amazingly random. It returned every sunny day for about four months. I've even written a poem about it and taken pictures and videos of its antics. At one point, one of the pictures was of a cross that I hadn't been able to see until I began to look at the newest pictures I had taken.

There were other pictures with lines that hadn't been there, and one video in which a light began bouncing into areas where it couldn't have gone. I asked myself, "Am I being visited?"

I've always felt that, when it came time to publish this book, something odd would happen to bring it to the attention of others. I immediately thought about YouTube. It is strange enough to see the videos and pictures, but they are only one dimensional. To be in the room as this is happening is something else. I'm in the process of writing a poem to go along with the video.

There You Have It

I've told you as much as I can about my failures, successes, hopes, and dreams. Now it is up to me to make my world as balanced, complete, and happy as possible.

I do want you to know before I end my final chapter that I don't see any of the people throughout my life's journey as monsters. It would be better if they were because they'd be easier to hate. I can't do that. They missed the mark, and I was caught in the trickle-down current of what they were doing. In some ways, there's a monster in all of us. I found this out for myself as I moved my mother from one place in my life and mind to another. Just as I had to sort our her possessions in her house, I had to do what was necessary to open our personal emotional baggage and toss out what no longer pertained to or was important to our relationship. If you think about it, I'm sure you know exactly what I mean. It's called growing up.

My grandfather is the one I see as being the most destructive. I wish I knew what happened to him to create his behavior. Maybe it was chemical or genetic; no one will ever know. When I think about him, which isn't often, I regret I wasn't able to learn more about his trickle-down past.

When my stepfather came into my life, he took from me the only shred of my mother I had. When they were married, she became his wife and stopped being my mother. At that point, he isolated me from my father's family and hers. Then it trickled down until he isolated her from not only me, but from her grandchildren.

The people in my life weren't any different than some of the people in your own life. They are parents, grocers, teachers, clergy, neighbors, Sunday school teachers, sales clerks, and so forth. You'll never convince me that most people who damage their children do it on purpose. I know if any of our own original family was caught in my own personal drama, it was without intention on my part. Further, I don't feel Mother meant for me to be hurt. I understand she had her own issues and chose to handle them in her own way. I recognize that, at times, she took the easy way out. I try to remember that she didn't have a choice when it came to her father. Her mother overcompensated and became enmeshed with Mother in a way that made their relationship unnatural, unnecessary, and codependent. Grandmother wasn't any better at protecting Mother than Mother was at protecting me. This is how it happens with trickle-down childhoods.

Instead of allowing my own issues to continue to filter into the lives of not only our sons but also the generations to follow, I decided to change. That is the choice I made for myself and for my family. I've never been sorry for the way I'm still attempting to end these trickle-down issues. As a matter of fact, I feel I've done a good job helping our family regroup and reshape their lives. This is the one thing no one was able to do for me. I had to do it by changing everything about myself. Once I decided to put away those things that happened to me as a child, I knew I could finish growing up.

I have done everything possible to find my freedom, and for this I will forever feel grateful for my journey. If anyone other than me has profited from my journey, then it has been my joy to help.

CHAPTER EIGHT

The Rules I Abide By Today

Here are a few beliefs that have enabled me to begin managing my behavior in a more productive way. I present them here in no particular order, and I use them daily because they are in many ways remain my salvation. Enjoy!

1. I have given up any expectation that others will behave the way I want them to simply because it seems right to me. Their free will is outside my control, and how they choose to think, behave, and speak is no longer my business.

2. It is foolish to feel or believe I am in control of my behaviors or the behavior of others. Instead, I have come to realize that I can manage only my own world in a moment-by-moment way. Control of anything or anyone (even myself) is a myth. I have given myself permission to manage my thoughts, behaviors, and language in a way that enables me to be more pliable and accepting of others as well as myself.

3. It is well known that anytime you change yourself, others must comply and change as well. Those changes may not be what I hoped for, but I realize that the only thing that matters is that I continue to manage my own changes in an acceptable way. If those changes don't comply with what others want, then that's not my problem.

4. I've taught myself that who I am and what I do are two different things. I can never change my authentic self, but I can change my thoughts, behaviors, and language in a way that enables me to be the best I can possibly be.

5. I've accepted that I was never to blame for what happened to me as a child. I've found it isn't necessary to blame or excuse the part others played in the person I could have been. I've accepted the person I am today as my normal, and I no longer care how I fit in the minds of others.

6. I've been able to change linguistically so I can now stop using words that can be easily misunderstood. Language is the most powerful tool any of us has to communicate not only with others but also with ourselves.

7. I've found that I need to respect my memory and know it has chosen to allow me to soldier on without needing to know or remember what happened. I also know that, if in the future memories surface, I will have both the courage and knowledge to realistically deal with them without needing to dissociate.

8. It has become apparent to me that writing is a productive way to dig into my mind and let go of things I don't remember. Everything I have written has always ended in way that seemed to enable me to make a final tune into the heaven of my mind to lift me up.

9. As for what I've referred to as my internal family, I've learned to appreciate the part they played. They enabled me to move forward without consciously carrying the burden alone. I know they aren't real, but they seemed real enough when I needed a family that cared about and loved me.

10. I feel it is important to never stop learning about myself and my past. Learning to respect my journey has shown me that I'm stronger than I realized. Growing my mind by exposing myself to information has enabled me to stay sharp. It is one of those things that will help keep me mentally young and alert.

11. Thinking outside the box and trying questionable ideas enabled me to trust myself and not be concerned about what others might think or to see these ideas as "evil."

12. Not taking myself too seriously has been a wonderful way to allow things to move forward without judgment. I like it when I can say, "Hmmm that's interesting." By doing this I have neither inflated nor deflated my past or what I might be doing to heal myself.

13. I've taught myself that when and if my mind begins acting like a naughty child, I can tell it to stop. This seems to give me enough time to point myself in another direction.

14. Hopefully I can tell my mind "Quiet" or "Listen" when I feel I need to change the subject or interrupt. Those two words should be what I need to recognize and respect the conversation others would like to have with me.

15. I have a very deep belief in the right thing happening at the right time. As my journey went off track, I allowed myself to remember that wherever I found myself was still exactly where I needed to be. "When the student is ready the teacher will appear." I listen for what my journey might be trying to tell me.

16. Because of the way Mother treated me, I try to remember that children aren't pieces of property we own; rather, they are small adults in children's clothing. I avoid the word *my* when referring to our children.

17. When I doubt that my story might be of value to others, I remind myself: This is the book I wish I could have read when I started my journey.

18. I try to be mindful about who or what I allow to influence me. As a mother, I told our children that being a follower is an important job because you need to know who to follow.

19. Existing isn't living. Since I have only one life, I need to live it to the fullest. I remind myself that Mother was twenty-four when I was born and lived to be ninety-seven, so I still have time.

20. I know stepping out of my feelings of safety isn't a bad thing. Only by pushing my envelope am I going to find my true calling.

21. I always try to listen to what my body tells me. Hopefully I can catch it as it whispers instead of waiting until it is screaming at me. Disease in my body begins with my own dis-ease.

22. I try not to judge too harshly. There have been times I've been harder on myself than necessary.

23. When I am unable to sleep and my mind won't stop ruminating or planning, I tell myself to get up and write things down so my paper can remember. I also tell myself it is the middle of the night, no one wants or needs anything, and I need sleep more than I need to be awake. Sometimes I tell myself, "Instead of taking a nap later—take it now!" This also applies to unreal conversations I might have with others in my mind. If the people aren't in front of me at that moment, I need to save my words until they are physically present.

24. Telling someone they "made me" mad or "made me" do something is incorrect. No one can make me do anything. I do things to myself through the choices I make.

25. I try to avoid the words *wrong* and *right*. Now I say "I may be mistaken" or that something is "correct." They are softer words with a less-harsh meaning.

26. I have taught myself to self-comfort. I talk to myself the way one might talk to a child. I begin by using the words "I love you" and end every conversation by saying "thank you." In other words, I show myself respect.

27. When my mind begins to ruminate in a way that isn't productive, I tell it, "Stop!" In my case, it seems to temporarily surprise my mind. It reminds me of someone turning around and asking "What?" It isn't unusual for the mind to ignore the directive and begin its conversation again. When this happens, I tell myself, "Stop!" After repeatedly doing this, I am generally able to get my mind to move on to a different thought.

28. I have had quite a lot of success seeing my mind as a child in need of direction. Sometimes I use a picture of me as a child so I can have a better visual image. Just

because I'm grown doesn't mean I can't retrain my inner self. I avoid tactics such as shame, fear, or guilt when dealing with this part of myself. I treat this mind image with respect.

29. I know that talking about my past to show how I've changed is healthy. Rehashing my past and not putting it behind me is unhealthy.

30. I try to remember the word *disremember* when I'm dealing with people who make promises they may not keep. I remind myself that, when they made a promise, they more than likely meant to follow through, but life got in the way, and they became distracted to the point of forgetfulness. I try to be careful of the promises I make. I write my plans, appointments, and promises on a calendar and keep it on my desk in plain sight. As I finish one item, I remove it and check what comes next. Promises made should be kept, but realistically that doesn't always happen, and I need only to notice and move on.

31. I know the trick to following some of the above-mentioned thoughts is to keep them soft and pliable. They aren't written in stone. I try to stay firm in the way I want to handle my life. These ideas have served me well and are still my go-to thoughts and lessons when I need them. This way I don't need to repeat a lesson simply because I have forgotten how it came into my life and how it relieved my pain.

32. I always try to keep my words like marshmallows—soft and sweet—because I never know when I might need to eat them.

33. Lastly I've taught myself to change the word *panic* into the words *high anxiety*. This, in turn, has enabled me to eventually drop the word *high* and just use the word *anxiety*. Now instead of having feelings of unreasonable, irresolvable panic, I have only the same level of anxiety as others. The step from panic toward peace has become shorter simply by doing away with the word *panic* and replacing how I view it.

ABOUT THE AUTHOR

Mary Davenport was born in 1942 and has lived in Iowa, Illinois, Missouri, California, Michigan, and North Carolina.

She graduated from high school in 1961, but claims to have diplomas from the University of Life. When the Universe is your teacher, the lessons are tough, and the tests tougher. She claims she will always be mentally prepared to dig deeper so she can climb higher toward the summit of her life.

Mary and her husband graduated from the same high school and have been married since 1962. Together they have four sons, six grandchildren, and four great-grandchildren.

Her hobbies are yard work, reading, cooking, sewing, antique shopping, and of course, writing.

You may contact her at mtdcmaryd@outlook.com.

REFERENCES

Barbara Ann Brennon: Hands of Light, A Guide to Healing Through the Human Energy Field A Bantam Book, New York, 1987 (pg. 105)

David E. Comings, M.D. Did Man Create God? Is Your Spiritual Brain at Peace With Your Thinking Brain?, Hope Press, Duarte, CA, 2008 (pg. 167)

Orrin Devinsky, M.D. Epilepsy (Third Edition) Patient and Family Guide, Demos Medical Publishing, LLC, New York 2008

Jack Dreyfus, A Remarkable Medicine Has Been Overlooked, Continuum Publishing Co, N.Y. 1981 (pg. 100)

Alice W. Flaherty, M.D., The Midnight Disease. The Drive to Write, Writer's Block, and the Creative Brain. A Mariner Book Houghton Mifflin Company Boston/New York 2005 (pg. 169)

Louise Hay, You Can Heal Your Life, Hay House, 1984, 1987, 2004 (pg. 102)

Dharma Singh Khalsa, M.D. with Cameron Stauth, Warner Books, N.Y. 1997 (pg. 70)

Jacquelyn Small, Transformers, Personal Transformation. The Way Through, DeVorss and Company, Del Rey, CA (pg. 105)

Printed in the United States
By Bookmasters